MW00564302

The Sailing Navy, 1775–1854

The U.S. Navy Warship Series

The Sailing Navy, 1775–1854

Paul H. Silverstone

Naval Institute Press

Annapolis, Maryland

Naval Institute Press
291 Wood Road
Annapolis, MD 21402

© 2001 by Paul H. Silverstone
All rights reserved. No part of this book may be reproduced or uti-
lized in any form or by any means, electronic or mechanical, including photocopying and recording, or by any information storage and
retrieval system, without permission in writing from the publisher.

Library of Congress Cataloging-in-Publication Data
Silverstone, Paul H.
    The sailing navy, 1775–1854 / Paul H. Silverstone.
        p.   cm. — (The U.S. Navy warship series)
    Includes bibliographical references and index.
    ISBN 1-55750-893-3 (alk. paper)
    1. Warships—United States—History—18th century.
2. Warships—United States—History—19th century.   3. United
States. Continental Navy—Lists of vessels.   4. United States. Navy—
Lists of vessels.   5. Navies—United States.   I. Title.   II. Series.

VA61 .S567 2000
359.8′32′097309033—dc21

                                                    00-048198

Printed in the United States of America on acid-free paper ∞
08 07 06 05 04 03 02 01   9 8 7 6 5 4 3 2
First printing

CONTENTS

Preface   vii

Explanation of Data   ix

List of Abbreviations   xi

U.S. Naval Ordnance, 1773–1854   xiii

1   The Continental Navy, 1775–1783   1

2   State Navies, 1775–1783   18

3   The United States Navy, 1797–1854   21

4   United States Revenue Cutter Service   79

5   Texas Navy   88

Appendix: Royal Navy Losses in North
American Waters   91

Bibliography   95

Index   97

PREFACE

This book provides a single comprehensive source of definitive information on the ships of the United States Navy during the age of sail from its beginning with the Continental Navy in 1775. No such source has previously been available focusing on this period of U.S. naval history.

From these times there is much conflicting information and lack of information. Systems of measuring ships, both tonnage and dimensions, varied so that the numbers given differ from source to source. The dimensions of a ship were more meaningful than tonnage. There is occasionally confusion about a ship's rig. Ships' batteries were changeable and different armaments are often found for the same ship. One has little assurance that these figures are right or wrong or merely reporting different systems of measurement. Some judgment has been required to choose which of these various measurements should be used.

Similarly it has been difficult to identify some acquired ships as to their prior identity and place or date of construction. Most of the records are handwritten, leading to a variety of spellings or readings of the names of ships and other data.

For illustrations from this era before photography it has been necessary to use line drawings, contemporary prints, and artists' impressions.

Appreciation is extended to Ernest Arroyo, William Jurens, Norman Polmar, and Charles R. Haberlein for assistance in obtaining information and photographs. And further appreciation to the editors, including Jack Brostrom, for many helpful suggestions.

EXPLANATION OF DATA

This book is divided into three main sections, covering the Continental Navy, the United States Navy from 1797, and the Revenue Cutter Service.

The ships of the Continental Navy, which lasted from 1775 to 1783, are divided into four basic groups: those authorized and built by Congress, those existing ships purchased and converted, those acquired abroad, and those captured and put into service. The ships which served on Lake Champlain are in a separate section and there is a brief listing of ships owned by the individual states.

The United States Navy was formally established in 1797. Most of its ships are listed by type—ships-of-the-line, frigates, brigs, and schooners—but again, the ships that served on the lakes are in separate sections. Also, the newly developed steamships are grouped together in another section.

Records from these early days are often sparse and nonexistent, and where they do exist they are unclear or conflicting. Reputable sources, as often as not, do not agree. Too often, basic information has been lacking altogether.

Particulars are given for each ship as follows. For certain types of ships, these are given in a single line without explanation.

For ships remaining on the Navy List after 1855, historical details and changes in the ship or its armament after that date, as well as its subsequent history, will be found in the succeeding volume of this series, *Civil War Navies, 1855–1883* (Annapolis, Md.: Naval Institute Press, 2001).

Name: Navy name as completed, with former names given below. Further changes of name, if any, are indicated in the service record, with new Navy names in bold type. If a ship retained its merchant name in Navy service, no former name is given.

Builder: Place where the ship was built, followed by the builder's name, if known, in parentheses.

Construction dates: For Navy-built ships, dates given are for laying down of keel, launching, and commissioning. For acquired vessels, dates given are date of launching, acquisition by the Navy, and commissioning.

Rate: Sailing ships were rated by number of guns, although this may not coincide with the number of guns actually carried. It was customary to append the rate to the name of the ship, thus denoting its strength and size.

Dimensions: Standard dimensions, given in feet (') and inches ("), are length × beam × draft (or depth of hull, prefixed with "d"). Figures varied widely and were often published without explanation of the method of measurement. The usual length given was between perpendiculars, that is to say, between the fore side of the stem and the aft side of the rudder post. Others measured the length overall, on deck, or on the keel.

Tonnage: Tonnage is not a good indicator of size in these early ships. It is mainly useful in comparing one ship to another. Measurement was often expressed in *tons burden*, an expression of the carrying capacity of a ship rather than weight, and rules of its calculation varied widely. Other measurements used are indicated in the text by: bm = burden, D = displacement.

Machinery (for steamships): The early steamships of the Navy had simple engines but with many variations as engineers experimented with new ideas. Side wheels were the principal mode of propulsion, but experimental screw propellers were developed by Ericsson, Hunter, and others. The mode of propulsion; number, type, and size of engines; number of boilers; horsepower; and speed are given. The diameter of the cylinder(s) and the length of the stroke of the piston are shown, the former in inches and the latter in feet, e.g., (50″ × 2′), following the type of engine. The maker of the machinery is noted in parentheses, if known ("bldr" indicates machinery manufactured by the builder).

Complement: Normal figure for officers and crew. For many ships, where sources vary, a range is given (e.g., 50/75). There was often a large variance in peacetime and wartime complements.

Battery: Original number and type of guns are given first, with later significant changes noted by date. A description of ordnance of this period is described in a separate section.

Notes: Additional information pertaining to design, construction or later modifications, acquisition, or earlier historical notes of interest, not included in other categories. The name of the designer and type of figurehead are noted here.

Service record: A capsule history of each ship's naval service, showing assignment by station or squadron and war service, including participation in engagements, major damage to vessel, or loss. The number of crewmen killed is noted in parentheses. Changes in Navy name are given here with date. Also listed is the final disposition by the Navy—loss, sale, or transfer to another agency. Other than final disposition, details of the service record after about 1855 are given in *Civil War Navies.*

Ships captured: Names and dates of merchant ships captured or sunk. Some prizes were credited to several ships acting together and so appear more than once.

Later history: Brief details of the ship's career after leaving naval service, including later merchant names and service in other government departments or in foreign navies. The ultimate fate is given where known, or the year the ship disappeared from shipping registers (RR) or was sold to foreign buyers (S/F). Occasionally a date is given for the last published reference. SE = still existing.

British naval losses during the Revolution and the War of 1812 are listed in the appendix to show both the importance and cost of these wars to Britain.

LIST OF ABBREVIATIONS

bldr	builder		oa	overall
bm	burden		pdr	pounder
bp	length between perpendiculars		R	rifle
BU	broken up		recomm	recommissioned
comm	commissioned		RN	Royal Navy (Great Britain)
crde	carronade		RR	removed from shipping registers
CSN	Confederate States Navy		rtnd	returned
CSS	Confederate States Ship		SB	smoothbore
D	displacement (tonnage)		schr	schooner
FFU	further fate unknown		SE	still existing
H	howitzer		S/F	sold foreign
HP	horsepower		sqn	squadron
LofM	Letter of Marque		trfd	transferred
M	mortar		(U)	information unknown
MLR	muzzle loading rifle		USCS	United States Coast Survey
NHP	normal horsepower		USNA	United States Naval Academy
NYd	Navy Yard		USRCS	United States Revenue Cutter Service

U.S. NAVAL ORDNANCE, 1773–1854
by W. J. Jurens

The U.S. Navy participated in two major conflicts during the period covered by this volume, the War of Independence (1776–83) and the War of 1812 (1812–15). Although many rifled guns firing elongated projectiles were employed later during the Civil War, ordnance prior to 1855 consisted almost exclusively of smoothbore muzzle-loaded guns firing spherical projectiles and employing black powder as a propellant.

Because the British actively discouraged the production of ordnance in the colonies, Colonial ordnance at the outbreak of the American Revolution consisted of a miscellany of vintage English and other foreign guns, often of uncertain and irregular pedigree. Although a few cannons were produced domestically prior to 1770, American ordnance production did not become significant until 1774, and even then bronze was in such short supply that manufacture was supported largely by recycling old bells and door knockers. Although about three dozen foundries produced cannons during the American Revolution, data concerning the number, characteristics, and utilization of the resulting weapons are almost nonexistent. Most evidence seems to suggest that the guns that were produced were most often near variants of contemporary British designs, primarily of iron.

At the outset of the war, the American fleet consisted of fewer than thirty ships, mounting in total only about 550 relatively small-caliber guns. During the course of the conflict, these guns were augmented by the capture of numerous British weapons and a large number of cannons—many obsolete—obtained from the French.

Guns of the period were highly variant, and the samples that have survived represent a mixed and quite probably nonrepresentative lot which, taken individually, rarely match official specifications. Guns were invariably designated by projectile weight—a 24 pdr would fire a 24-pound iron round shot. Though these designations had been discarded by the time of the Revolutionary War, early cannoneers typically divided guns into categories by length as well: *mortars* were less than three calibers long, *perriers* (the ancestors of our modern howitzers) from eight to sixteen calibers long; *cannons* from fifteen to twenty calibers long, and *culverins* from twenty-five to thirty calibers long.[1] Most naval guns of

the Revolutionary War were developed from cannons and culverins; the Carronade, intermediate in length between a perrier and a mortar, was an entirely new development.

The table on page xiv (which must be considered approximate) is adapted from a variety of sources and gives information on typical guns of the period. As noted earlier, all of these were smoothbore muzzle loaders.

REGULAR GUNS
The typical cannon of the period was mounted to a sturdy four-wheeled carriage or "truck," which, equipped with a fairly elaborate arrangement of lines and lashings, allowed the gun to recoil into the ship upon firing and to be hauled back up to the gunport after (or sometimes before) loading was complete. Early cannons were typically cast bronze, but by the time of the American Revolution, iron guns were common and the bore, instead of being cast, was often drilled out of the solid blank. Train, which was rather rarely changed in action, was adjusted by manhandling the gun from side to side with crowbars; elevation was adjusted by driving wedges under the breech. A small hole was drilled from a point on the breech right through to the powder chamber, which was, in many guns, slightly smaller than the bore proper. This hole was filled with a flammable mixture that was, in earlier guns, ignited by torch or a piece of smoldering rope; later guns were equipped with mechanical mechanisms similar to those used on flintlock or matchlock small arms. The rate of fire was typically slightly less than one round per minute.

THE CARRONADE
In 1778 the Carron Company, a Scottish ironworks, began producing a short, light, large-caliber gun, which came to be known as a Carronade or "Smasher." Careful manufacture made it possible to reduce the windage to about one-fiftieth the caliber, a figure so small that a small internal muzzle taper was required in order to allow the projectile to be inserted and rammed against trapped air. This greatly improved the efficiency, and although the range of a Carronade was relatively short—perhaps half that of a cannon—the gun gave good accuracy and great hitting power close in, which was where most of the important fighting was done anyway. First provided to privateers and merchant ships, the Carronade quickly made its way into more conservative naval circles.

---

[1] The diameter of the bore is known as the *caliber* of the weapon. A cannon twenty calibers long would thus have a bore length equal to twenty times the diameter of the shot.

Size	Length (inches)	Weight (gun) (lbs)	Weight (all-up) (lbs)	Shot diameter (inches)	Caliber* (inches)	Range** (yards)
10 pdr	78	890	1,200*	c. 10	2.9–3.0	1,850
42 pdr	120	5,537	7,504	6.70	7.04	1,940
32 pdr	114	5,398	6,216	6.12	6.43	2,080
24 pdr	113	4,800	5,600	5.56	5.84	1,800
18 pdr	108	4,133	4,704	5.05	5.30	1,800
12 pdr	108	3,278	3,808	4.42	4.64	1,580
9 pdr	101	2,352	3,528	4.01	4.21	1,620
6 pdr	96	1,739	2,000	3.50	3.68	(U)
3 pdr	77	1,100	1,200	2.78	2.91	(U)
68 pdr Carronade	59	4,032	4,760	7.90	8.06	1,280
42 pdr Carronade	52	2,485	2,930	6.70	6.83	1,170
32 pdr Carronade	48	1,915	2,260	6.12	6.24	1,087
24 pdr Carronade	36	1,288	1,520	5.56	5.67	1,050
18 pdr Carronade	28	952	1,120	5.05	5.15	1,000
12 pdr Carronade	26	661	780	4.42	4.51	870

* Based on "windage" of $1/20$ shot diameter for regular guns. Carronades, which were more carefully made and shorter, had a windage of about $1/50$ shot diameter.

** Ranges are based on 5° elevation with a charge equal to $1/3$ shot weight.

With a shot travel of only six or seven calibers and a weight (in U.S. service) of only about sixty-five pounds per pound of shot, the Carronade also used an unusual carriage. Manufactured without trunnions, the Carronade was equipped with a vertical pin cast into the bottom of the barrel; the pin penetrated through a wooden bed, which recoiled over a wooden slide that was itself attached to the ship by a frontal pivot anchored to the side.

PROPELLANTS

The propellant of choice—in fact, the only propellant used—during this period was "black powder," a mixture of potassium nitrate, charcoal, and sulfur. Yielding a specific force of about 110,000 foot-pounds per pound, black powder is, on a pound-for-pound basis, only about one-quarter as powerful as modern smokeless powders. The strength of a given powder lot was determined in a *prouvette*, a small mortar that tested how far a one-ounce charge could propel a solid twenty-four-pound ball. (Good powder would propel the ball almost three hundred yards.)

Black powder in its original form has a relatively small grain size and is unsuitable for cannon use; cannon powders were therefore made by "corning," a process whereby larger grains were broken by rollers or pelleted and separated for size by sieve. The presence of solid reaction products resulted in large volumes of smoke and a corrosive residue when the powder was fired, which required that the gun be cleaned out often, sometimes after every round. Charges—generally weighing about one-third of the shot weight—were usually made up in the form of cartridges, that is, pre-prepared cloth or parchment packages carried from magazine to gun by young boys known as "powder monkeys." The first powder mills were not established in America until 1775. The gunpowder they produced was of relatively low quality, and during the Revolutionary War most propellant had to be obtained from foreign sources.

PROJECTILES

The variety of projectiles fired from smoothbore guns was remarkable. *Round shot*, essentially a solid cast iron ball, could be fired either at ambient temperature or as "hot shot," that is, heated to red heat in order to start fires on the target. (Hot shot required the installation of a wet tamper wad to separate the shell from the powder and was often fired at low velocity because excessive penetration retarded the incendiary effect.) *Cored shot* was round shot cast with an interior cavity which, surprisingly, was usually filled with water or left empty.

Shell, employed only after about 1800, was simply round shot hollowed out and equipped with a black powder explosive charge at the center. A fuze was needed, and in order to orient this correctly, the shell was often strapped to a squat cylindrical (usually wooden) guide, known as a *sabot*. Fuzes throughout the period were rudimentary, usually some sort of tapered plug filled with powder, which was cut off at various lengths to vary the burning time and hammered into a hole in the shell just before firing. All round shot suffered from aerodynamic instabilities, which rendered accuracy problematical.

Grapeshot, as its name implied, resembled a bunch of grapes, simply a bundle of one- to four-pound lead or iron balls wrapped in tarred cloth or canvas that turned the gun into what amounted to a very large shotgun. Later, light metal frameworks were included to hold the balls more firmly in place. Grapeshot was effective out to about 600 yards.

Case shot, also known as "common case," "Langrel," "Langridge," or "Lagrange" shot, originally consisted on conveniently sized pieces of scrap iron contained in a case filled with sawdust. As time went on—and ammunition became more "formal"—cannonballs tended to be substituted for scraps. *Canister shot*—a later development effective out to about 350 yards—was similar, except that the balls were much smaller, usually weighing less than a pound, and packed in a light metal can.

Dismantling shot, designed to expand in flight in order to wreck rigging and clear decks, came in a remarkable number of variants, although many were apparently little-used. One common type, *chain shot*, was made by splitting a single ball in half and coiling chain inside or between the two halves, or—more often—by simply linking two balls together with a length of chain five or six calibers long. *Bar shot*, also known as double-headed shot or "Stang balls," was similar, but used an eight- to fourteen-inch-long solid bar instead of chain to connect two half-balls; a variant allowed two bars coupled together to expand in length while in flight. *Star shot* consisted of an iron ring with five or six eyebolts swiveling on its perimeter. All of these items were short-ranged and by all accounts wildly inaccurate.

Especially near the beginning of an action, guns were often "double-shotted" with either two balls, or one ball and grapeshot. Especially at short range, this required some reduction in the powder charge and the acceptance of a great decrease in accuracy. "Triple shotting," while not unheard of, was relatively rare.

The allowances regarding the type of shell and the number of rounds provided per gun varied widely over time. In general, peacetime loads tended to be about seventy-five rounds per gun of round shot and twenty-five rounds per gun of other shot; in war, these numbers were typically increased by 30 to 40 percent.

The Sailing Navy, 1775–1854

1
THE CONTINENTAL NAVY, 1775–1783

The long-simmering dispute between the American colonies and England over taxes and self-government erupted into a shooting war at Lexington and Concord in April 1775. Military operations grew in scope during the year but it was not until autumn that the Continental Congress began authorizing funds for a navy.

At first, ships were acquired and fitted out for war purposes. Local commanders obtained some ships, George Washington acquired schooners in Massachusetts, and Benedict Arnold captured three ships on Lake Champlain. Individual colonies formed local navies by purchasing or building ships, but most of these vessels were small and poorly armed. Massachusetts and Pennsylvania were more successful than the others.

Vessels obtained by authority of Congress included two serviceable ships renamed *Alfred* and *Columbus*. Fourteen other vessels included the brigs *Andrew Doria*, *Cabot*, and *Lexington*. A Marine Committee was established.

On 13 December 1775, Congress authorized the construction of thirteen frigates: five of 32 guns, five of 28, and three of 24. Allocation of where to build these ships was assigned politically with little sense of the colonies' ability to construct them. In the event, most of them did not get to sea. On 22 December the first officers were commissioned, with Esek Hopkins named commodore. A few months later privateering was authorized and letters of marque and reprisal issued.

An attempt at fleet action took place in early 1776 when a squadron under Hopkins raided New Providence Island in the Bahamas to take guns, ammunition, and supplies. Mention should also be made of the first submersible, built by David Bushnell, which actually attacked the British flagship in New York harbor in September 1776.

Following the failure of their attack on Quebec, Continental forces retreated to Fort Ticonderoga. Both sides commenced building ships to take control of Lake Champlain, the strategic key to the area. The battle of Valcour Island on 11 October 1776 resulted in a defeat for the Americans and almost complete destruction of their fleet. However, this action upset British plans sufficiently to lead to the American victory at Saratoga in October 1777.

After the British occupied New York in September 1776, they set out to capture Philadelphia. A series of land battles ensued as Washington fell back through New Jersey. The British fleet with transports sailed up the Delaware River to Philadelphia, eventually leading to the loss of many American vessels in the fall of 1777.

In June 1778 France declared war on England and French aid to the colonies included the support of the French fleet in North America and the West Indies. Use of bases in France enabled Ameri-

The sloop *Ranger*, 18, receiving the first recognition of the American flag by a foreign government in Quiberon Bay, France, 14 February 1778. (U.S. Naval Historical Center)

can ships under captains such as John Paul Jones in *Ranger* and Gustavus Conyngham in *Revenge* to harass English shipping and ports in and near the British Isles. American successes in the war were chiefly in single-ship actions that laid the foundations of an American naval pantheon. John Paul Jones, called the father of the American Navy, defeated HMS *Serapis* in *Bonhomme Richard*. Other commanders of note included John Barry (*Lexington*) and Lambert Wickes (*Reprisal*).

The British capture of Savannah in December 1778, and later of Charleston, led to further losses of American ships. Often single American ships were kept in port for long periods by superior British squadrons cruising offshore. During the summer of 1779 an ambitious but poorly planned attack on the British in Penobscot Bay (now in Maine) led to the complete destruction of an American fleet of forty-two warships and transports. The Continental Navy frigate *Warren*, sloop *Providence*, and brig *Diligent*—together with state ships, privateers, and transports—were all burned or captured.

The French fleet under DeGrasse ultimately checkmated the Royal Navy, enabling Washington to gain his great victory at Yorktown in 1781. By blockading the coast with a large number of heavy ships, the

An impression of ship-of-the-line *America*, as presented to France in 1782. Painting by John S. Blunt in 1834. (U.S. Naval Historical Center)

French prevented supplies from getting through to Cornwallis's army in Virginia, forcing him to surrender.

At the end of the war, all the ships of the Navy were sold. The *Alliance*, one of the finest ships and most successful ships of the Continental Navy, was the last to be sold in 1785.

SHIPS BUILT FOR THE NAVY

SHIPS-OF-THE-LINE

Name	Builder	Laid down	L	Comm
America	Portsmouth, N.H. (James Hackett)	May 1777	5 Nov 1782	never

Tonnage	3,400 tons D; 1,564 tons B
Rate	74 guns
Dimensions	182′6″ (deck), 150′ (keel) × 50′6″ × d23′6″; also reported as d22′
Tonnage	1,982 tons
Complement	626
Battery	30–18pdr, 32–12pdr, 14–9pdr (projected)

Notes: Probably designed by William Hackett. One of three ships-of-the-line (74) authorized on 9 Nov 1776 by Congress, the others to be

USS *Hancock*, 32, the first to go into service of the frigates authorized by Congress. A month later she was captured and commissioned in the Royal Navy as *Iris*. Painting by E. Tufnell. (U.S. Naval Historical Center, Naval Historical Foundation)

built at Boston and Philadelphia, but the latter were never built. Offered to France to replace *Magnifique*, which had been wrecked near Boston on 11 Aug 1782 and whose fittings and cannon were used to equip this ship. Figurehead: female figure crowned with laurels.
Service record: Much delayed by lack of funds, shortage of materials, and skilled workmen. Given to France, 3 Sep 1782. Completed 24 Jun 1783.
Later history: French *L'America*. Scrapped in France, 1786.

FRIGATES

Thirteen frigates were authorized by the Continental Congress on 13 Dec 1775.

Name	Builder	Laid down	L	Comm
Hancock	Newburyport, Mass. (Jno. Greenleaf)	1776	10 Jul 1776	May 1777

Rate	32 guns
Dimensions	136′7″ (deck), 115′10″ (keel) × 35′6″ × 11′
Tonnage	763 tons
Complement	290
Battery	24–12pdr, 10–6pdr

Notes: Authorized 13 Dec 1775. Based on a design by Joshua Humphreys. Figurehead: John Hancock.
Service record: Captured HMS *Fox*, 28, off New England with *Boston*, 27 Jun 1777; later (8 Jul) both recaptured by HMS *Rainbow*, 44, and *Flora*, 32, after a 29-hour chase (8 casualties).
Ships captured: (With *Boston*) small brig, 29 May 1777.
Later history: HMS *Iris*. Captured by French in Chesapeake Bay, 11 Sep 1781. Converted to hulk, 1792. Blown up by RN at Toulon, 18 Dec 1793.

Name	Builder	Laid down	L	Comm
Boston	Newburyport, Mass. (Stephen & Ralph Cross)	1776	3 Jun 1776	spring 1777

Rate	24 guns
Dimensions	114'3" (deck), 94'3" (keel) × 32' × d10'3"
Tonnage	514 tons
Complement	(U)
Battery	5–12pdr, 19–9pdr, 2–6pdr, 4–4pdr

Notes: Authorized 13 Dec 1775. Designed by Joshua Humphreys. Figurehead: Indian with bow and arrow.
Service record: Engaged British squadron and escaped, 8 Jul 1777. Operated in North Atlantic west of Spain, 1778. Captured by British at Charleston, S.C., 12 May 1780.
Ships captured: Three prizes, 1777; ship *Martha*, 11 Mar 1778; brig *John & Rebecca*, 19 Jun 1778; brig *Britannia*, 23 Jun 1778; brig *Elizabeth*, 25 Jun 1778. (With *Providence* and *Ranger*) brig *Sally*, 24 Aug 1778; brig *Friends*, 9 Sep 1778, snow *Adventure*, 10 Sep 1778. (With *Confederacy*) privateer *Poole*, 24, schr *Patsey*, sloop *William*, 6 Jun 1779. (With *Deane*) schr *Tryall*, 10 (LofM), *Glencairn*, 20 (LofM), ship *Sandwich*, 16, brig *Venture*, 2, ship *Thorne*, 14, schr *Flying Fish*, 10 (LofM), 2 Aug–24 Sep 1779.
Later history: HMS *Charleston*. Sold 24 Apr 1783.

Name	Builder	Laid down	L	Comm
Raleigh	Portsmouth, N.H. (James Hackett)	21 Mar 1776	21 May 1776	Aug 1777

Rate	32 guns
Dimensions	131'5" (deck), 110'7" (keel) × 34'5" × 11'
Tonnage	697 tons
Complement	180
Battery	32–12pdr; also reported as 26–12pdr, 6–6pdr

Notes: Authorized 13 Dec 1775. Designed by William Hackett. Figurehead: Sir Walter Raleigh.
Service record: Action with sloop HMS *Druid*, 20, at 40°33'N 30°17'W, 4 Sep 1777. With *Alfred*, attacked British convoy, 25 Sep, and went aground during action with British ships *Experiment*, 50, and *Unicorn*, 26, off Boston and was captured, 27 Sep 1778. (25 casualties)
Ships captured: (With *Alfred*) one schr (burned), 15 Aug 1777; brig *Nancy*, one other, 2 Sep 1777.
Later history: HMS *Raleigh*. Sold 17 Jul 1783.

Name	Builder	Laid down	L	Comm
Warren	Providence, R.I. (Sylvester Bowers)	1776	15 May 1776	Apr 1778

Rate	32 guns
Dimensions	132'1" (deck) × 34'5" × 11'
Tonnage	(U)
Complement	250
Battery	12–18pdr, 14–12pdr, 8–9pdr

Notes: Authorized 13 Dec 1775.
Service record: Blockaded by British, 1776–78. Expedition up Penobscot River, 25 Jul–14 Aug 1779. Burned to prevent capture in Bagaduce River, Maine, 15 Aug 1779.
Ships captured: Ship *Neptune*, one other, Mar 1778. (With *Ranger* and *Queen of France* off Cape Henry) privateer schr, Mar 1779; schr *Hibernia*, 8, 6 Apr 1779; ship *Jason*, 20, ship *Maria* (LofM), brig *Prince Frederick*, brig *Patriot*, brig *Bachelors John*, schr *Chance*, 7 Apr 1779.

The frigate *Raleigh*, 32, was one of 13 frigates authorized by the Continental Congress in 1775. She was captured by the British in 1778. Painting by Capt. James F. Rowe. (U.S. Naval Historical Center)

Name	Builder	Laid down	L	Comm
Providence	Providence, R.I. (Sylvester Bowers)	1776	18 May 1776	Dec 1776

Rate	28 guns
Dimensions	126'6" × 33'8" × 10'5"
Tonnage	632 tons
Complement	170
Battery	26–12pdr, 6–4pdr

Notes: Authorized 13 Dec 1775. Designed by Sylvester Bowers.
Service record: Blockaded in Providence River for more than a year, 1777. Attacked Jamaica fleet, Jul 1779. Captured by British at Charleston, S.C., 12 May 1780.
Ships captured: (With *Boston* and *Ranger*) brig *Sally*, 24 Aug 1778; brig *Friends*, 9 Sep 1778; snow *Adventure*, 10 Sep 1778.
Later history: HMS *Providence*. Sold 11 Mar 1784.

Name	Builder	Laid down	L	Comm
Trumbull	Chatham, Conn. (John Cotton)	Mar/Apr 1776	5 Sep 1776	20 Sep 1779

Rate	28 guns
Dimensions	(U)
Tonnage	700 tons
Complement	199
Battery	24–12pdr, 6–6pdr

Notes: Authorized 13 Dec 1775. Probably designed by Joshua Humphreys. After launching, draft was too great to get ship to sea; freed by lifting ship over the bar, 1779. Fitted out at New London.
Service record: Nearly dismasted in action with *Watt*, 32 (LofM), both ships damaged (8 killed), 2 Jun 1780. Inactive at Philadelphia until 1781. Captured in action with former U.S. ships HMS *Iris*, 32, and *General Monk*, 18, off Delaware Capes after masting/damaged in storm (5 killed), 29 Aug 1781.

Later history: Not taken into RN because of damage. FFU.

Name	Builder	Laid down	L	Comm
Congress	Poughkeepsie, N.Y. (Lancaster Burling)	1775	29 Oct 1776	never

Rate	28 guns
Dimensions	126′ (bp) × 34′10″ × 10′6″
Tonnage	(U)
Complement	(U)
Battery	26–12pdr, 2–6pdr

Notes: Authorized 13 Dec 1775. Designed by Joshua Humphreys. Burned before completion to prevent capture after British capture of New York, 6 Oct 1777.

Name	Builder	Laid down	L	Comm
Montgomery	Pougkeepsie, N.Y. (Lancaster Burling)	7 Mar 1776	Oct 1776	never

Rate	24 guns
Dimensions	(U), probably 126′6″ × 32′6″ × 10′6″
Tonnage	(U)
Complement	(U)
Battery	24–9pdr?

Notes: Authorized 13 Dec 1775. Designed by Joshua Humphreys. **Service record:** Burned incomplete to prevent capture after British capture of New York, 6 Oct 1777.

Name	Builder	Laid down	L	Comm
Randolph	Philadelphia (Wharton & Humphreys)	1775	10 Jul 1776	1776
Washington	Philadelphia (Benj. Eyre)	1776	7 Aug 1776	never

Rate	32 guns
Dimensions	132′9″ (bp) × 34′6″ × 10′6″
Tonnage	(U)
Complement	315
Battery	26–12pdr, 10–6pdr

Notes: Authorized 13 Dec 1775. Designed by Joshua Humphreys.
Service records:
Randolph: Accident to masts during first sailing forced ship to return to port, Feb 1777. Left Charleston, 16 Aug 1777. Blew up during action with HMS *Yarmouth*, 64, off South Carolina (311 killed), 7 Mar 1778.
Ships captured: Two schrs, summer 1777; privateer *True Briton*, 20, *Severn*, brig *Charming Peggy*, brig *L'Assumption*, 4 Sep 1777.
Washington: Sunk incomplete to prevent capture, 2 Nov 1777; raised, 1778. Burned below Bordentown, N.J., 7 May 1778.

Name	Builder	Laid down	L	Comm
Effingham	Philadelphia (Grice)	1776	7 Nov 1776	never

Rate	28 guns
Dimensions	(U)
Tonnage	(U)
Complement	(U)
Battery	26–12pdr, 2–6pdr

Notes: Authorized 13 Dec 1775. Designed by Joshua Humphreys.
Service record: Sunk incomplete at Bordentown, N.J., 2 Nov 1777. Burned to waterline to prevent capture, 7 May 1778.

Name	Builder	Laid down	L	Comm
Delaware	Philadelphia (Warwick Coates)	1776	12 Jul 1776	1777

Rate	24 guns
Dimensions	119′ (bp), 117′10″ (deck) × 32′10″ × 9′8″
Tonnage	563 tons
Complement	(U)
Battery	22–12pdr, 6–6pdr

Notes: Authorized 13 Dec 1775.
Service record: Defense of Philadelphia, summer 1777. Went aground under fire in Delaware River and was captured, 27 Sep 1777.
Later history: HMS *Delaware*. Sold 14 Apr 1783.

Name	Builder	Laid down	L	Comm
Virginia	Fells Point, Md. (Geo. Wells)	1776	12 Aug 1776	spring 1777

Rate	28 guns
Dimensions	126′4″ (deck) × 34′10″ × 18′, d10′5″
Tonnage	682 tons
Complement	315
Battery	24–12pdr, 2–6pdr (or 6–4pdr)

Notes: Authorized 13 Dec 1775. Designed by Joshua Humphreys.
Service record: Blockaded in Chesapeake Bay. Went aground at Hampton, Va., while trying to run blockade, 31 Mar 1778. Lost rudder and was refloated but surrendered to HMS *Emerald*, 32, and *Conqueror*.
Later history: HMS *Virginia*. BU Dec 1782.

Name	Builder	Laid down	L	Comm
Alliance ex-*Hancock* (29 May 1778)	Salisbury, Mass. (J & W Hackett)	1777	28 Apr 1778	1778

Rate	36 guns
Dimensions	151′ (bp) × 36′ × 12′6″
Tonnage	900 tons
Complement	300
Battery	28–12pdr, 12–9pdr

Notes: Designed by William Hackett. Finest ship in the Continental Navy.
Service record: Took Lafayette to France, Jan 1779. Unit of John Paul Jones's squadron, 1779; flagship, 1780. Collided with *Bonhomme Richard*, 19 Jun 1779. Returned to U.S., 1780. Sailed under John Barry, Feb 1781. Repaired at Boston. Action with HMS *Sybille*, 28, in West Indies (3 killed), 7 Mar 1783. Stranded in Narragansett Bay, requiring repairs, 20 Jun 1783. Sold merchant, unrepaired, 3 Jun 1785; last ship of Continental Navy.
Ships captured: Several ships with *Bonhomme Richard* (q.v.), 1779. One brig, 8 Jan 1780; one ship, 12 Jan 1780; one bark, 5 Feb 1780; privateer *Alert*, 10, and prize (which was released), 4 Mar 1781; privateer *Mars*, 26, privateer *Minerva*, 10, off French coast, 2 Apr 1781; ship HMS *Atalanta*, 20, brig HMS *Trepassy*, 14, in North Atlantic (11 killed), 29 May

The frigate *Alliance*, 36, was one of the most successful ships of the Continental Navy and, in 1785, the last to be sold. (U.S. Naval Historical Center)

1781; one brig, one snow, 2 May 1781; recaptured brigantine *Adventure* in Long Island Sound, 4 Aug, 1782; schr *Polly*, 10 Aug 1782; recaptured sloop *Fortune*, 25 Aug 1782; whaler *Somerset*, 10 Sep 1782; ships *Britannia, Anna, Commerce,* and *Kingston,* 24–28 Sep 1782.

Name	Builder	Laid down	L	Comm
Confederacy	Norwich, Conn. (J. Willets)	1777	8 Nov 1778	Apr 1779

Rate	36 guns
Dimensions	160′; also reported as 154′9″ (deck) × 37′ × 12′3″
Tonnage	959 tons
Complement	260
Battery	28–12pdr, 8–6pdr

Notes: Galley-frigate. Authorized 13 Dec 1775. Completed at New London. Had a complete row of oar ports on lower deck. Figurehead: Greek warrior.
Service record: Voyaged to France with French minister and John Jay, U.S. minister to France, Sep 1779. Captured by HMS *Roebuck*, 44, and *Orpheus*, 32, off Delaware River, 14 Apr 1781.
Ships captured: (With *Boston*) privateer *Poole*, 24, schr *Patsey*, sloop *William*, 6 Jun 1779. Brigantine *Elizabeth & Nancy* in Atlantic, 5 Jan 1781.
Later history: HMS *Confederate*. BU Mar 1782.

Name	Builder	Laid down	L	Comm
Bourbon	Chatham, Conn. (John Cotton)	1779	31 Jul 1783	never

Rate	28 guns
Dimensions	(U)
Tonnage	about 900 tons
Complement	(U)
Battery	(U)

Notes: Authorized by Congress 23 Jan 1777. Little known of this ship. Too deep to cross bar at mouth of Connecticut River. Sold incomplete, Sep 1783.

SLOOPS

Name	Builder	Laid down	L	Comm
Ranger ex-*Hampshire* (1777)	Portsmouth, N.H. (James Hackett)	1777	10 May 1777	Oct 1777

Rate	18 guns
Dimensions	116′ (deck) × 34′ × 13′6″
Tonnage	308 tons
Complement	140
Battery	18–6pdr

Notes: Designed by William Hackett.
Service record: First ship to raise the "Stars and Stripes," 4 Jul 1777. Sailed for France under J. P. Jones, 1 Nov 1777. Received first official salute to an American warship in Europe in Quiberon Bay, France, 14 Feb 1778. Attack on Whitehaven, England; took sloop HMS *Drake*, 14, off Carrickfergus (2 killed), 24 Apr 1778. Captured by British at Charleston, S.C., 11 May 1780.
Ships captured: Brig *Mary*, brig *George*, 23–25 Nov 1777; one brig (sunk) off Cape Clear, 14 Apr 1778; ship *Lord Chatham*, in St. George's Channel, 17 Apr 1778; one schr (sunk), one sloop off Ireland, 20 Apr 1778; brig *Patience* off Ireland, 25 Apr 1778. (With *Boston* and *Providence*) brig *Sally*, 24 Aug 1778; brig *Friends*, 9 Sep 1778; snow *Adventure*, 10 Sep 1778. (With *Queen of France* and *Warren* off Cape Henry) privateer schr, Mar 1779; schr *Hibernia*, 8, 6 Apr 1779; ship *Jason*, 20, ship *Maria* (LofM), brig *Prince Frederick*, brig *Patriot*, brig *Bachelors John*, schr *Chance*, 7 Apr 1779. (With *Queen of France* and *Providence*) ships *Holderness, Dawes, George, Friendship, Blenheim, Thetis, Fort William, Neptune,* and two others off Newfoundland Banks, 15 Jul 1779.
Later history: HMS *Halifax*. Sold 13 Oct 1781.

The sloop *Ranger (left)* engaging HMS *Drake*, 23 April 1778. (U.S. Naval Historical Center, Norman Polmar Collection)

Name	Builder	Laid down	L	Comm
Saratoga	Philadelphia (Wharton & Humphreys)	1779	10 Apr 1780	Aug 1780

Rate	18 guns
Dimensions	68′ (keel) × 25′4″ × 12′
Tonnage	150 tons
Complement	86
Battery	16–9pdr, 2–4pdr

Notes: Ship/sloop.
Service record: Action with brig HMS *Keppel*, 9 Sep 1780. Disappeared at sea off Cap Francais, West Indies, after capturing two ships, 15 Mar 1781.
Ships captured: Ship *Charming Molly*, 22 (LofM), brig *Elizabeth*, 12, *Nancy*, 14, one other, 8 Oct 1780 (all retaken next day by HMS *Intrepid*); ship *Sarah*, 12 Sep 1780; schr *Two Brothers*, *Providence*, 11 Oct 1780; privateer *Resolution*, 20 Dec 1780; *Tonyn*, 20 (LofM), 9 Jan 1781; armed brig *Douglas*, 16 Jan 1781.

SHIPS ACQUIRED IN AMERICA

Name	Builder	Built	Acquired	Comm
Alfred ex–*Black Prince* (8 Nov 1775)	Philadelphia	1774	4 Nov 1775	3 Dec 1775

Rate	24 guns
Dimensions	(U)
Tonnage	440 tons
Complement	220
Battery	24–9pdr; (later) 20–9pdr

Notes: Ship. Philadelphia merchant ship. First U.S. warship to fly the national flag.
Service record: Flagship of Esek Hopkins. Expedition to New Providence Island (6 killed), 17 Feb–7 Apr 1776. Captured by HMS *Ariadne*, 20, and *Ceres*, 14, off Barbados, 9 Mar 1778.
Ships captured: Brig *Active*, 6, off New England, 10 Nov 1776; troop transport *Mellish*, 10, 13 Nov 1776; snow *Hetty* off New England coast, 16 Nov 1776; transport ship, aground at Sable Island (burned), 22 Nov 1776; ship *Surprise*, *Betty*, *Polly*, 24 Nov 1776; ship *John*, 10 (LofM), off Isle Royal, 26 Nov 1776; privateer schr, 16, off Isle Royal, 30 Nov 1776. (With *Raleigh*) one schr (burned), 15 Aug 1777. (With *Raleigh*) brig *Nancy*, one other, 2 Sep 1777.
Later history: HMS *Alfred*, 20. Sold 1782.

Name	Builder	Built	Acquired	Comm
Columbus ex–*Sally*	Philadelphia	1774	Nov 1775	4 Jan 1776

Rate	24 guns
Dimensions	(U)
Tonnage	200 tons
Complement	220
Battery	18–9pdr, 10–6pdr

Notes: Merchantman. Ship. First Continental Navy vessel to capture a British warship.
Service record: Expedition to New Providence Island, 17 Feb–7 Apr

The ship *Alfred* was the first warship to fly the national flag. A converted merchantman, she took several ships before being captured by the British in March 1778. (National Archives)

1776. Captured schr HMS *Hawk*, 6, 4 Apr 1776. Chased ashore at Point Judith, Del., by British squadron and burned, 27 Mar 1778.
Ships captured: Ship *Royal Exchange* off New England coast, 29 Aug 1776; three vessels, Aug 1776.

Name	Builder	Built	Acquired	Comm
Andrew Doria ex–*Defiance*	(U)	(U)	Nov 1775	Jan 1776

Rate	14 guns
Dimensions	(U)
Tonnage	(U)
Complement	112
Battery	14–4pdr

Notes: Brig. Purchased Nov 1775. Converted at Philadelphia.
Service record: Expedition to New Providence Island, 17 Feb–7 Apr 1776. Received first salute to an American flag at St. Eustatius, 16 Nov 1776. Captured sloop HMS *Racehorse*,[1] 8, off Puerto Rico (4 killed), Dec 1776. Defense of Delaware River, Oct–Nov 1777. Burned to prevent capture at Red Bank, N.J., 21 Nov (or 8 Jul) 1777.
Ships captured: Recaptured schr *John and Joseph* off Montauk, 12 Apr 1776; sloop *Two Friends*, two brigs, one sloop off Providence, R.I., 21

[1] Later USS *Racehorse*.

The brig *Andrew Doria*, 14, was a converted merchantman and is celebrated as receiving the first salute to the American flag by a foreign power at St. Eustatius. Painting by W. N. Van Powell. (U.S. Naval Historical Center)

USS *Cabot*, 14, a brig of the Continental Navy captured by the British in 1777. (U.S. Naval Historical Center)

May 1776; transports *Oxford* and *Crawford* off Newfoundland (latter recaptured by HMS *Cerberus*, the former by soldiers on board), 3 Jun 1776; ship *Nathaniel and Elizabeth*, in North Atlantic, 11 Jul 1776; ship *Molly*, brig *Maria* off New England coast, Aug 1776; brig *Peggy*, brig *Lawrence*, brig *Elizabeth*, Sep 1776; snow *Thomas* off U.S. coast, 12 Dec 1776.

Name	Builder	Built	Acquired	Comm
Cabot ex-*Sally*?	(U)	(U)	Nov 1775	1775

Rate	14 guns
Dimensions	74'10" (deck), 53'7" (keel) × 24'8" × d11'4"
Tonnage	189 tons
Complement	80
Battery	14–6pdr

Notes: Brig. Merchant ship.
Service record: Expedition to New Providence Island (4 killed), 17 Feb–7 Apr 1776. Damaged in action with HMS *Glasgow*, 20, off Block Island, Apr 1776. Forced ashore by HMS *Milford*, 32, off Nova Scotia, 3 (or 26) Mar 1777; captured.
Ships captured: Ship *True Blue*, 6, off U.S. New England coast, 26 May 1776; ship *Lowther*, 41°30'N 45°00'W, 27 Sep 1776; ship *Esther* (released), 27 Sep 1776; brig *Watson* off New England coast, 27 Sep 1776; brig *Clarendon*, 2 Oct 1776; brig *Georgiana*, 5 Oct 1776.
Later history: Refloated by British and comm as HMS *Cabot*. Sold 25 Jun 1783.

Name	Builder	Built	Acquired	Comm
Providence ex-*Katy* (1775)	(U)	(U)	3 Dec 1775	9 Jan 1776

Rate	12 guns
Dimensions	70' × (U)
Tonnage	(U)
Complement	90
Battery	12–4pdr; (1776) 12–6pdr; (1779) 6–6pdr, 6–4pdr, 2–2pdr

Notes: Sloop. As *Katy*, used by Rhode Island Committee of Safety, 1775.
Service record: Expedition to New Providence Island, 17 Feb–7 Apr 1776. With *Alfred*, captured brigantine HMS *Active*, 10 Nov 1776. Ran blockade out of Narragansett Bay, Feb 1777. Attacked Fort Nassau, New Providence Island, 27 Jan 1778. Sailed under J. P. Jones until Sep 1776. Took brig HMS *Diligent*,[2] 12, in action off Sandy Hook (4 killed), 7 May 1779. Expedition up Penobscot River, 25 Jul–14 Aug 1779. Destroyed (blown up) in Penobscot River to prevent capture, 14 Aug 1779.
Ships captured: Brigantine *Britannia* off New England coast, 27 Aug 1776; brigantine *Sea Nymph*, 3 Sep 1776; brigantine *Favourite* (later recaptured), 6 Sep 1776; ship *Alexander*, at Canso, N.S., 22 Sep 1776; brig *Kingston Packet*, at Canso, 22 Sep 1776; brig *Success*, at Canso, 22 Sep 1776; brig *Portland*, brig *Defiance*, sloop *Adventure*, ship *Friendship*, schr *John*, schr *Betsey*, schr *Sea Flower*, schr *Ebenezer*, schr *Hope* (the last seven burned), at Madame, N.S., 23 Sep 1776. (With *Alfred*) transport *Mellish*, 10, 13 Nov 1776; snow *Hetty*, 16 Nov 1776. One Jamaica privateer, five others, at Nassau, 27–28 Jan 1778. (With *Queen of France* and *Ranger*) ships *Holderness*, *Dawes*, *George*, *Friendship*, *Blenheim*, *Thetis*, *Fort William*, *Neptune*, and two others off Newfoundland Banks, 15 Jul 1779.
Later history: HMS *Providence*, 12. RR 1781.

---

[2] Later USS *Diligent*.

The sloop *Providence*, 12, which was under command of John Paul Jones in 1776, had a short but successful career. (U.S. Naval Historical Center)

USS *Independence*, a 10-gun sloop of 1775. (U.S. Naval Historical Center)

Name	Builder	Built	Acquired	Comm
Independence	(U)	(U)	1775	(U)

Rate	10 guns
Dimensions	(U)
Tonnage	(U)
Complement	30
Battery	10–9pdr

Notes: Sloop. Rerigged as brig, 1777.
Service record: Defense of Delaware River, Oct–Nov 1777. Wrecked off Ocracoke Inlet, N.C., 24 Apr 1778.
Ships captured: Ship *Sam*, 4 (with $20,000 in coin), 26 Nov 1776.

Name	Builder	Built	Acquired	Comm
Hornet ex-*Falcon*	Baltimore	(U)	Dec 1775	1776

Rate	10 guns
Dimensions	(U)
Tonnage	100 tons
Complement	(U)
Battery	8– or 10–4pdr

Notes: Sloop. Chartered.
Service record: Damaged, unable to go on expedition to New Providence Island, Feb 1776. Defense of Delaware River, Oct–Nov 1777. Either burned on 8 Jul 1777 or blown up in Delaware River in Nov 1777.

Name	Builder	Built	Acquired	Comm
Reprisal ex-*Molly*	(U)	(U)	28 Mar 1776	spring 1776

Rate	16 guns
Dimensions	100' × 30' × (U)
Tonnage	(U)
Complement	130
Battery	16–6pdr

Notes: Brig. Merchantman.
Service record: Action with HMS *Shark*, 16, off St. Pierre, Martinique, 27 Jul 1776. Under Lambert Wickes, first Continental Navy ship to arrive in Europe, bringing Benjamin Franklin to France, 29 Nov 1776. Foundered off Newfoundland (1 survivor), Oct 1777.
Ships captured: Ship *Friendship* at 33°N 57°W, 11 Jul 1776; schr *Peter*, 13 Jul 1776; *Neptune*, *Duchess of Leinster*, Jul 1776; two brigs en route to France, Nov 1776; brig *Hibernia*, brig *Generous Friends*, Feb 1777; snow *Swallow* (1 killed), 5 Feb 1777; *Polly & Nancy*, ship *Betty*, Feb 1777. (With *Lexington* and *Dolphin* in Bay of Biscay) sloop *Merrion*, brig *Expedition* (sunk), ship *Belleisle*, 19 Jun 1777; brig *Jenny & Sally*, sloop *Jason*, sloop *Jenny & Peggy* (sunk), sloop *Edward & Ann*, 20 Jun 1777; bark *John & Thomas*, 21 Jun 1777; brig *Graystock*, brig *Favorite* (sunk), 22 Jun 1777; ship *Grace* (sunk), brig *Peggy*, brig *Crawford*, 23 Jun 1777.

Name	Builder	Built	Acquired	Comm
Lexington ex-*Wild Duck*	Bermuda	(U)	13 Mar 1776	Mar 1776

Rate	14 guns
Dimensions	86' (bp) × 24'6" × 9'
Tonnage	(U)
Complement	84 or 110
Battery	16–4pdr; (1777) 2–6pdr, 14–4pdr

Notes: Brigantine. Purchased at St. Eustatius by Maryland Committee of Safety. Turned over to Continental Navy, 13 Mar 1776.

The sloop *Hornet* was one of several ships lost when the fleet was trapped by the British in the Delaware River during 1777. (U.S. Naval Historical Center)

Service record: John Barry, captain. Action against and captured sloop HMS *Edward*,[3] 6, off Virginia Capes (2 killed), 7 Apr 1776. Captured by frigate HMS *Pearl*, 32, off Delaware Capes, 20 Dec 1776; later retaken by crew. Blockaded in Brittany, but ordered to leave and captured by HMS *Alert*, 10, off Ushant, 19 Sep 1777. (7 killed)

Ships captured: Privateer *Lady Susan*, 27 Jul 1776; sloop *Betsey*, Sep 1776. (With *Reprisal* and *Dolphin* in Bay of Biscay) sloop *Merrion*, brig *Expedition* (sunk), ship *Belleisle*, 19 Jun 1777; brig *Jenny & Sally*, sloop *Jason*, sloop *Jenny & Peggy* (sunk), sloop *Edward & Ann*, 20 Jun 1777; bark *John & Thomas*, 21 Jun 1777; brig *Graystock*, brig *Favorite* (sunk), 22 Jun 1777; ship *Grace* (sunk), brig *Peggy*, brig *Crawford*, 23 Jun 1777.

Name	Builder	Built	Acquired	Comm
Hampden	(U)	(U)	summer 1776	Sep 1776

Rate	14 guns
Dimensions	(U)
Tonnage	(U)
Complement	(U)
Battery	(U)

[3] Later USS *Sachem*.

The Continental brigs *Reprisal* and *Lexington*, which operated together in 1777. (U.S. Naval Historical Center)

Notes: Brigantine. Merchantman purchased in 1776; converted at New Haven, Conn.
Service record: Sold after running ashore, late 1777.

Name	Builder	Built	Acquired	Comm
Resistance	(U)	(U)	24 Apr 1777	Aug 1777

Rate	10 guns
Dimensions	(U)
Tonnage	(U)
Complement	(U)
Battery	10–4pdr

Notes: Brigantine/brig. Purchased at Stonington, Conn.
Service record: Captured by British squadron off Cape Cod, 27 Aug 1778.
Ship captured: One prize, Dec 1777.

Name	Builder	Built	Acquired	Comm
Wasp	Baltimore	1775	Dec 1775	Dec 1775/ Jan 1776
ex-*Scorpion*				

Rate	8 guns
Dimensions	(U)
Tonnage	(U)
Complement	(U)
Battery	8–2pdr

Notes: Schooner.
Service record: With *Hornet*, was one of first two Continental Navy ships to go to sea, 14 Jan 1776. Expedition to New Providence Island, 17 Feb–7 Apr 1776. Defense of Delaware River, Oct–Nov 1777. Either burned on 8 Jul 1777 or run aground and destroyed in Delaware River in Nov 1777.
Ships captured: Brig *Betsey*, in Delaware Bay, 9 May 1776; ship *Leghorn Galley*, 4 Oct 1776; schr *Two Brothers*, one unnamed schr, Dec 1776. Recaptured ship *Success*.

SHIPS ACQUIRED IN EUROPE

Name	Builder	Laid down	L	Comm
L'Indien	Amsterdam	1777	1777	never

Rate	40 guns
Dimensions	172'6" (bp), 154' (deck) × 43'3" × 16'6"
Tonnage	1,430 tons; also reported as 1,186 tons
Complement	550
Battery	28–36pdr, 12–12pdr

Notes: Frigate. Her unusually heavy armament caused her to hog (the ends to droop). Built for U.S. but British diplomatic pressure forced sale to France.
Service record: Chartered to South Carolina and renamed **South Carolina**, 30 May 1780. Captured by HMS *Astraea*, *Diomede*, and *Quebec* off Delaware Capes, 20 Dec 1782.
Ships captured: One cutter, one privateer, brig *Venus*, seven other vessels, Aug–Oct 1781.

The schooner *Wasp*, 8, was one of the first Continental ships to go to sea in 1776. (U.S. Naval Historical Center)

Name	Builder	Built	Acquired	Comm
Queen of France	Lorient, France	(U)	1777	1778
ex—*La Brune*				

Rate	28 guns
Dimensions	(U)
Tonnage	(U)
Complement	(U)
Battery	(U)

Notes: Frigate. Purchased in France; arrived in Boston, Dec 1778. Sunk to prevent capture at Charleston, S.C., 11 May 1780.
Ships captured: (With *Ranger* and *Warren* off Cape Henry) privateer schr, 14, Mar 1779; privateer schr *Hibernia*, 8, 6 Apr 1779; ship *Jason*, 20, ship *Maria* (LofM), brig *Prince Ferdinand* (or *Frederick*), brig *Patriot*, brig *Bachelors John*, schr *Chance*, 7 Apr 1779. (With *Providence* and *Ranger*) ships *Holderness, Dawes, George, Friendship, Blenheim, Thetis, Fort William, Neptune*, and two others off Newfoundland Banks, 15 Jul 1779. Privateer *Dolphin*, 12, 5 Dec 1779.

Name	Builder	Laid down	L	Comm
Deane	Nantes, France	1777	1777	Jan 1779

Rate	32 guns
Dimensions	96' (keel) × 32' × (U)
Tonnage	517 tons
Complement	550
Battery	24–12pdr, 2–6pdr, 8–4pdr

Notes: Frigate. Built in France and taken to U.S. for completion.
Service record: Arrived at Philadelphia, May 1778. Renamed **Hague** Sep 1782. Sold 1783.

USS *Bonhomme Richard*, 42, as depicted by E. Tufnell. The frigate under John Paul Jones scored the Navy's most important victory of the Revolution. (U.S. Naval Historical Center)

Ships captured: Armed ship *Viper*, Apr 1779. (With *Boston*) schr *Tryall*, 10 (LofM), *Glencairn*, 20 (LofM), ship *Sandwich*, 16, brig *Venture*, 2, ship *Thorne*, 14, schr *Flying Fish*, 10 (LofM), 2 Aug–24 Sep 1779. Several vessels, Mar 1780; ship *Regulator*, 18, ship *Mary*, brig *Swallow*, 16, schr HMS *Jackal*, 14, 1782; ship *Baille*, Jan 1783.

Name	Builder	Built	Acquired	Comm
Bonhomme Richard ex–*Duc de Duras*	France	1765	4 Feb 1779	Feb 1779

Rate	42 guns
Dimensions	152′ (deck), 128′ (keel) × 40′ × d19′
Tonnage	998 tons
Complement	375
Battery	6–18pdr, 28–12pdr, 8–9pdr

Notes: Frigate. Built for French East India Co. Served in French Navy, 1769–71 and 1778–79. Presented (or loaned) to U.S.
Service record: Under J. P. Jones, defeated HMS *Serapis*, 44, in action off Flamborough Head, 23 Sep, and sank as a result of damage (49 killed), 25 Sep 1779. During the battle, Jones said, "I have not yet begun to fight."

Ships captured: (With *Alliance*, *Pallas*, and *Vengeance*) ship *Die Verwagting* (prize) in English Channel, 18 Aug 1779; brig *Mayflower*, 21 Aug 1779; brig *Fortune* off Cape Clear, 24 Aug 1779; ship *Betsey*, off coast of Scotland, 31 Aug 1779; privateer *Union*, 22, off Cape Wrath, 1 Sep 1779; one brig, two sloops, 3 Sep 1779; one ship, one brigantine, 14 Sep 1779; one brig, two sloops off Cape Leith, 19 Sep 1779; one sloop, two brigantines off Flamborough Head, 20 Sep 1779.

Name	Builder	L	Acquired	Comm
Ariel ex-HMS *Ariel*	Blackwall (Perry)	7 Jul 1777	spring 1780	1780

Rate	20 guns
Dimensions	108′ × 30′ × (U)
Tonnage	435 tons
Complement	45
Battery	16–9pdr; also reported as 26–9pdr

Notes: British sloop of war captured 10 Sep 1779 by French frigate *Amazone*. Given to U.S.

Service record: Commanded by J. P. Jones. Dismasted and damaged in severe storm off Lorient, 8 Oct 1780. Action with British privateer *Triumph*, 20, in Atlantic, Dec 1780. Returned to France, Jun 1781.
Later history: French *Ariel*. Lost in the Escaut, 21 Mar 1793.

Name	Builder	Built	Acquired	Comm
Revenge	(U)	(U)	May 1777	Jul 1777

Rate	14 guns
Dimensions	(U)
Tonnage	(U)
Complement	106
Battery	14–6pdr

Notes: Cutter. Purchased in France.
Service record: Under Conyngham, conducted successful commerce raids. Captured a total of 60 British vessels and destroyed 33 during 1777. Sold 12 Mar 1779.
Ships captured: *Black Prince* and about 20 small vessels off British and French coasts, Jul 1777; schr *Happy Return* (burned), 21 Jul 1777; brig *Maria* (burned), 23 Jul 1777; brig *Patty*, 25 Jul 1777; brigantine *Northampton* (later recaptured), 26 Jul 1777; two privateers and several other ships, Nov 1777.
Later history: Captured as privateer by HMS *Galatea* off New York, 27 Apr 1779.

Name	Builder	Built	Acquired	Comm
Dolphin	(U)	U	Feb 1777	May 1777

Rate	10 guns
Dimensions	(U)
Tonnage	(U)
Complement	(U)
Battery	(U)

Notes: Cutter. Purchased at Dover, England; outfitted at Nantes, France.
Ships captured: (With *Reprisal* and *Lexington* in Bay of Biscay) sloop *Merrion*, brig *Expedition* (sunk), and ship *Belleisle*, 19 Jun 1777; brig *Jenny & Sally*, sloop *Jason*, sloop *Jenny & Peggy* (sunk), sloop *Edward & Ann*, 20 Jun 1777; bark *John & Thomas*, 21 Jun 1777; brig *Graystock*, brig *Favorite* (sunk), 22 Jun 1777; ship *Grace* (sunk), brig *Peggy*, brig *Crawford*, 23 Jun 1777.
Later history: Converted to packet at St. Malo, France, Jul 1777. Later seized by British as prize at Lorient.

Name	Builder	Built	Acquired	Comm
Surprize ex–*Admiral Pocock*	(U)	(U)	Apr 1777	1777

Rate	10 guns
Dimensions	67′8″ × 28′11″ × 9′
Tonnage	(U)
Complement	(U)
Battery	(U)

Notes: Sloop. Purchased in England; fitted out at Dunkerque, France. Possibly a former Royal Navy sloop built in 1779.
Service record: Sailed under Conyngham. Seized by French, May 1777.

Ships captured: Brig *Joseph* off Holland (released), 4 May 1777; packet brig *Prince of Orange* off Holland (released), 3 May 1777.

Name	Builder	Built	Acquired	Comm
Vengeance	France	(U)	1779	1779

Rate	12 guns
Dimensions	(U)
Tonnage	(U)
Complement	(U)
Battery	12–6pdr

Notes: Brig. Fitted out by French government. Former merchantman and dockyard tender.
Service record: Sailed with squadron under J. P. Jones, 19 Jun 1779. Returned to France, 1783.
Ships captured: Several ships with *Bonhomme Richard* (q.v.), 1779.

Name	Builder	Built	Acquired	Comm
Duc de Lauzun	(U)	(U)	Oct 1782	Jan 1783

Rate	20 guns
Dimensions	(U)
Tonnage	(U)
Complement	(U)
Battery	(U)

Notes: Ship. Purchased at Dover, England; outfitted at Nantes, France.
Service record: Transported 72,000 Spanish dollars from Havana, 1783. Loaned to France, Apr 1783.

Name	Builder	Built	Acquired	Comm
Pallas	France	1778	1779	spring 1779

Rate	30 guns
Dimensions	(U)
Tonnage	(U)
Complement	(U)
Battery	26–9pdr, 6–4pdr

Notes: Ship. French privateer. Turned over to U.S., 1779.
Service record: Part of J. P. Jones's squadron that captured a number of vessels (see *Bonhomme Richard*). Attacked a large convoy and captured sloop HMS *Countess of Scarborough*, 23 Sep 1779. Returned to France at end of war.

PRIZES TAKEN INTO SERVICE

Name	Builder	Built	Acquired	Comm
Sachem ex-HMS *Edward*	(U)	(U)	2 May 1776	Jun 1776

Rate	10 guns
Dimensions	(U)
Tonnage	(U)
Complement	(U)
Battery	10–9pdr

Notes: Sloop. Captured by USS *Lexington* off Virginia Capes, 7 Apr 1776.
Service record: Defense of Delaware River, Oct–Nov 1777. Believed burned to prevent capture in Delaware River, Nov 1777.
Ship captured: Brig *Three Brothers*, 6 (LofM), off the Delaware River (3 killed), 6 Jul 1776.

Name	Builder	Built	Acquired	Comm
Racehorse	(U)	(U)	Dec 1776	1777
ex-HMS *Racehorse*, ex–*Marquis de Vaudreuil* (1757)				

Rate	10 guns
Dimensions	96′6″ × 30′ × (U)
Tonnage	385 bm
Complement	(U)
Battery	10–9pdr

Notes: Sloop. Captured by USS *Andrew Doria* off Puerto Rico, Dec 1776. Former French privateer captured by British in 1757.
Service record: Blockaded at Philadelphia. Defense of Delaware River, Oct–Nov 1777. Burned to prevent capture at Philadelphia, 15 Nov 1777. Reportedly renamed ***Surprize***.

Name	Builder	Built	Acquired	Comm
General Gates	Bristol, England	1764	19 Dec 1777	24 May 1778
ex–*Industrious Bee*				

Rate	18 guns
Dimensions	(U)
Tonnage	160 tons
Complement	100
Battery	16–4pdr

Notes: Brig. British merchantman, captured by USS *Lee* en route from Gibraltar to Newfoundland, 29 Aug 1777.
Service record: Ordered sold, 2 Jun 1779. Conveyed prisoners from Boston to New York, Aug 1779, then sold.
Ships captured: (With privateer *Hawk*) ship *Jenny*, brigantine *Thomas*, brigantine *Nancy*, Aug 1778. Schr *Polly*, Aug 1778; brigantine *Montague* after 5 hour engagement (captain killed), 3 Aug 1778; schr *Friendship* off Casco, Maine, 4 Dec 1778; schr *General Leslie* off Bermuda, Feb 1779. (With *Hazard*) brig *Active*, brig *Union*, 16 Mar 1779.

Name	Builder	Built	Acquired	Comm
Argo	(U)	(U)	spring 1779	(U)
ex-HMS *Pigot*				

Rate	8 guns
Dimensions	(U)
Tonnage	200 tons
Complement	45
Battery	8–12pdr

Notes: Brig purchased by Royal Navy in U.S., Jul 1778; armed by British and cut down to galley. Taken by Maj. Silas Talbot in U.S. sloop *Hawke* in Narragansett Bay, 28 Oct 1778. Possibly later burned.

Name	Builder	Built	Acquired	Comm
Diligent	U.S.	1776	1779	(U)
ex-HMS *Diligent*				

Rate	12 guns
Dimensions	88′5″ (deck) × 24′8″ × d10′10″
Tonnage	236 tons
Complement	50
Battery	(in RN) 10–3pdr; (in USN) 14–4pdr

Notes: Brig. Captured by USS *Providence* off Newfoundland, 7 May 1779.
Service record: Expedition up Penobscot River, 25 Jul–14 Aug 1779. Run ashore and burned to prevent capture near Castine, Maine, 14 Aug 1779.

MISCELLANEOUS VESSELS

Name	Builder	Built	Acquired	Comm
Hannah	(U)	(U)	24 Aug 1775	5 Sep 1775

Rate	4 guns
Dimensions	(U)
Tonnage	78 tons
Complement	(U)
Battery	4–4pdr

Notes: Schooner. First armed vessel to sail under Continental Navy flag.
Service record: Captured first prize of war, 7 Sep 1775. Run ashore during engagement with sloop HMS *Nautilus* near Beverly, Mass., 10 Oct 1775; refloated and later sold.
Ship captured: Sloop *Unity*, 7 Sep 1775.

A model of the schooner *Hannah*, which was reputed to be the first armed vessel to sail under the Continental flag. (Smithsonian Institution)

"WASHINGTON'S SCHOONERS"

The following seven ships were acquired by Gen. George Washington and were not part of the Continental Navy.

Name	Builder	Built	Acquired	Comm
Hancock ex-*Speedwell*	(U)	(U)	Oct 1775	1775

Rate	6 guns
Dimensions	60′ × 20′ × (U)
Tonnage	72 tons
Complement	70
Battery	6–4pdr

Notes: Schooner. Returned to owner, 1777.
Service record: Ran ashore during engagement with HMS *Hope*, 14, off Plymouth, Mass., 30 Jan 1776; refloated.
Ships captured: Two transports, 25 Jan 1776; two brigs off Boston, 7 May 1776.

Name	Builder	Built	Acquired	Comm
Franklin	(U)	(U)	1775	1775

Rate	6 guns
Dimensions	(U)
Tonnage	60 tons
Complement	21
Battery	(U)

Notes: Marblehead fishing schooner. Returned to owner, 1776.
Ship captured: Ship *Hope*, 17 May 1776.

Name	Builder	Built	Acquired	Comm
Harrison ex-*Triton*	(U)	1761	22 Oct 1775	1775

Rate	6 guns
Dimensions	(U)
Tonnage	(U)
Complement	(U)
Battery	4–4pdr

Notes: Schooner.
Service record: Decomm, early 1776.
Ships captured: Two British ships, 5 Nov 1775; two other prizes, Nov 1775.

Name	Builder	Built	Acquired	Comm
Washington ex-*Endeavor*	(U)	(U)	Oct 1775	Nov 1775

Rate	10 guns
Dimensions	(U)
Tonnage	160 tons
Complement	74
Battery	6–6pdr, 4–4pdr

Notes: Schooner, rerigged as brigantine. Acquired by Washington and converted at Plymouth, Mass.
Service record: Captured by HMS *Fowey*, 20, off Cape Ann, Mass., 3 Dec 1775.
Ship captured: Sloop *Britannia*, 25 Nov 1775.

Name	Builder	Built	Acquired	Comm
Warren ex-*Hawk*	Marblehead, Mass.	(U)	Oct 1775	Oct 1775

Rate	4 guns
Dimensions	(U)
Tonnage	64 tons
Complement	50
Battery	4–4pdr

Notes: Schooner.
Service record: Unsuccessful attack on troopship *Unity* off Cape Ann (3 killed), Jun 1776. Captured by HMS *Liverpool*, 28, off Nova Scotia, 26 Aug 1776.
Ships captured: Schr *Rainbow*, 27 Nov 1775; recaptured brig *Sally* (prize), 24 Dec 1775.
Later history: Tender to HMS *Milford*. Ran aground in storm near Portsmouth, N.H., end of Dec 1776.

Name	Builder	Built	Acquired	Comm
Lee (U) ex–*Two Brothers*	(U)	Oct 1775	28 Oct 1775	

Rate	(U)
Dimensions	(U)
Tonnage	74 tons
Complement	(U)
Battery	4–4pdr, 2–2pdr, 10 swivels

Notes: Schooner. Purchased as replacement for *Hannah*. Returned to owner, Nov 1777.
Ships captured: Sloop *Polly*, 27 Nov 1775; prize British brig *Nancy*, 29 Nov 1775; ship *Concord*, early Dec 1776. (With *Franklin*) sloop *Rainbow*, 29 Jan 1776; brigantine *Henry and Esther*, 1 Feb 1776. (With squadron under Manley) merchant *Susannah*, transport *Stokesby*, Feb 1776; transport *Anne*, 7 Jun 1776; brig *Elizabeth*, Nov 1776. Schr *Hawke*, 13 Apr 1777; sloop *Betsey*, 3 May 1777; brigantine *Charles* (later recaptured), 10 May 1777; brigantine *Capelin*, brigantine *Industry*, May 1777; brig *Industrious Bee*,[4] 29 Aug 1777; snow *Lively* (later recaptured), 30 Aug 1777; brigantine *Dolphin*, Sep 1777.

Name	Builder	Built	Acquired	Comm
Lynch	(U)	(U)	26 Jan 1776	1 Feb 1776

Rate	4 guns
Dimensions	(U)
Tonnage	(U)
Complement	(U)
Battery	2–4pdr, 2–2pdr

Notes: Schooner, chartered.
Service record: Joined Manley's squadron at Cape Ann, Feb 1776. Escaped capture by British fleet, 27 Sep 1776. Captured by HMS *Foudroyant*, 80, off Belle Isle while sailing from France to America with dispatches, 19 May 1777.
Ships captured: (With squadron under Manley) brig *Elizabeth*, 2 Apr 1776; transport *Anne*, 7 Jun 1776.

[4] Later USS *General Gates*.

LOCAL OR SUBSIDIARY VESSELS

Name	Rate	Type	Built	Acquired	Battery
Active		brigantine		Jul 1779	
Argo	12	schr		24 Mar 1779	12–6pdr
ex-*Sally*					
Baltimore	12	brigantine	1777	1777	
Champion	8	xebec		1777	2–24pdr, 2–18pdr, 4–9pdr
Despatch		packet		1778	
Enterprise	8	schr		20 Dec 1776	
Fame		schr			
Fly	6	schr		Jan 1776	6–9pdr
General Arnold		schr		1776	
General Mifflin		sloop		Apr 1776	
General Schuyler		sloop		1776	
General Washington	32	ship		Aug 1782	24– or 18–9pdr, 2–6pdr
ex-*Congress*, ex-*General Monck*					
Georgia Packet				Nov 1776	
Hawke		sloop		Oct 1778	
Hornsnake		schr		1775	
Lady Washington	10	galley	1776	1776	
Mercury		ketch	1776	1780	
Mercury		schr	1781		
Morris	24	ship	1778	Feb 1779	16–6pdr, 8–4pdr
ex-*Rebecca*					
Morris		schr		1779	
Mosquito	4	sloop		late 1775	
Phoenix	2	packet		1778	
Repulse	8	xebec	1775	1777	2–24pdr, 2–18pdr, 4–9pdr
Retaliation		brigantine		1778	
Spitfire	1	galley	1775	Jan 1776	1–18pdr
Spy		schr		1776	
Washington	1	galley	1775	Jan 1776	1–18pdr
West Florida	14	sloop		Sep 1779	

The schooner *Fly*, 8, and sloop *Mosquito*, 4. (U.S. Naval Historical Center)

Notes and service records:

Active: Captured by HMS *Proserpine* off Havana, 23 Mar 1782.

Argo: Rhode Island privateer, 14 Apr 1780.

Baltimore: Dispatch vessel. Lost near Cape Henry, 29 Jan 1780.

Champion: Pennsylvania State Marine, loaned to Continental Navy. Defense of Philadelphia, 1777. Burned to prevent capture in Delaware River, 21 Nov 1777.

Delaware: Defense of Delaware River, Oct–Nov 1777. Destroyed at Philadelphia, 21 Nov 1777.

Enterprise: LofM purchased. Operated in Chesapeake Bay, 1776–77. Returned to owner, Feb 1777.

Fly: Purchased at Baltimore as dispatch vessel. Sometimes called **Cruizer**. Expedition to New Providence Island, 17 Feb–7 Apr 1776. Damaged in engagement with enemy ship, 1776; repaired at Philadelphia. Defense of Delaware River, Oct–Nov 1777. Burned to prevent capture in the Delaware, late 1777.

General Arnold: Purchased to carry dispatches. Out of service after 1778.

General Mifflin: Acquired for local defense of New York.

General Schuyler: Purchased at New York. Probably destroyed in Hudson River after British captured New York in Aug 1776. Comm in state navy. Trfd to Gen. Washington, Apr 1776.

Ships captured: Recaptured five prizes taken by British, Jun 1776.

General Washington: Rhode Island privateer, 1780. Captured by British, renamed *General Monck*, Sep 1781. Captured by Pennsylvania state gunboat *Hyder Aly* off Cape May, 8 Apr 1782. Renamed **General Washington**, 1782. Employed as packet to France. Sold to owner, summer 1784.

Georgia Packet: Despatch vessel, 1776–77.

Hawke: Under Talbot, captured HMS *Pigot*[5] in Narragansett Bay, 28 Oct 1778.

Hornsnake: Chartered 1775–76.

Lady Washington: Borrowed from New York Committee of Safety for defense of New York. FFU.

Mercury: Captured off Newfoundland Banks by HMS *Vestal* and *Fairy* while carrying despatches to America, 10 Sep 1780. Built at Philadelphia by Wharton & Humphrey. Dimensions: 72'6" (deck) × 20'6" × 8'9".

Mercury: Dispatch vessel. Built at Plymouth, Mass., by John Peck. FFU.

Morris: Captured on Mississippi River, 1778? Wrecked in hurricane (11 killed), 18 Aug 1779.

Morris: Presented to American forces for use on Mississippi River. Captured by British sloop *West Florida* in Lake Pontchartrain, Sep 1779.

Mosquito: Destroyed to prevent capture in Delaware Bay, 1777.

Repulse: Pennsylvania State Marine, loaned to Continental Navy. Defense of Philadelphia, 1777. Burned to prevent capture in Delaware River, Jul or 21 Nov 1777.

Retaliation: Operated in Philadelphia area, 1778.

Spitfire and *Washington:* Built by Rhode Island. Recaptured British prizes brigantine *Georgia Packet* and sloop *Speedwell*, 11 Apr 1776. Fought action with British *Phoenix* and *Rose*. At New York, 3 Aug 1776. Destroyed before 1778.

West Florida: British sloop taken by USS *Morris* on Lake Pontchartrain, Sep 1779. Sold at Philadelphia, 1780.

Ship captured: One small vessel in Gulf of Mexico, 1780.

[5] Later USS *Argo*.

SUBMARINE

Name	Builder	Built	Acquired	Comm
Turtle (or *American Turtle*)	Saybrook, Conn.	1775	(U)	(U)

Dimensions	7'6" long, 6' deep
Complement	1
Armament	1 "torpedo"

Notes: Designed by David Bushnell in 1771.
Service record: Attempted attack on British flagship *Eagle*, 64, in New York harbor, 7 Sep 1776; unsuccessful because of failure of the "torpedo." Two further attempts also failed. Lost on board a sloop sunk by the British squadron during the fall of Fort Washington, N.Y., 9 Oct 1776.

LAKE CHAMPLAIN SQUADRON

Congress authorized an attack on Quebec in August 1775 but the American force under Benedict Arnold was weak and undersupplied and the result was a disastrous defeat. The Americans retreated the following spring to Fort Ticonderoga, and both sides immediately began assembling a fleet to control Lake Champlain, the strategic key to the northeast.

A shipbuilding yard was erected at Skenesboro, N.Y. (now Whitehall), but the lack of supplies and men as well as a divided command seriously hindered construction. Arnold took charge and soon two schooners, a sloop, and seven gundalows were ready. The gundalow was a form of river barge with a high curved bow and lateen mainsail, propelled by oars.

The British brought some ships down from the St. Lawrence River. Two schooners, a gundalow, and twenty gunboats were stripped bare and hauled overland to Saint-Jean (now in Quebec). The 180-ton *Inflexible* on the stocks at Quebec and not yet planked was broken up and hauled over as well. By the end of August the British fleet consisted of the ship *Inflexible*, 18; schooners *Maria*, 14, and *Carleton*, 12; gundalow *Loyal Consort*, 7; the twenty gunboats; and radeau *Thunderer*, 12, built at Saint-Jean.

On 11 October 1776 the fleets joined battle off Valcour Island. The British fleet under Sir Guy Carleton was manned by experienced sailors, in contrast to Arnold's motley crews. After a seven-hour engagement, most of the American ships were out of action The surviving ships were destroyed in a second action two days later. Although the battle was lost, the delay caused British plans to be held over until the following year, enabling the Americans to reinforce their troops and defeat their enemy at Saratoga.

Name	Builder	Built	Acquired	Comm
Enterprise	(U)	(U)	May 1775	May 1775

Rate	12 guns
Dimensions:	(U)
Tonnage	70 tons
Complement	50
Battery	12–4pdr

Notes: British supply sloop. Captured by Arnold at Saint-Jean, Richelieu River, Quebec, 19 May 1775.
Service record: Expedition to capture Montreal, Aug 1775. Battle of Valcour Island, 11 Oct 1776. Run aground and burned (or blown up) to prevent capture at Skenesboro, N.Y., 5 Jul 1777.

Name	Builder	Built	Acquired	Comm
Liberty	Skenesboro, N.Y.	(U)	11 May 1775	(U)

Rate	8 guns
Dimensions	(U)
Tonnage	(U)
Complement	(U)
Battery	2–4pdr, 4–2pdr

Notes: Schooner. Captured by Arnold, 11 May 1775.
Service record: Raid on St. Jean, Quebec, 16 May 1775. Destroyed, summer 1777.

Name	Builder	Built	Acquired	Comm
Revenge	Fort Ticonderoga (Baldwin)	(U)	1776	1776

Rate	8 guns
Dimensions	(U)
Tonnage	(U)
Complement	35
Battery	4–4pdr, 4–2pdr

Notes: Schooner.
Service record: Battle of Valcour Island, 11 Oct 1776. Captured with Fort Ticonderoga, Jul 1777. Or sunk to prevent capture.

Name	Builder	Built	Acquired	Comm
Royal Savage ex–*Brave Savage*	Saint-Jean, Quebec	1775	1775	1776

Rate	12 guns
Dimensions	50' × 15' × (U)
Tonnage	70 tons
Complement	40/50
Battery	4–6pdr, 8–4pdr

Notes: British schr. Sunk in Oct 1775 during siege of Saint-Jean; raised and repaired by U.S.
Service record: Ran aground and was burned, Battle of Valcour Island, 11 Oct 1776. (Also reported sunk by American batteries in Richelieu River.)

Name	Builder	Built	L	Comm
Congress	Skenesboro, N.Y.	(U)	1776	1776
Trumbull	Skenesboro, N.Y.	(U)	10 Sep 1776	Sep 1776
Washington	Skenesboro, N.Y.	(U)	fall 1776	Sep 1776

Rate	10 guns
Dimensions	72'4" × 19'7" × 6'2"
Tonnage	123 tons
Complement	80
Battery	1–18pdr, 1–12pdr, 2–9pdr, 6–6pdr, except *Congress*: 2–12pdr, 2–8pdr, 4–6pdr

THE CONTINENTAL NAVY, 1775–1783 17

Notes: Galleys. Two-mast lateen rig. Built by Arnold.
Service records:
Congress: Battle of Valcour Island (20 killed), 11 Oct 1776; damaged and run ashore. Burned to prevent capture, 12 Oct, or near Crown Point, 15 Oct 1776.
Trumbull: Battle of Valcour Island, 11 Oct 1776. Captured by British and destroyed, 1777.
Washington: Battle of Valcour Island, 11 Oct 1776; heavily damaged. Captured by British at Valcour, 13 Oct 1776; taken into British service and rerigged as brig.

Name	Builder	Built	Acquired	Comm
Gates	Skenesboro, N.Y.	1776	1776	late 1776

Rate	8 guns
Dimensions	60'6″ × 19' × 6'2″
Tonnage	123 tons
Complement	80
Battery	4–18pdr

Notes: Galley.
Service record: Blown up to prevent capture at Skenesboro, N.Y., 1777.

Name	Builder	Built	Acquired	Comm
Lee	Skenesboro, N.Y.	1775	Oct 1775	6 Sep 1776

Rate	6 guns
Dimensions	43'9″ (deck) × 16'3″ × 4'8″
Tonnage	48 tons
Complement	86
Battery	1–12pdr, 1–9pdr, 4–4pdr

Notes: Galley. Begun by British at Saint-Jean, Quebec, captured there, and taken to Skenesboro for completion.
Service record: Battle of Valcour Island, 11 Oct 1776; run aground near Crown Point, 13 Oct 1776.
Raised and taken into Royal Navy, 1777.

Name	Builder	Built	Acquired	Comm
Boston	Skenesboro, N.Y.	1776	1776	1776
Connecticut	Skenesboro, N.Y.	1776	1776	1776
Jersey	Skenesboro, N.Y.	1776	1776	1776
New Haven	Skenesboro, N.Y.	1776	1776	1776
New York	Skenesboro, N.Y.	1776	1776	1776
Philadelphia	Skenesboro, N.Y.	1776	1776	1776
Providence	Skenesboro, N.Y.	1776	1776	1776
Spitfire	Skenesboro, N.Y.	1776	1776	1776
Success	Skenesboro, N.Y.	1776	1776	1776

Rate	3 guns
Dimensions	53'4″ × 15'6″ × 3'10″
Battery	1–12pdr, 2–9pdr or 6pdr

Notes: Gundalows. Small wooden warships carrying a single gun in the bows and propelled by oars, built under the direction of Benedict Arnold.
Service records:
Boston: Battle of Valcour Island, 11 Oct 1776. Burned to avoid capture at Buttonmold Bay, N.Y., 13 Oct 1776.
Connecticut: Battle of Valcour Island, 11 Oct 1776. Burned to prevent capture after Battle of Split Rock, N.Y., 17 Oct 1777.
Jersey: Battle of Valcour Island, 11 Oct 1776; abandoned and captured by British, 13 Oct 1776.
Providence: Battle of Valcour Island, 11 Oct 1776; sunk, 13 Oct 1776.
New Haven: Battle of Valcour Island, 11 Oct 1776; burned, 13 Oct 1776.
New York: Battle of Valcour Island, 11 Oct 1776; burned, 13 Oct 1776.
Philadelphia: Battle of Valcour Island, 11 Oct 1776; sunk. Raised in 1935. On display at Smithsonian Institution.
Spitfire: Battle of Valcour Island, 11 Oct 1776. Burned to prevent capture, 13 Oct 1776.

2
STATE NAVIES, 1775–1783

Among the original thirteen states, only New Jersey and Delaware had no navy. The vessels of the other eleven states are listed below. The state navies' vessels were smaller and less well armed than those of the Continental Navy.

CONNECTICUT

Name	Rate	Type	Builder	Built
Oliver Cromwell	18	ship	Saybrook, Conn.	Aug 1776
Minerva		brig		
Defence	14	brigantine		
Guilford	8	sloop		
Schuyler		sloop		
Mifflin		schr		
Spy	6	schr		
Crane		row galley		
Shark		row galley		
Whiting		row galley		

Notes and service records:
Defence: Wrecked off Connecticut, Mar 1779.
Oliver Cromwell: Captured off Sandy Hook, 5 Jun 1779.
　Ships captured: Brigantine *Honor*, packet *Weymouth*, summer 1777; *Admiral Keppel* (LofM), 1778.

GEORGIA

Name	Rate	Type	Builder	Built
Bulloch		row galley		
Congress				
Lee				
Washington				

MARYLAND

Name	Rate	Type	Builder	Built
Defence	22	ship		
Defence		brig		
Dolphin		brig		
Reformation		brig		
Revenge		brig		
Experiment		brig		
Fearnought		brig		
Intrepid		brig		
Protector		brig		
Somerset		brig		
Terrible		brig		
Venus		brig		
Dolphin		schr		
Resolution		schr		
Annapolis		row galley		
Baltimore		row galley		
Chester		row galley		
Conqueror		row galley		
Independence		row galley		
Johnson		row galley		
Plater		armed boat		
Amelia		tender		

MASSACHUSETTS

On 2 Feb 1776, the Massachusetts legislature authorized the building of ten sloops of war of 110–115 tons burden. By 1779 all the vessels acquired starting in 1775 had been sold or lost. In addition to the vessels listed below, Massachusetts also had vessels named *Adams, Bunker Hill, Compte d'Estang, Duc de Chartres, Nantes, Penet, Reprisal, Union,* and *Versailles.*

Name	Rate	Type	Builder	Built
Machias Liberty	4	sloop		1775
Diligent		schr		1775
Tyrannicide	14	sloop	Salisbury	Jul 1776
Rising Empire		brigantine	Dartmouth	Jul 1776
Independence		brigantine	Kingston	Jul 1776
Republic		sloop	Swanzey	Sep 1776
Freedom		sloop	Swanzey	Sep 1776
Massachusetts		sloop	Salisbury	Sep 1776
Hazard	14	brigantine		fall 1777
Active	14	brigantine		spring 1779
Protector	28	frigate	Newburyport	fall 1779
Mars		ship		Mar 1780
Defence		sloop		summer 1781
Tartar	20	ship		1781–82
Winthrop	12	sloop		spring 1782
Lincoln		galley		1779

Service records:
Machias Liberty: RR Oct 1776.
Diligent: RR Oct 1776.
Tyrannicide: Lost at Penobscot, Aug 1779.
Rising Empire: Sold Mar 1780.
Independence: Captured, Spring 1777.
Republic: RR 1777.
Freedom: Taken by HMS *Apollo,* Oct 1777.
Massachusetts: RR 1778.
Hazard: Lost at Penobscot, Aug 1779.
Active: Lost at Penobscot, Aug 1779.
Protector: Action with privateer frigate *Admiral Duff,* 32, which blew up, 9 Jun 1780. Captured by HMS *Roebuck,* 44, and *Medea,* 28, 5 May 1781.
   Later history: HMS *Hussar,* 6th rate. Sold 14 Aug 1783.
Mars: RR 1781.
Defence: RR 1781.
Tartar: RR 1782.
Winthrop: RR 1783.
Lincoln: RR 1781.

NEW HAMPSHIRE

Name	Rate	Type	Builder	Built
Hampden	22	ship		

Service record: Damaged by running aground, Aug 1776. Lost at Penobscot, Aug 1779.

NEW YORK

Name	Rate	Type	Builder	Built
General Putnam		schooner		
General Schuyler		sloop (see p. 15)		
Montgomery		sloop		

NORTH CAROLINA

Name	Rate	Type	Acquired	Disposition
King Tammany	12	brigantine	17 Jan 1776	later merchant
Pennsylvania Farmer	16	brigantine	Feb 1776	scuttled Jun 1778
General Washington		brigantine	Feb 1776	to be destroyed, Feb 1781
Caswell	16	galley	Apr 1777	
Washington	16	galley		

Notes: First three purchased. Second pair lateen-rigged, built at Ocracoke Inlet.

PENNSYLVANIA

Name	Rate	Type	Builder	Built
Hyder Aly	16	sloop		
Montgomery	14	ship		
General Greene	16	ship		
Convention		brig		
Delaware		schr		
Bulldog		row galley		
Burke		row galley		
Camden		row galley		
Chatham		row galley		
Congress		row galley		
Dickinson		row galley		
Effingham		row galley		
Experiment		row galley		
Franklin		row galley		
Hancock		row galley		
Ranger		row galley		
Warren		row galley		
Washington (or *General Washington*)		row galley		

Notes:
Hyder Aly: Privateer.
Ships captured: British sloop *General Monck* (formerly American privateer *General Washington*) in Delaware Bay, 8 Apr 1782.

Other Pennsylvania vessels included:
- guard boats *Argus, Basilisk, Brimstone, Dragon, Eagle, Fame, Firebrand, Hawk, Hornet, Lion, Porcupine, Racehorse, Revolution, Repulse, Salamander, Terror, Thunderer, Tormentor, Viper, Vulture,* and *Wasp*
- floating batteries *Arnold* and *Putnam*
- fire ships: sloops *Aetna* and *Strombello;* brigantine *Blast;* and brigs *Comet, Hecla, Hellcat, Volcano,* and *Vesuvius*
- shallop *Black Duck*
- accommodation/provision sloops *Defiance, Hetty, Industry, Liberty, Lydia, Sally,* and *Speedwell*

RHODE ISLAND

Name	Rate	Type	Builder	Built
Argo	12	sloop		
Katy	10	sloop		
Rover		sloop		
Washington		sloop		
Pigot		row galley		
Spitfire	1	row galley		
Washington	1	row galley		

Notes:

Katy: Later USS *Providence* (see p. 7).
Spitfire: See p. 15.
Washington: See p. 15.

SOUTH CAROLINA

Name	Rate	Type	Builder	Built
Bricole	44	ship		
South Carolina	40	ship		
Prosper		ship		
Truite	26	ship		
Ballony		brigantine		
Beaufort		brigantine		
General Lincoln		brigantine		
Notre Dame	16	brigantine		
General Moultrie	18	schr		
Fair American	16	schr		
Polly	16	schr		
Anthony		schr		
Comet		schr		
Defence		schr		
Eshe		schr		
Lovely Julia		schr		
Nancy		schr		
Peggy		schr		
Polly	16	schr		
Rattlesnake		schr		
Sally		schr		
Three Friends		schr		
Commerce		sloop		
Count de Kersaint		sloop		
Beaufort		row galley		
Carolina		row galley		
Congress		row galley		
Lee		row galley		
Marques de Bretigny		row galley		
Revenge		row galley		
Rutledge		row galley		
South Edisto		row galley		

Notes:

Bricole and *Truite* purchased from France.
South Carolina: Ex-*L'Indien* (see p. 10). Captured 20 Dec 1782.

VIRGINIA

Virginia's naval vessels were poorly armed, incompletely manned, and ill fitted for service. These vessels included:

- ships *Caswell, Dragon, Gloucester, Protector, Tartar, Tempest, Thesis, Virginia,* and *Washington*
- schooner *Adventure*
- brigs *Adventure, Greyhound, Hampton, Jefferson, Liberty, Mosquito, Northampton,* and *Raleigh*
- sloop *Scorpion*
- galley *American Congress* (14 guns)
- row galleys *Accomac, Diligence, Henry, Hero, Lewis, Manly, Norfolk Revenge, Page,* and *Safeguard*
- armed boats *Dolphin, Experiment, Fly, Liberty, Nicholson, Patriot*
- *Dispatch, Thames*

3

THE UNITED STATES NAVY, 1797–1854

Following the sale of the *Alliance* in 1785, there was only the Revenue Cutter Service, founded in 1790, to guard the coasts. American merchant ships were being subjected to attacks by pirates from the Barbary Coast of North Africa, while French ships seized neutral American merchantmen for violation of wartime trade laws. On 27 March 1794 Congress passed an act providing for the building of four frigates of 44 guns and two of 36 guns, thus founding the United States Navy.

The first of the new ships, the frigate *United States*, was launched at Philadelphia on 10 May 1797, followed shortly by the *Constellation* and *Constitution*. In 1798 Congress established a Navy Department and authorized acquisition of ships to protect American trade.

An undeclared war at sea with France ensued, beginning with the capture of the privateer *Le Croyable* by the USS *Delaware* on 7 July 1798. In the years following, until a peace treaty was ratified in 1801, more than eighty French ships were captured and U.S. ocean trade increased significantly.

Following the peace, all but fourteen Navy ships were sold, but almost immediately the United States again found itself in conflict with the Barbary pirates, particularly Tripoli. A squadron under Edward Preble was dispatched to the Mediterranean. In 1803 the frigate *Philadelphia* was captured after running aground in Tripoli harbor. In the most notable exploit of the period, a detachment led by Stephen Decatur entered the harbor and burned the captured ship. During 1804 there was heavy fighting in the area. In May 1805 a detachment of seamen and Marines captured the Tripolitanian fortress of Derna (whence "to the shores of Tripoli").

Relations with Britain deteriorated as American ships were stopped at sea by British ships impressing seamen into the Royal Navy. In 1807 HMS *Leopard* fired on the frigate USS *Chesapeake*, killing three men and taking off four men. In 1811 the USS *United States* exchanged shots with HMS *Little Belt* off Cape Henry, Va. In addition, the Napoleonic wars led Britain to order a blockade of Europe and France to prohibit commerce. Competing decrees aimed at neutral (American) ships led to President Jefferson in December 1807 prohibiting all foreign commerce, an embargo which remained in force until 1809.

The Navy during this time was greatly diminished in size. Its ships were to be replaced by 257 small gunboats to provide protection to the bays and harbors, a "defensive Navy" concept propounded by Thomas Jefferson.

On 18 June 1812 the United States declared war on Great Britain in reaction to a series of overt acts against American commerce, including impressment of seamen, seizing of ships, and restraint of trade by new theories of belligerent rights. The trade war incidents leading up to the War of 1812 were also hurting Britain, but proposals to end the problem arrived in Washington too late. The U.S. Navy at the time consisted of just seventeen seaworthy ships.[1]

The war at sea resulted in the capture of many American ships, but was enlivened by spectacular successes in several single-ship actions, which galvanized the public in both America and Britain. First, the USS *Constitution* took the British *Guerriere* in August; then the *United States* captured HMS *Macedonian* in October. In December the *Constitution* took the *Java*. Meanwhile the *Essex* was causing the British problems off the western coast of South America, capturing many ships. Isaac Hull, William Bainbridge, Stephen Decatur, David Porter, and their victories were important in establishing the traditions and credibility of the U.S. Navy.

American privateers were also very active and, with U.S. Navy ships, operated in and around the British Isles, capturing many merchant ships and disrupting trade.[2]

An important American success occurred on Lake Erie in 1813 when a squadron under Oliver Hazard Perry defeated a British squadron, ending British supremacy in the Western territories. The following year, Thomas MacDonough won a victory on Lake Champlain, causing the British Army to retreat back to Canada.

The American cause declined during 1814 when a British army occupied and burned the capital city of Washington. The British blockade had crippled U.S. trade. Nevertheless, American privateers were a serious threat to British commerce, forcing the introduction of a convoy system. Both sides wanted to end the war and a peace treaty was finally signed on 28 December 1814. Before the news reached America, however, the Americans won the Battle of New Orleans and the frigate *President* was captured by a British squadron off New York.

The War of 1812 reinforced the need for a strong Navy. No sooner was it over than a new conflict arose in the Mediterranean with Algiers. In 1816 Congress authorized the construction of nine 74-gun ships-of-the-line and twelve 44-gun frigates. During the following years, the Navy was occupied with eliminating pirates in and around

---

[1] The frigates *Adams, Chesapeake, Congress, Constellation, Constitution, Essex, John Adams, President,* and *United States;* sloops *Hornet* and *Wasp;* brigs *Argus* and *Siren;* and schooners *Enterprise, Nautilus, Viper,* and *Vixen.*

[2] A privateer license gave one authority to arm a ship to capture enemy merchant ships; letters of marque and reprisal authorized a merchant vessel to capture an enemy merchant vessel. The Declaration of Paris of 1856 abolished privateering and letters of marque, although the United States did not ratify it until after the Civil War.

"The U.S. squadron parting from Port Mahon," Minorca I., Spain, 25 January 1825. Left to right, *North Carolina*, *Constitution*, *Brandywine*, *Erie*, and an unidentified ship. Watercolor by A. Carlotta. (U.S. Naval Historical Center, Naval Historical Foundation)

Florida, the Gulf of Mexico, and Caribbean Sea. In the 1830s there were actions against the Seminole Indians in Florida. American frigates and sloops of war now regularly appeared in foreign ports around the world for the protection of American interests and shipping.

Expeditions of exploration and scientific discovery commenced when Charles Wilkes sailed in 1838 to explore the Pacific Ocean, ranging from the Philippines to Antarctica and Fiji.

The first experimental steam-driven warship, the *Fulton*, was launched in 1814. In 1841 the first steam warships, the sidewheel frigates *Mississippi* and *Missouri*, were launched. Ships were now able to move regardless of wind and tide. The early ships propelled by paddle wheels were soon supplanted by propeller-driven vessels. During the next ten years, more of the ungainly steamers joined the fleet, belching black smoke and changing the aspect of the Navy forever.

Starting in 1842 the United States, in cooperation with Great Britain, regularly maintained patrols off the coast of Africa for the suppression of the slave trade.

Some setbacks occurred, such as the explosion and fire which destroyed the new frigate *Missouri* in 1843. In 1844 a new gun exploded on board the gunboat *Princeton*, killing the secretaries of state and the Navy.

In 1845 the U.S. Naval Academy was opened at Annapolis.

The Navy was very active in the war with Mexico, which began in 1846 and lasted two years. Expeditions on both the Atlantic and Pacific coasts were mounted to attack Mexican ports and land troops.

During the 1850s a survey expedition under Cadwallader Ringgold was conducted in the Northern Pacific and China Seas. Search expeditions to find the Franklin Expedition were sent to the Arctic. A squadron under Matthew Perry arrived in Japan in 1853, leading to negotiations for opening Japanese ports to American trade that concluded in 1854. In 1855 the USS *Water Witch*, surveying in the Paraguay River, was fired upon. This incident led to an expedition of a squadron of eighteen ships to Paraguay in 1858–59 to demand retribution for the attack.

DISPOSITION OF THE NAVY, 1 NOVEMBER 1851

Home Squadron: sloops *Albany*, *Cyane*, *Decatur*; paddle frigate *Saranac*; steamers *John Hancock*, *Vixen*

Mediterranean: razee *Independence*; paddle frigate *Mississippi*

Brazil: frigate *Congress*; sloop *Jamestown*; storeship *Relief*

Coast of Africa: sloops *Dale*, *Germantown*, *John Adams*; brigs *Bainbridge*, *Perry*, *Porpoise*

Pacific: frigates *Raritan*, *Savannah*; sloops *Falmouth*, *St. Mary's*, *Vandalia*, *Vincennes*, *Warren*; storeships *Lexington*, *Southampton*, *Supply*; steamer *Massachusetts*

East Indies: sloops *Marion*, *Plymouth*, *Saratoga*; paddle frigate *Susquehanna*

Annapolis: sloop *Preble* (practice ship)

Baltimore: sloop *Ontario* (receiving ship)

Boston: ship-of-the-line *Ohio* (receiving ship); frigate *Cumberland* (in ordinary); sloop *Portsmouth* (repairing); steamer *Princeton* (rebuilding)

Great Lakes: steamer *Michigan*

New York: ship-of-the-line *North Carolina* (receiving ship); frigates *Brandywine* (in ordinary), *Constitution* (in ordinary), *Macedonian* (repairing), *Potomac* (in ordinary), *St. Lawrence* (repairing); schooner *Petrel* (repairing); storeship *Fredonia* (equipping); steam frigate *San Jacinto* (equipping); steamer *Fulton* (equipping)

Norfolk: ships-of-the-line *Columbus* (in ordinary), *Delaware* (in ordinary), *Pennsylvania* (receiving ship); frigates *Columbia* (repairing), *Constellation* (in ordinary), *United States* (in ordinary); sloops *Fairfield* (in ordinary), *St. Louis* (in ordinary); steamer *Engineer*

Pensacola: steamer *General Taylor* (tender)

Philadelphia: steamer *Union* (receiving ship)

Portsmouth, N.H.: ships-of-the-line *Franklin* (testing drydock), *Vermont* (in ordinary)

Special Service: brig *Dolphin*

Coast survey: schooners *Wave, Phoenix*

Under construction: Boston: *Virginia*; Hoboken, N.J.: *Stevens*; New York: *Sabine*; Norfolk: *New York*; Portsmouth, N.H.: *Alabama, Santee*; Sacket's Harbor, N.Y.: *New Orleans.*

SHIPS-OF-THE-LINE

COLUMBUS CLASS

Name	Builder	Laid down
Columbus	Portsmouth NYd	never
Franklin	Philadelphia NYd	10 Jun 1800
(unknown)	Boston NYd	never
(unknown)	New York NYd	never
(unknown)	Washington NYd	never
(unknown)	Norfolk NYd	never

Rate	74 guns
Dimensions	183′ (bp) × 48′6″ × 19′6″
Tonnage	1,859 tons
Battery	74–32pdr

Notes: Designed by Joshua Humphreys. Authorized by Act of Congress, 25 Feb 1799, but all canceled during 1800. Only one laid down, none completed. Names speculative. They would have been more heavily armed than European contemporaries.

INDEPENDENCE CLASS

Name	Builder	Laid down	L	Comm
Independence	Boston NYd (E. Hartt & J. Barker)	18 Aug 1813	22 Jun 1814	Jul 1815
Washington	Portsmouth, N.H. (Hartt & Badger)	Mar 1814	1 Oct 1814	26 Aug 1815

Rate	74 guns
	Independence: (1836) 54 guns
Dimensions	*Independence:* (1836) 188′ (bp) × 51′6″ × 24′4″
	Washington: 190′10″ (bp) × 54′7″ × 24′4″
Tonnage	2,257 tons
	Independence: (1836) 1,891 tons
Complement	750
Battery	*Independence:* (1817) 63–32pdr, 24–32pdr crde; (1836) 8–8″, 48–32pdr; (1854) 10–8″, 46–32pdr
	Washington: (1820) 62–32pdr, 20–32pdr crde

The ship-of-the-line *Washington*, 74, had a short career, going into reserve in 1820. Watercolor by A. Roux. (U.S. Naval Historical Center)

Notes: Reportedly designed by Edmund Hartt as modifications of the *Columbus* class. Well-built but unsatisfactory, as they floated too low for the battery with only 3′10″ freeboard to lower gunports when fully loaded. They were the poorest of the first four ships. *Independence* was more satisfactory as razee, a smart sailer.

Service records:

Independence: First ship-of-the-line commissioned in USN. Mediterranean Squadron 1815 (flagship). Home Sqn 1815–22 (flagship). Razee recommended in 1817. In ordinary, 1822–36. Razeed to 54-gun frigate at Boston NYd, 1836; recomm 26 Mar 1837. Flagship on voyage to Europe, visiting Portsmouth, Copenhagen, and Kronstadt, 1837. Brazil Station 1837–40 (flagship). Home Sqn 1842 (flagship). Pacific Sqn 1846–49 (flagship). Capture of Mazatlan, 11 Nov 1847. Mediterranean Sqn 1849–52 (flagship). Pacific Sqn 1854–57 (flagship). Receiving ship, Mare Island, 1857–1912. Stricken 3 Sep 1913.

The *Independence*, 54, in 1837 after her conversion to a razee frigate. Painting by J. W. Schmidt. (U.S. Naval Historical Center)

Ship captured: Ship *Correo* in Pacific, 9 May 1847.
Washington: Cruised in Mediterranean, 1816–18 (flagship of Chauncey). Reserve 1820. BU 1843.

FRANKLIN

Name	Builder	Laid down	L	Comm
Franklin	Philadelphia NYd (Humphreys & Penrose)	1815	25 Aug 1815	1815

Rate 74 guns
Dimensions 187′10″ (bp), 155′ (keel) × 50′ × 24′4″, d19′9″
Tonnage 2,243 tons
Complement 786
Battery (1820) 58–32pdr, 24–32pdr crde; (1850) 64–32pdr, 20–32pdr crde

Notes: Designed by Samuel Humphreys. Similar to *Independence* and also had insufficient displacement for battery. It was intended to razee her at one time but she was not found worth preserving and was instead "rebuilt" as a large screw frigate.
Service record: Mediterranean Sqn, 1817–20 (flagship). Pacific Station 1821–24 (flagship). Laid up 1824–43. Receiving ship, Boston, 1843. BU at Portsmouth, 1853.

COLUMBUS

Name	Builder	Laid down	L	Comm
Columbus	Washington NYd	Jun 1816	1 Mar 1819	7 Sep 1819

Rate 74 guns
Dimensions 193′3″ (bp) × 53′6″ × 26′6″, d21′10″
Tonnage 2,480 tons
Complement 780
Battery 68–32pdr, 24–42pdr crde; (1842) 8–8″, 56–32pdr, 22–32pdr crde; (1850) 12–8″, 68–32pdr

Notes: Designed by William Doughty. Poor sea boat. Most successful of the war-built 74s.
Service record: Mediterranean Sqn 1820–21 (flagship). Receiving ship, Boston, 1833–42. Mediterranean Sqn 1842 (flagship). Brazil Station 1843–44 (flagship). Far East 1845. First U.S. visit to Japan, 20 Jul 1846. Laid up 1848. Destroyed at Norfolk NYd, 20 Apr 1861.
Ship captured: (With *Erie* and *Warren*) British schr *William* at Monterey, Calif., 22 Mar 1847.

USS *Columbus*, 74, a ship-of-the-line, was in active service from 1819 to 1848. (U.S. Naval Historical Center)

DELAWARE CLASS

Name	Builder	Laid down	L	Comm
Alabama	Portsmouth NYd	1 Jun 1819	23 Jan 1864	13 May 1864
Delaware	Norfolk NYd	Aug 1817	21 Oct 1820	Feb 1828
New York	Norfolk NYd	May 1820	never	never
North Carolina	Philadelphia NYd	Jun 1816	7 Sep 1820	27 May 1825
Vermont	Boston NYd	Sep 1818	15 Sep 1848	30 Jan 1862
ex-*Virginia* (27 Apr 1827), ex-*Massachusetts* (1818)				
Virginia	Boston NYd	May 1822	never	never
ex-*Vermont* (27 Apr 1827)				

Rate	74 guns
Dimensions	*Delaware:* 197′1″ (bp) × 54′6″ × 20′6″, d21′7″
	North Carolina: 196′3″ (bp) × 53′6″ × 21′6″
Tonnage	*Delaware:* 2,602 tons
	North Carolina: 2,633 tons
Complement	820
Battery	*Delaware:* (1833) 32–42pdr, 32–32pdr, 28–42pdr crde;
	(1841) 8–8″, 28–42pdr, 30–32pdr, 22–42pdr crde;
	(1850) 12–8″, 72–32pdr
	North Carolina: 34–42pdr, 36–32pdr, 24–42pdr crde;
	(1841) 32–42pdr, 34–32pdr, 24–42pdr crde; (1850)
	12–8″, 72–32pdr; (1862) 4–9″, 1–30pdr MLR
	Vermont: (1864) 4–8″, 20–32pdr

Notes: Nine ships "to rate not less than 74 guns each" authorized by Congress, 29 Apr 1816. Designed by William Doughty. Highly successful vessels. *Alabama, New York, Vermont,* and *Virginia* were completed ready for launch and kept as a reserve until needed; *Vermont* and *New Hampshire* (ex-*Alabama*) were eventually used as storeships.

Service records:

Alabama: Renamed **New Hampshire** 28 Oct 1863. Launched as storeship. Renamed **Granite State** 30 Nov 1904. Sold 1921.

The USS *Vermont* as receiving ship at Brooklyn Navy Yard after the Civil War. She retains some of her armament. (U.S. Naval Historical Center)

Delaware: Mediterranean Sqn 1828–30 (flagship). Laid up 1830–33. Recomm 15 Jul 1833. Mediterranean Sqn 1833–36 (flagship). Laid up 1836–41. Brazil Station 1841–43 (flagship). Mediterranean 1843–44. Laid up 1844–61. Burned at Norfolk NYd, 20 Apr 1861.

New York: Burned on stocks at Norfolk NYd, 21 Apr 1861.

North Carolina: Completed by Norfolk NYd. Mediterranean Sqn 1825–27 (flagship). In ordinary 1827–36. South America 1837–39 (flagship). Receiving ship, New York, 1840–66. Sold 1 Oct 1867.

Vermont: Ready for launching in 1825 but only launched to clear slip in 1848. Comm as store and receiving ship. Sold 17 Apr 1902.

The ship-of-the-line *North Carolina*, completed in 1825, as receiving ship in New York during the 1860s. (U.S. Naval Historical Center)

The ship-of-the-line *Delaware*, 74, as she appeared in 1833 en route to Europe. Painting by A. Roux. (U.S. Naval Historical Center)

The ship-of-the-line *Ohio* as receiving ship at Boston during the 1870s.

The ship-of-the-line *Pennsylvania*, 120, the largest sailing warship built for the Navy, as she appeared in 1853 off the Norfolk Navy Yard. She saw little service because of her huge size. (U.S. Naval Historical Center)

Virginia: Ready for launching, 1825, but never launched. BU on stocks, 1874.

OHIO

Name	Builder	Laid down	L	Comm
Ohio	New York NYd	Nov 1817	30 May 1820	16 Oct 1838

Rate	74 guns
Dimensions	197'2" (bp) × 53'10" × 26'6"
Tonnage	2,757 tons
Complement	820
Battery	32–42pdr, 34–32pdr, 24–42pdr crde; (1846) 12–8", 78–32pdr; (1847) 12–8", 28–42pdr, 44–32pdr; (1850) 12–8", 72–32pdr

Notes: Designed by Henry Eckford. Good sea boat; fast. Considered one of finest 74s in the world. Carried guns high. Laid up unfinished, 1820–36. Figurehead: Hercules.
Service record: Mediterranean Sqn 1838–40 (flagship). Receiving ship, 1842–46. Mexico 1847. Pacific Sqn 1847–50. Receiving ship, Boston, 1851–75. Sold 27 Sep 1883.

PENNSYLVANIA

Name	Builder	Laid down	L	Comm
Pennsylvania	Philadelphia NYd	Sep 1821	18 Jul 1837	1841

Rate	120 guns
Dimensions	210' (bp) × 56'9" × d24'3"
Tonnage	3,241 tons
Complement	1,100
Battery	16–8", 90– to 104–32pdr

Notes: Largest sailing warship built for USN, with four complete gundecks and no poop. Designed by Samuel Humphreys. Probably the most powerful vessel in the world when completed. A powerful ship of enormous displacement without grace. Poor reputation as a sailer, although design revised to improve sailing qualities. With a huge complement, the enormous cost of manning her made her expensive to operate and she saw little service.
Service record: Receiving ship, Norfolk, 1842. No active service. Burned to prevent capture at Norfolk NYd, 20 Apr 1861.

FRIGATES

UNITED STATES CLASS

Name	Builder	Laid down	L	Comm
Constitution	Boston (G. Claghorne)	1795	21 Oct 1797	Jul 1798
President	New York (Wm. Doughty & C. Bergh)	(U)	10 Apr 1800	Jul 1800
United States	Philadelphia (J. Humphreys)	1795	10 May 1797	11 Jul 1797

Rate	44 guns
Dimensions	175' (bp), 157'10" (keel) × 43'6" × 23', d14'3"
Tonnage	1,576 tons
Complement	467/480
	United States: 364
Battery	*Constitution:* 30–24pdr, 22–12pdr; (1804) 30–24pdr, 14–12pdr, 8–32pdr crde; (1812) 30–24pdr, 1–18pdr, 24–32pdr crde; (1814) 31–24pdr, 20–32pdr crde; (1840) 32–24pdr, 20–32pdr crde; (1848) 4–8", 46–32pdr

The frigate *United States* capturing HMS *Macedonian*, 25 October 1812. Painting by E. Tufnell. (U.S. Naval Historical Center, Norman Polmar Collection)

President: (1813) 32–24pdr, 1–18pdr, 22–42pdr crde
United States: 30–24pdr, 14–12pdr; (1812) 32–long 24pdr, 24–42pdr
    crde; (1841) 32–32pdr, 20–32pdr crde; (1848) 4–8″,
    42–32pdr

Notes: Authorized by Congress, 27 Mar 1794. Designed by Joshua Humphreys. Fast, weatherly, and good sea boats. Extremely heavily armed and strongly built. Approximated the size of contemporary 74s. The largest frigates built to this date, having an extraordinary rig with skysails on all masts. Construction delayed because of alterations in plans. Work on *President* stopped in 1796 but resumed in 1798; as completed by Christian Bergh, she was slightly heavier than the others. Figureheads: *Constitution*, Hercules with club raised; *United States*, the goddess of Liberty, (1834) Andrew Jackson; *President*, George Washington.

Service records:

Constitution: Patrolled off U.S. coast, then Santo Domingo, 1798–99. Mediterranean (under Preble) 1803–07. Attacks on forts at Tripoli, Aug–Sep 1804. In collision with *United States*, 12 Sep 1804. N. Atlantic Sqn 1809–12 (flagship). Action with British sqn (*Africa*, 64, *Shannon*, 38, *Guerriere*, 38, *Belvidera*, 36, and *Aeolus*, 32), evaded enemy while becalmed by rowing and kedging for two days, 17–20 Jul 1812. Took HMS *Guerriere*, 38 (burned), in action off Gulf of St. Lawrence (7 killed), 19 Aug 1812. Took HMS *Java*, 38 (burned), in action off Brazil (9 killed), 29 Dec 1812. Destroyed schr HMS *Pictou*, 14, off Barbados, 15 Feb 1814. Took HMS *Cyane*, 22, and *Levant*, 18, in action off Madeira, 20 Feb 1815; latter was recaptured (3 killed), 11 Mar 1815. Laid up 1815–21. Mediterranean Sqn 1821–28 (flagship of Jacob Jones). Rebuilt 1833; recomm 1835. Mediterranean Sqn 1835–38 (flagship). S. Pacific Sqn 1839–41 (flagship). Home Sqn 1842–43 (flagship). Circumnavigated the world (under Percival), 1844–46. Mediterranean Sqn 1848–51 (flagship). Anti-slaver patrol off Africa, 1852–55. Laid up 1855–60. Training ship, USNA, 1860; moved USNA to Newport, R.I. Rebuilt at Philadelphia, 1871. Receiving ship, Portsmouth, N.H., 1884. Decomm 1897. Saved from demolition by public subscription, 1905. Bore name **Old Constitution** 1 Dec 1917–24 Jul 1925. Recomm. 1 Jul 1931. Made tour of 90 U.S. ports, 1931–34. Returned to Boston as museum ship, 1934.

Ships captured: Privateer *Niger*, 24, 8 Sep 1798; French schr *Spencer* (or *Spender*), 16 Jan 1799; schr *Neutrality*, 27 Mar 1799; French *Carteret*, 3 Apr 1799; *Amelia*, 15 Sep 1799; *Swift*, 1 Feb 1800; privateer *Ester*, brig *Nymph*, 8 May 1800; sloop *Sally*, 9 May 1800; ship *Sand-*

U.S. Frigate *President*, 44, as she appeared when captured in 1815. (U.S. Naval Historical Center)

The U.S. Frigate *Constitution* during the 1930s after being restored to her original appearance.

wich (LofM), 10 May 1800; two polacres, 11 Sep 1804; three xebecs, 24 Apr 1805; *Golconda, Rose,* 10 Aug 1810; brig *Lady Warren* (burned) off Cape Race, 10 Aug 1812; brig *Adeona,* 11 Aug 1812; bark *Harriet* (burned), brig *Adeline,* 15 Aug 1812; brig *South Carolina,* 9 Nov 1812; ship *Lovely Ann,* 14 Feb 1814; schr *Phoenix* (burned), 17 Feb 1814; brig *Catherine* (burned), 19 Feb 1814; brig *Lord Nelson* (scuttled) east of Bermuda, 24 Dec 1814; ship *Susannah* off Lisbon, 18 Feb 1815; slaver schr *N. H. Gambrill,* 7.33S, 12.42E, off Africa, 3 Nov 1853.

President: Mediterranean Sqn 1801–02 (flagship of Dale). Mediterranean Sqn 1803–05 (flagship of Barron). Actions against Tripoli, 1804. East coast of U.S., 1809–12. Controversial action with HMS *Little Belt,* 22, off Cape Henry, 16 May 1811. Action with HMS *Belvidera,* 36, off New York (3 killed), 23 Jun 1812. Took schr HMS *Highflyer,* 5, in Atlantic, 23 Sep 1813. Captured off New York under Decatur by British sqn (*Endymion,* 40, *Majestic,* 58, *Pomone & Tenedos,* 38) after a running fight of 6 hours; surrendered to *Majestic* razee (24 killed), 15 Jan 1815.

Ships captured: One xebec off Tripoli, Oct 1804; brig *Traveller* (burned), 2 Jul 1812; brig *Duchess of Portland* (burned), 4 Jul 1812; *John of Lancaster,* 16, 24 Jul 1812; brig *Argo,* 10, 12 Aug 1812; schr *Adeline,* 17 Aug 1812; schr *Betsey* (prize), 25 Aug 1812; packet *Swallow,* 12, near Grand Banks, 17 Oct 1812; brig *Kitty,* 2, packet brig *Duke of Montrose,* 12, brig *Maria,* 14 (LofM), schr *Falcon,* 2, north of Azores, 9–12 Jun 1813; brig *Jean & Ann* (burned), 12 Jul 1813; brig *Daphne* in Irish Channel (sunk), 18 Jul 1813; ship *Eliza Swan,* 24 Jul 1813; brig *Alert* (burned), 29 Jul 1813; bark *Lion,* 2 Aug 1813; brig *Shannon* (later recaptured), 30 Aug 1813; brig *Fly* (later recaptured), 9 Sep 1813; schr *Comet* (prize), off New York, 5 Dec 1813; ship *Wanderer,* 7, *Edward,* 6, schr *Jonathan* (sunk), off Barbados, 5–9 Jan 1814.

Later history: HMS *President,* 60, 4th rate. BU Jun 1818.

United States: West Indies under Barry, 1799. Decomm 6 Jun 1801. Laid up 1801–10. Under Decatur, took HMS *Macedonian,* 38,[3] in action 500 miles south of Azores (6 killed), 25 Oct 1812. Blockaded in New London, Conn., 1813–15. Mediterranean 1815–19. Laid up 1819–24. Pacific Sqn 1824–27. Modernized 1830–32. Mediter-

[3] Later USS *Macedonian.*

ranean 1833–38. Home Sqn 1839–40. Pacific Sqn 1842–44 (flagship). Under Commo. Thomas Jones, seized Monterey, Calif., in error, 21 Oct 1842. Africa and Mediterranean 1846–48. Decomm 24 Feb 1849. Sunk at Norfolk NYd, 20 Apr 1861. Comm in CSN as CSS *Confederate States.* BU 1865.

Ships captured: (With *Delaware*) French privateer schr *Sans Pareil,* 16, 22 Aug 1798; French privateer schr *Jalouse,* 14, 4 Sep 1798. Privateer *Amour de la Patrie,* 6 (sunk), off Martinique, 3 Feb 1799; British ship *Cicero* (LofM), 26 Feb 1799; *La Tartuffe* (LofM) with prize *Vermont, Le Bonaparte* (LofM), 26 Mar 1799; ship *Mandarin,* 11 Oct 1812.

CONSTELLATION CLASS

Name	Builder	Laid down	L	Comm
Congress	Portsmouth, N.H. (Jas. Hackett)	1796	15 Aug 1799	Dec 1799
Constellation	Baltimore (D. Stodder)	1796	7 Sep 1797	spring 1798

Rate	36 guns
Dimensions	*Congress:* 163'3" (bp) × 41'6" × d14'3" *Constellation:* 164' (bp) × 40'6" × d13'6"; (1812) beam 42'2"
Tonnage	1,268 tons
Complement	340

The frigate *Constellation* as she appeared during the War of 1812. Painting by J. W. Schmidt. (U.S. Naval Historical Center, Norman Polmar Collection)

Spar and sail plan of the frigate *Congress* of 1799. (U.S. Naval Historical Center)

The frigate *Constellation*, 36, depicted leaving Annapolis harbor, 3 January 1813. Painting by Donald Stewart. (U.S. Naval Historical Center)

Battery | *Congress:* 28–18pdr, 12–9pdr; (1800) 24–18pdr, 12–12pdr; (1812) 24–18pdr, 20–32pdr crde
Constellation: 28–24pdr, 10–12pdr; (1799) 28–24pdr, 10–24pdr crde; (1812) 2–32pdr, 24–18pdr, 18–32pdr crde; (1815) 2–32pdr, 28–18pdr, 18–32pdr crde; (1840) 16–32pdr, 30–18pdr; (1850) 6–8″, 32–32pdr

Notes: Probably designed by Joshua Humphreys. Authorized 27 Mar 1794. Construction of *Congress* ceased from 1796 to 1798. Original armament too heavy for displacement. *Constellation* beam increased during rebuilding in 1812. Classified as 2nd class frigates after 1815. Plan to convert *Constellation* to screw sloop in 1845 not carried out. Figureheads: *Congress:* unknown; *Constellation:* a female head representing Nature.

Service records:

Congress: Under command of Sever, sailed for East Indies with *Essex* in Dec 1799, but, totally dismasted in a gale, was obliged to return. West Indies 1800–01. Laid up 1801–04. Mediterranean (under John Rodgers and Decatur) 1804–05. Laid up 1805–11. Repaired and lengthened, 1811. Made three cruises, 1812–14. Europe 1815. West Indies 1816–17. Brazil 1818. East Indies (under Henley) 1818–21. First U.S. warship to visit China, Dec 1820. Last cruise, special service to Spain and West Indies, 1822–24. Laid up 1824. BU at Norfolk, 1836.

Ships captured: Brig *Experiment* (later recaptured), 29 Aug 1800; two prize ships off Tripoli, 24 Apr 1805; ship *Argo*, 10, 1 Nov 1812; brig *Jean* (burned), 19 May 1813; brig *Diana*, 22 May 1813; ship *Rose* off Brazil (burned), 25 Oct 1813; brig *Atlantic* in North Atlantic, 5 Dec 1813.

Constellation: Under Truxtun, captured French *L'Insurgente*, 40, in action off Nevis (2 killed), 9 Feb 1799. Action with French *La Vengeance*, 52, off Guadeloupe (14 killed), 2 Feb 1800. Went aground in ebb tide in Delaware Bay, 10 Apr 1801. Mediterranean 1802–05. Action with nine gunboats off Tripoli, sinking two, 22 Jul 1802. Laid up 1805–12. Rebuilt 1812–13. Action with ship *Mashouda*, 46, and brig *Esledio*, 22, off Cape de Gatt, Spain, 17–19 Jun 1815. Brazil Station 1819–20 (flagship). Pacific Sqn 1820–22. West Indies 1827 (flagship). Mediterranean 1829–34. Gulf of Mexico, Seminole War, 1835–38. Far East, 1841–43. Laid up 1845–53. BU 1854.

Ships captured: Privateers *La Diligente, L'Union,* Feb 1799; schr *Charming Betsey* (prize), off Guadeloupe, Jul 1800; one xebec off Tripoli, 10 Sep 1804.

ALGERIAN TRIBUTE SHIPS

Four vessels were built by the U.S. in 1797 as tribute for the Dey of Algiers:
- Frigate *Crescent*, 32, designed by Josiah Fox and launched 29 Jun 1797 by Josiah Hackett at Portsmouth, N.H. Dimensions: 122′ (deck) × 32′ × d10′2″.
- Brig *Hassan Bashaw*, 22, built 1797 by Samuel Humphreys at Philadelphia. Dimensions: 93′2″ (bp) × 27′ × 11′6″. Tonnage: 287 tons.
- Schr *Skjoldebrand*, 20, designed by Benjamin Hutton, Jr., and built at Philadelphia. Dimensions: 77′6″ (bp) × 23′ × 10′6″.
- Schr *Lelah Eisha*, 18, designed by Samuel Bowers.

CHESAPEAKE

Name	Builder	Laid down	L	Comm
Chesapeake	Norfolk NYd	10 Dec 1798	2 Dec 1799	May 1800

Rate | 36 guns
Dimensions | 152′6″ (bp) × 40′11″ × 13′9″
Tonnage | 1,244 tons
Complement | 340
Battery | 30–18pdr, 12–32pdr crde; (1813) 28–18pdr, 20–32pdr crde

Notes: Authorized 17 Mar 1794. Originally ordered as 44 guns. Designed by Josiah Fox.

Service record: U.S. southern coast (under Barron) 1800–01. Mediterranean Sqn 1802–03 (flagship). Laid up 1803–07. Attacked and damaged by HMS *Leopard*, 50, off U.S. coast during search for deserters (3 killed, 5 seamen impressed), 22 Jun 1807. West Indies 1812–13. Captured off Boston by HMS *Shannon*, 38 (165 casualties, including the captain, Lawrence, who uttered the famous "Don't give up the ship."), 1 Jun 1813.

Ships captured: French privateer *La Jeune Creole* off Barbuda, 1 Jan 1801; ship *Volunteer*, 12 Jan 1813; brig *Liverpool Hero* (burned), 14 Jan 1813; brig *Julia*, 1 Feb 1813; brig *Earl Percy* (run ashore on Long Is-

The frigate *Chesapeake* under sail. It was during her last fight that her captain, James Lawrence, mortally wounded, said, "Don't give up the ship!" Painting by F. Muller. (U.S. Naval Historical Center)

land), 5 Feb 1813; schr *Valeria* (or *Nystead*), 7 Apr 1813; schr *Ellen*, Apr 1813.
Later history: HMS *Chesapeake*. Sold 18 Aug 1819.

GANGES

Name	Builder	Built	Acquired	Comm
Ganges	Philadelphia (Penrose)	1794	3 May 1798	24 May 1798

Rate	24 guns
Dimensions	116′4″ × 31′4″ × 15′8″
Tonnage	504 tons
Complement	220
Battery	26–9pdr

Notes: Ex-Indiaman (merchant). First man-of-war out to sea of the "New Navy."
Service record: Patrolled off East Coast, 1798. Damaged in storm near St. Kitts, Feb 1801. Found "unfit" and sold before Dec 1801.
Ships captured: Privateer *La Vainqueur*, 16 Jun 1799; *Eliza*, Jul 1799; *La Rabateuse* (LofM), 5 Aug 1799. (With *Merrimack* and *Pickering*) recaptured American schr *John*, 16 Aug 1799. Unidentified LofM, 20 Aug 1799; *L'Eugene*, Sep 1799; *L'Esperance* (ex-American *Laurel*), 2 Oct 1799; schr *Prudent*, 19 Jul 1800; recaptured brigantine *Dispatch*, 20 Jul 1800; schr *Phoebe*, 21 Jul 1800; French privateer *La Fortune, Louise*, 28 Jul 1800.

PHILADELPHIA

Name	Builder	Laid down	L	Comm
Philadelphia	Philadelphia (Humphreys, Hutton, & Delavue)	14 Nov 1798	28 Nov 1799	5 Apr 1800
ex–*City of Philadelphia*				

USS *Philadelphia*, 36, captured by Berbers after running aground off Tripoli in October 1803. Sketch by Fred S. Cozzens. (U.S. Naval Historical Center)

Rate | 36 guns
Dimensions | 157' (bp), 130' (keel) × 39' × 13'6"
Tonnage | 1,240 tons
Complement | 307
Battery | 28–18pdr, 10–9pdr; (1803) 28–18pdr, 16–32pdr crde

Notes: Built by public subscription. Designed by Josiah Fox; built by Samuel Humphreys, Nathaniel Hutton, and John Delavue. Fast and well-built. Designed as 44 guns; rerated during construction. Figurehead: Hercules slaying the Hydra.

Service record: West Indies (under Decatur) 1800–01. Mediterranean (under Barron) 1801–02, 1802–03. Captured Berber ship *Mirboka*, 22, near Cape de Gatt, Spain, 26 Aug 1803. Ran aground on uncharted reef off Tripoli and was captured, captain Bainbridge and crew taken prisoner, 31 Oct 1803. Boarded and burned by U.S. detachment under Decatur in Tripoli harbor, 16 Feb 1804.

Ships captured: *La Levrette, L'Union, La Magdalen, La Guerre, L'Amphitrite*, 1801.

NEW YORK

Name	Builder	Laid down	L	Comm
New York	New York (Peck & Carpenter)	Aug 1798	24 Apr 1800	Oct 1800

Rate | 36 guns
Dimensions | 144'2" (bp) × 37' × 11'9"
Tonnage | 1,130 tons
Complement | 340
Battery | 26–18pdr, 14–9pdr

Notes: Designed by Samuel Humphreys. Built by public subscription. Beautiful and well-built vessel.

Service record: West Indies 1800–01. Mediterranean 1802–03. Damaged by powder explosion off Malta (4 killed), 25 Apr 1803; returned to U.S. and was laid up, 1803. Unfit for sea in 1812. Sheer hulk burned to prevent capture at Washington, 24 Aug 1814.

BOSTON

Name	Builder	Laid down	L	Comm
Boston	Boston (Edmund Hartt)	22 Aug 1798	20 May 1799	Jun 1799

Rate | 28 guns
Dimensions | 136'6" (deck), 134' (bp) × 34'6" × 11'6"
Tonnage | 400 tons
Complement | 220
Battery | (1801) 24–12pdr, 12–9pdr

Notes: Designed by Edmund Hartt. First vessel in Navy with a copper bottom. Well built, very fast.

Service record: Cruised in West Indies, Jul 1799–Jun 1800. One of Talbot's Sqn under Little, 1800. Action with Picaroons off St. Marks, West Indies, 28 Mar 1800. Captured French *Berceau*, 24, northeast of Guadeloupe (4 killed), 12 Oct 1800. Mediterranean 1801–02. Action with seven Tripolitanian gunboats, 16 May 1802. Unworthy of repair in 1812. Burned to prevent capture at Washington, 24 Aug 1812.

Ships captured: (With *Norfolk* and *General Greene*) schr *Flying Fish*, 1 Dec 1799. *Les Deux Anges*, 20, *La Fortune, L'Heureux*, 1800. (With *Norfolk*) *La Gourde, Le Pelican*, 1800. (With *Augusta*) *L'Espoir*, 24 Jun 1800.

GENERAL GREENE

Name	Builder	Laid down	L	Comm
General Greene	Warren, R.I.	1798	21 Jan 1799	Jun 1799

Rate | 28 guns
Dimensions | 139' (bp), 124'3" (deck) × 34'8" × 17'4"
Tonnage | 654 tons
Complement | 250
Battery | 24–12pdr, 8–9pdr

Notes: Probably designed by Benjamin Talman. Authorized 1798.

Service record: Damaged in storm, Jul 1799; returned to Newport with yellow fever (20 dead). San Domingo Station, Oct 1799–Jul 1800. Under command of C. R. Perry, attached to Talbot's Sqn in West Indies, 1800; supported Toussaint in Haiti. Laid up 1801. Sheer hulk at Washington in 1805. Hulk burned at Washington, 24 Aug 1814.

Ships captured: Schr *Flying Fish* (with *Boston* and *Norfolk*), American schr *Weymouth*, 1 Dec 1799; *L'Industrie*, one Danish brig, 1800.

ADAMS

Name	Builder	Laid down	L	Comm
Adams	New York	30 Jul 1798	8 Jun 1799	Sep 1799

Rate | 28 guns
Dimensions | 113' (bp) × 34' × 10'9"; (1812) 128' length
Tonnage | 530 tons
Complement | 220
Battery | 24–12pdr, 4–9pdr; (1812, as sloop) 26–18pdr, 1–12pdr

Notes: Authorized 1798. Designed by William Sheffield. Fast, with deep draft. Rebuilt as sloop, flush-deck corvette, 1812. Cut in half and lengthened 15'; new design by Josiah Fox.

Service record: Cruise in West Indies in sqns of Truxtun and Decatur, 1799 and 1800. Ordered laid up, 23 Mar 1801. Mediterranean 1802–Nov 1803. Cruised U.S. East Coast, 1805–06. Laid up in Washington, 1806. Receiving ship, Washington, Aug 1811. Rebuilt 1812; launched 24 Dec 1812. Blockaded in Chesapeake Bay until Jan 1814. Damaged by grounding on Haute Island, 17 Aug 1814; refloated and reached Hampden, Maine. Burned to prevent capture in Penobscot River at Camden, Maine, 3 Sep 1814.

Ships captured: Recaptured brig *Zylpha*, Oct 1799. (With *Insurgent*) captured a 4-gun privateer, Oct 1799; recaptured British brig *Margaret*, 14, 12 Nov 1799; privateer *Le Douze Vendémiaire*, 15 Nov 1799. (With *Eagle*) French schr *La Fougueuse*, 10 Jan 1800. Recaptured schr *Alphia*, Jan 1800; French schrs *L'Heureuse Rencontre* and *Isabella*, Feb 1800; recaptured sloop *Nonpareil*, Mar 1800; recaptured schr *Priscilla*, Apr 1800; unidentified schr, schr *Nancy, Grinder*, an unidentified brig, brig *Dove*, schr *Renommee*, May 1800; recaptured British schr *Grendin*, late 1800; *General Massena*, 6, *Flambeau*, 4, also in 1800; schr *Prince Regent* in North Atlantic (burned), 29 Jan 1814; schr *Industry* (burned), 9 Feb 1814; sloop *Nayntine Fairy* off Africa, 4 Mar 1814; brig *Roebuck* off Africa, 11 Mar 1814; ship *Woodbridge* (later escaped), 25 Mar 1814; brig *Hunter*, 10 (destroyed), 24 Jun 1814; brig *Mary* (destroyed), 28 Jun 1814; schr *Favorite* (destroyed) off England, 28 Jul 1814; ship *Paris* (destroyed) off Ireland, 7 Aug 1814; schr *Maria* (destroyed), 16 Aug 1814.

JOHN ADAMS

Name	Builder	Laid down	L	Comm
John Adams	Charleston, S.C. (Pritchard)	(U)	5 Jun 1799	Sep 1799

Rate	28 guns
Dimensions	139′ (bp), 127′9″ (gun deck) × 33′3″ × 16′10″
Tonnage	544 tons
Complement	220
Battery	24–12pdr, 2–9pdr, 6–24pdr crde; (1804) 24–12pdr, 8–24pdr crde; (1820) 4–18pdr, 20–32pdr crde

Notes: Designed by Josiah Fox. Built by public subscription. Stuck on the ways on first attempt at launch.
Service record: Cruise in West Indies in sqns of Truxtun and Decatur, 1799 and 1800. Mediterranean (under J. Rodgers and Chauncey) 1802–05. Action near Tripoli with Berber *Mishouda*, 22, which blew up, 22 Jun 1803. Attacks on Tripoli, Aug 1803–1804. Brought Preble home, 1805. In ordinary 1805–12. Laid up until 1814. Europe 1814. Mediterranean 1815–16. U.S. coast and West Indies in 1817 and 1818. Obtained surrender of pirates on Amelia Island, 22 Dec 1817. South America (under O. H. Perry and Claxton) 1818–19. Brazil 1820. West Indies 1821–29; operations against pirates. BU at Norfolk, 1829.
Ships captured: Brig *Dolphin*, Jan 1800; recaptured brig *Hannibal*, 22 Mar 1800; recaptured brig *Atlantic*, 23 Mar 1800; French privateer *La Jason*, 8, 3 Apr 1800; recaptured schrs *Dispatch* and *William*, May 1800; recaptured brig *Olive*, spring 1800; schr *Decade*, 13 Jun 1800.

PORTSMOUTH

Name	Builder	Laid down	L	Comm
Portsmouth	Portsmouth, N.H. (J. K. Hackett)	1798	11 Oct 1798	1798

Rate	24 guns
Dimensions	(U)
Tonnage	593 tons
Complement	220
Battery	(U)

Notes: Designed by Josiah Fox.

The small frigate *Merrimack*, 24, was built by public subscription in 1804. (U.S. Naval Historical Center)

Service record: Cruised in West Indies, 1798–99. Sent to France for U.S. minister, 1800. Sold 1801.
Ship captured: *Le Fripon*, 6, 1799.

MERRIMACK

Name	Builder	Laid down	L	Comm
Merrimack	Newburyport, Mass. (Cross & Clark)	9 Jul 1798	12 Oct 1798	Dec 1798

Rate	24 guns
Dimensions	(U)
Tonnage	460 tons
Complement	220
Battery	20–9pdr, 8–6pdr

Notes: Ship. Built by public subscription and presented to the Navy. Reputed to be the best of the small frigates.
Service record: West Indies in sqns of Barry and Decatur, 1799–1801. Captured *Magicienne* (ex-USS *Retaliation*), 28 Jun 1799. Sold 1801.
Ships captured: Schr *La Bonaparte* (LofM), 7 Aug 1799. (With *Ganges* and *Pickering*) recaptured schr *John*, 16 Aug 1799. Recaptured brig *Ceres*, 6 Jun 1800; French privateer *Phénix*, 14, 20 Oct 1800; schr *Brillante*, later in 1800.
Later history: Merchant *Monticello*. Lost off Cape Cod.

CONNECTICUT

Name	Builder	Laid down	L	Comm
Connecticut	Middletown, Conn. (Overton)	1798	6 Jun 1799	Oct 1799

Rate	24 guns
Dimensions	(projected) 93′ × 31′ × 13′6″
Tonnage	492 tons
Complement	220
Battery	24–12pdr

Notes: Hull leaked and she sank soon after launching, delaying completion. Reputed to be very fast.
Service record: West Indies with sqns of Truxtun and Decatur, 1799 and 1800. Sold at New York, 1801.
Ships captured: *La Conquête*, 29 Oct 1799; *Le Piège*, 12, *L'Unité*, 2, *Le Chou Chou*, 1800.

TRUMBULL

Name	Builder	Laid down	L	Comm
Trumbull	Norwich, Conn.	1799	1799	Mar 1800

Rate	24 guns
Dimensions	(U)
Tonnage	400 tons
Complement	220
Battery	18–12pdr

Notes: Built by public subscription.
Service record: West Indies 1800–01. Sold, summer 1801.
Ships captured: Schr *Peggie*, May 1800; *La Vengeance*, 10, with refugees from Haiti, 3 Aug 1800; *La Tulipe* (or *Cullie*), 4 Aug 1800.

The frigate *Essex*, 32, made a historic cruise off the Pacific coast of South America under David Porter. She was the first U.S. warship to double both the Cape of Good Hope and Cape Horn. Painting by E. Tufnell. (U.S. Naval Historical Center)

WARREN

Name	Builder	Laid down	L	Comm
Warren	Newburyport, Mass. (Webster)	1799	26 Sep 1799	Nov 1799

Rate	24 guns
Dimensions	(U)
Tonnage	385 tons
Complement	160
Battery	(U)

Service record: West Indies 1800–01. Sold 1801.

ESSEX

Name	Builder	Laid down	L	Comm
Essex	Salem, Mass. (Enos Briggs)	13 Apr 1799	30 Sep 1799	17 Dec 1799

The frigate *Essex* during the War of 1812. Drawing by Capt. William Bainbridge Hoff. (U.S. Naval Historical Center)

Rate	32 guns
Dimensions	141'9" (bp), 118' (keel) × 37' × d12'3"
Tonnage	850 tons
Complement	300
Battery	26–12pdr, 10–6pdr; (1810) 6–12pdr, 40–32pdr crde

Notes: Designed by William Hackett. Built by public subscription. Large and fast. Rearmed in 1810 with carronades, which hampered her sailing qualities and reduced effectiveness. First U.S. vessel of war to double Cape of Good Hope and Cape Horn, the former in 1800 under Preble and the latter in 1813 under Porter.

Service record: Convoyed merchant ships, doubled Cape of Good Hope twice, 1800. Cruised in Mediterranean (under J. Barron, Bainbridge, Decatur, Stewart, Cox, and Campbell), 1802–05. Laid up 1805–09. Europe (under J. Smith) 1810. One of Rodgers's Sqn on the coast, 1811. Took sloop HMS *Alert*, 18, in action in Atlantic, 13 Aug 1812. South Atlantic, then west coast of South America (under Porter), 1812–13. Captured off Valparaiso, Chile, by HMS *Phoebe*, 36, and *Cherub*, 18, after a desperate resistance of 2½ hours and 154 casualties (89 killed), 28 Mar 1814.

Ships captured: Brig *Samuel & Sarah* near Bermuda, 11 Jul 1812; brig *Lamprey*, 13 Jul 1812; brig *Leander*, 5, off Newfoundland, 26 Jul 1812; brig *Hero*, 8 (burned), ship *Nancy*, 11, off Newfoundland, 2 Aug 1812; brig *Brothers*, 10, 3 Aug 1812; brig *King George*, 10, 8 Aug 1812; brig *Mary*, 9 (burned), 9 Aug 1812; packet brig *Nocton* (or *Noctor*), 10 (later recaptured), off Brazil, 12 Dec 1812; schr *Elizabeth* off Rio de Janeiro (burned), 29 Dec 1812; schr (Peruvian cruiser) *Nereyda*, 15, off Coquimbo, Chile, 26 Mar 1813; whaler *Barclay* (prize), 5 Apr 1813; whaler *Montezuma*, 2, *Policy*, 10, *Georgiana*, 6 (later recaptured), 29 Apr 1813; whalers *Atlantic*, 8,[4] *Greenwich*, 10,[5] *Catharine*, 8 (burned), *Rose*, 8, *Hector*, 11 (burned), in Pacific, 28 May 1813; whalers *Charlton*, *Seringapatam* (later recaptured), and *New Zealander* (recaptured 2 Apr), 13 Jul 1813; whaler *Sir Andrew Hammond*, 12 (recaptured 19 Jun 1814), 13 Sep 1813.

Later history: HMS *Essex*, 42, 5th rate. Convict ship, 1823. Sold 6 Jul 1837.

GEORGE WASHINGTON

Name	Builder	Built	Acquired	Comm
George Washington	Providence, R.I.	1793	12 Oct 1798	20 Dec 1798

Rate	24 guns
Dimensions	108' (keel) × 32'6" × 15'8"
Tonnage	624 tons
Complement	220
Battery	24–9pdr, 8–6pdr; (1801) 15–9pdr

Notes: Purchased merchant vessel.

Service record: West Indies 1798–99. Carried tribute to Algiers, Aug 1800, then was forced by the dey to take Algerian tribute to Constantinople. Sold at Philadelphia, May 1802.

Ships captured: Recaptured brig *Fair American*, 29 Apr 1799; schr *Francis*, 1 May 1799.

BALTIMORE

Name	Builder	Built	Acquired	Comm
Baltimore ex-*Adriana*	Baltimore (Joseph Caverly)	1798	23 May 1798	1798

---

[4] Later USS *Essex Jr.*
[5] Later USS *Greenwich.*

Rate	20 guns
Dimensions	103'9" (bp) × 30'8" × (U)
Tonnage	422 tons
Complement	180
Battery	18–9pdr, 6–4pdr; also reported as 20–9pdr

Notes: Purchased. Reputation as a slow ship. Figurehead: a woman.
Service record: Stopped by British sqn off Havana, 5 men impressed, 16 Nov 1798. Sold 1801.
Ships captured: Schr *La Sirène*, *L'Esperance*, 1799; *La Brillante Jeunesse*, 12, *La Laque Joinnolla*, 1800.

MONTEZUMA

Name	Builder	Built	Acquired	Comm
Montezuma	Virginia	1795	26 Jun 1798	Aug 1798

Rate	20 guns
Dimensions	(U) × (U) × 16'
Tonnage	347 tons
Complement	180
Battery	20–9pdr

Notes: Purchased merchant ship.
Service record: West Indies 1798–99. Sold to previous owner, 30 Dec 1799.
Ships captured: *L'Ami*, 6, 1799; recaptured brig *Fair American*, 20 Nov 1799; French brig *Les Amis*, 16, off Curaçao, 7 Mar 1800.
Later history: Merchant until about 1810.

DELAWARE

Name	Builder	Built	Acquired	Comm
Delaware ex–*Hamburgh Packet*	Philadelphia	1794	5 May 1798	Jun 1798

Rate	20 guns
Dimensions	94'9" (gun deck), 72'6" (keel) × 28' × 14'
Tonnage	321 tons
Complement	180
Battery	16–9pdr, 8–6pdr

Notes: Purchased.
Service record: Cruised in West Indies, one of first cruisers to get to sea, 1798–1801. Took French privateer schr *Croyable*, 14,[6] off Great Egg Harbor, Delaware Capes, 7 Jul 1798. Sold at Baltimore, Jun 1801.
Ships captured: (With *United States*) French privateer schr *Sans Pareil*, 16, 22 Aug 1798; French privateer schr *Jalouse*, 14, 4 Sep 1798. (With USRC *General Greene*) schr *Le Marsouin*, 5 Mar 1799. *Le Rénard*, *L'Ocean*, 1799.

HERALD

Name	Builder	Built	Acquired	Comm
Herald	Newburyport, Mass.	1798	15 Jun 1798	Aug 1798

Rate	18 guns
Dimensions	92'8" × 26'3" × 13'2"
Tonnage	279 tons
Complement	140
Battery	16–6pdr, 6–4pdr

[6] Later USS *Retaliation*.

Notes: Ship. Purchased at Boston.
Service record: Cruised in West Indies under Russel, 1799–1800. Sqns of Barry and Talbot; dispatched to recall U.S. forces in West Indies, 23 Mar 1801. Sold 1801.
Ship captured: (With *Augusta*) French privateer *La Mutiné*, 21 Jan 1800.

INSURGENT

Name	Builder	Built	Acquired	Comm
Insurgent ex-*L'Insurgente*	France	1793	1799	Aug 1799

Rate	36 guns
Dimensions	148' (bp) × 37'5" × 11'9"
Tonnage	950 tons
Complement	340
Battery	26–18pdr, 10–12pdr, 4–32pdr crde

Notes: French frigate, captured off St. Kitts by *Constellation*, 9 Feb 1799.
Service record: Europe 1799–1800. Sailed from Hampton Roads, 8 Aug 1800, and was lost at sea with all hands in North Atlantic; perhaps lost in storm in West Indies, 20 Sep 1800.
Ships captured: (With *Adams*) captured a 4-gun privateer, Oct 1799; recaptured British brig *Margaret*, 12 Nov 1799; French ship *Le Douze Vendémiaire*, 15 Nov 1799. *Aurora*, *Commerce*, *William & Mary*, 1799–1800.

MACEDONIAN

Name	Builder	L	Acquired	Comm
Macedonian ex-HMS *Macedonian*	Woolwich (England) Dockyard	2 Jun 1810	Dec 1812	Apr 1813

Rate	38 guns
Dimensions	158' (deck) × 40' × 18'4" (in USN); also reported as 154' × 39'6"
Tonnage	1,325 tons, 1,082 bm
Complement	362
Battery	28–18pdr, 2–12pdr, 2–9pdr, 16–32pdr crde, 1–18pdr crde; (1820) 26–18pdr, 2–9pdr, 10–32pdr crde

Notes: British 5th rate captured by USS *United States* 500 miles south of Azores, 25 Oct 1812.
Service record: Under command of Jacob Jones, blockaded in Thames River, Conn., 1813–15. Mediterranean, 1815–18. Pacific coast of South America, 1819–21. Africa Station 1822–26. Lost 103 to yellow fever during 1822 cruise. Pacific 1826–28. BU at Norfolk, 1835.

JAVA CLASS

Name	Builder	Laid down	L	Comm
Essex ex-*Columbia* (1813)	Washington NYd	1813	never	never
Guerriere ex-*Continental* (1813)	Philadelphia NYd	1813	20 Jun 1814	1814
Java	Baltimore (Flannigan & Parsons)	1813	1 Aug 1814	Aug 1815

Rate	44 guns
Dimensions	175' (bp), 145' (keel) × 44'6" × d13'6"
Tonnage	1,508 tons
Complement	400
Battery	*Guerriere*: (1817) 33–24pdr, 20–42pdr crde *Java*: 33–32pdr, 20–42pdr crde

Notes: Authorized 2 Jan 1813. Designed by William Doughty. Deteriorated rapidly because of poorly seasoned timber. Named after prizes.
Service records:

Essex/Columbia: Burned on stocks after Battle of Bladensburg, Aug 1814.

Guerriere: Mediterranean (under Decatur) 1814–15. Action with ship *Mashouda*, 46, and brig *Esledio*, 22, off Cape de Gatt, Spain (5 killed), 17–19 Jun 1815. Laid up 1815–18. Europe; returned to U.S. in 1820. Training ship, Norfolk, 1820–28. Pacific Sqn 1829–31 (flagship). Decomm 19 Dec 1831. BU 1841.

Java: Mediterranean (under O. H. Perry) 1815–17. Lost mast in gale (5 killed), 22 Jan 1816. Laid up 1817–27. Mediterranean 1827–31. Receiving ship, Norfolk, 1831. BU 1842.

CYANE

Name	Builder	L	Acquired	Comm
Cyane	Topsham, England (Bass)	14 Oct 1806	Apr 1815	1815
ex-HMS *Cyane*, ex-*Columbine*				

Rate	34 guns
Dimensions	120'4" × 31'6" × 17'3"; also reported as 110' (bp), 90' (keel) × 29' × d8'6"
Tonnage	540 tons
Complement	185
Battery	(1815) 4–9pdr, 22–32pdr crde, 9–18pdr crde, 1–12pdr crde; (1818) 2–12pdr, 2–9pdr, 22–32pdr crde, 6–18pdr crde, 2–12pdr crde

Notes: British 6th rate, 22, captured by *Constitution* in Atlantic off Madeira, 20 Feb 1815. Eckford recommended she be cut down into a flush-decked ship, but no funds were available. Rate raised to 34 guns after capture.
Service record: Africa Station 1819–20. West Indies 1820–21. Mediterranean 1824–25. Brazil Station 1825–27. Sunk at Philadelphia NYd, winter 1835. BU 1836.
Ships captured: Slaver schrs *Louisa, Dasher, Eliza, Endymion, Esperanza, Plattsburgh,* and *Sciena* off West Africa, 5–12 Apr 1820.

POTOMAC CLASS

Name	Builder	Laid down	L	Comm
Brandywine	Washington NYd	Sep 1821	16 Jun 1825	25 Aug 1825
ex-*Susquehanna* (1825)				
Columbia	Washington NYd	Nov 1825	9 Mar 1836	May 1838
Cumberland	Boston NYd	1825	24 May 1842	Nov 1843
Potomac	Washington NYd	9 Aug 1819	22 Mar 1822	15 Jun 1831
Raritan	Philadelphia NYd	Sep 1820	13 Jun 1843	1 Dec 1843
St. Lawrence	Norfolk NYd	1826	25 Mar 1847	17 Aug 1848
Savannah	New York NYd	Jul 1820	5 May 1842	15 Oct 1843

Rate	44 guns
Dimensions	175' (bp) × 45' × d14'5"
	Brandywine: 22' draft
	Potomac: 177'10" × 46'2" × 20'6"
Tonnage	1,726 tons
Complement	480
Battery	*Brandywine:* 30–32pdr, 24–32pdr crde; (1840) 4–8", 28–32pdr, 22–32pdr crde; (1847) 8–8", 42–32pdr
	Columbia: 4–8", 28–32pdr, 22–42pdr crde; (1853) 10–8", 40–32pdr

The razee frigate *Cumberland* at Portsmouth Navy Yard about 1860. (U.S. Naval Historical Center)

Cumberland: 4–8", 28–32pdr, 20–42pdr crde; (1847) 8–8", 42–32pdr; (1850) 10–8", 40–32pdr; (1856, as razee) 6–8", 16–32pdr; (1862) 1–10", 22–9", 1–70pdr MLR
Potomac: 4–8", 28–32pdr, 20–32pdr crde; (1846) 4–8", 26–32pdr, 20–32pdr crde; (1847) 4–8", 42–32pdr; (1850) 8–8", 42–32pdr; (1855) 10–8", 40–32pdr; (1861) 10–8", 22–32pdr

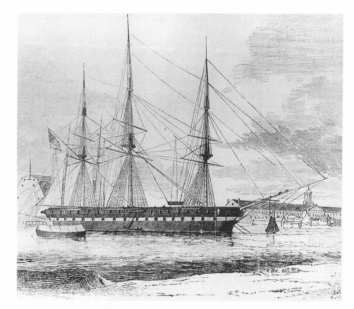

The frigate *Columbia*, 44, shown in a contemporary view, was first commissioned in 1838. (U.S. Naval Historical Center)

Raritan: 4–8″, 28–32pdr, 22–42pdr crde; (1848) 8–8″, 42–32pdr

St. Lawrence: 8–8″, 42–32pdr; (1856) 10–8″, 40–32pdr; (1858) 10–8″, 42–42pdr crde; (1861) 10–8″, 40–32pdr; (1863) 10–8″, 2–50pdr MLR, 34–32pdr; (1864) 8–9″, 2–32pdr, 1–30pdr MLR

Savannah: 4–8″, 28–32pdr, 22–42pdr crde; (1850) 8–8″, 42–32pdr; (1853) 10–8″, 40–32pdr; (1857) 2–10″, 8–8″, 14–32pdr; (1862) 2–10″, 6–8″, 12–32pdr; (1862) 1–11″, 2–9″, 4–32pdr

Notes: Authorized 29 Apr 1816. Designed by William Doughty; an improved *Java* class. Well-built, easy-to-handle, graceful ships. Formed the backbone of the Navy during the 1840s and 1850s. *Cumberland* razeed to corvette in 1850, improving sailing qualities.

Service records:

Brandywine: Mediterranean, sailed to France with Lafayette on board, 1825. Three cruises in Mediterranean, two in Pacific (flagship), also to Gulf of Mexico, East Indies, and Brazil, 1826–51. In ordinary, New York, 1851–60. Storeship, 1861–64. Destroyed by fire at Norfolk NYd, 3 Sep 1864. Wreck raised and sold, 26 Mar 1867.

Columbia: East Indies 1838–40 (flagship). Second attack on Kuala Batu, Sumatra, 1–2 Jan 1839. Home Sqn 1842 (flagship). Brazil Station 1842–44. Mediterranean 1844. Brazil Station 1845–47 (flagship). Home Sqn 1853–55. Burned at Norfolk NYd, 20 Apr 1861.

Cumberland: Mediterranean Sqn 1843–46 (flagship). Expedition against Alvarado, Mexico, 7 Aug 1846. Mediterranean 1849–51. Razee corvette, 1850. Mediterranean Sqn 1852–55 (flagship). African Sqn 1857–59 (flagship). Rammed and sunk by CSS *Virginia* in Hampton Roads, Va., 8 Mar 1862.

Potomac: World cruise, 1831–34. Attacked pirate stronghold at Kuala Batu, Sumatra (2 killed), 6 Feb 1832. Brazil Station 1834–37, 1840–42. West Indies 1844–45. Expedition against Alvarado, Mexico, 7 Aug 1846. Home Sqn 1855–56 (flagship). Storeship, 1862–65. Sold 24 May 1877.

Raritan: South Atlantic 1844–45 (flagship). Home Sqn 1846–48. West Indies Sqn 1849. Pacific Sqn 1850–52. Burned to prevent capture at Norfolk NYd, 20 Apr 1861.

St. Lawrence: Europe 1848–50. Took exhibits to London International Exposition, 1851. Pacific Sqn 1851–55. Brazil Station 1856–59. Paraguay Expedition, 1858. Sold 31 Dec 1875.

Savannah: Pacific Sqn 1844–47. Seizure of Monterey, Calif., 7 Jul 1846. Recapture of San Pedro and Los Angeles, 7 Oct 1846. Pacific Sqn 1849–52 (flagship). Brazil Station 1853–56. Home Sqn 1859–60 (flagship). Sold 27 Sep 1883.

SABINE CLASS

Name	Builder	Laid down	L	Comm
Sabine	New York NYd	Feb 1823	3 Feb 1855	23 Aug 1858
Santee	Portsmouth NYd	12 Feb 1823	16 Feb 1855	9 Jun 1861

Rate	44 guns
Dimensions	202′6″ (oa), 190′ (bp) × 47′ × 21′6″, d14′4″
Tonnage	1,726 tons
Complement	400
Battery	*Sabine:* 12–8″, 36–32pdr; (1862) 2–10″, 10–8″, 38–32pdr
	Santee: 2–64pdr, 10–8″, 20–32pdr/57, 16–32pdr/33, 2–heavy 12pdr; also reported as 10–8″, 26–32pdr; (1861) 12–8″, 36–32pdr

Notes: Improved *Brandywine* design. Lengthened during construction, but obsolete when launched. Well-built, easy to handle.

The frigate *Hudson* was purchased in 1826 when the Greek government was unable to pay for it. Engraving by W. J. Bennett. (U.S. Naval Historical Center)

Service records:

Sabine: Paraguay Expedition, 1858. Sold 23 Sep 1883.

Santee: Station ship, Annapolis, 1865–1912. Sold 2 Aug 1912

HUDSON

Name	Builder	Laid down	L	Comm
Hudson	New York (Smith & Dimon)	1825	Nov 1825	Sep 1828
ex-*Liberator* (Greek)				

Rate	44 guns
Dimensions	177′10″ (bp) × 45′ × d13′8″
Tonnage	1,728 tons
Complement	(U)
Battery	32–32pdr, 30–42pdr crde

The razee frigate *Macedonian* late in the Civil War while serving as practice ship for the U.S. Naval Academy, at Newport, R.I. (U.S. Naval Historical Center)

Notes: Built for Greece but purchased 23 Aug 1826 when Greek government was unable to pay for the ship. Pierced for 66 guns. Designed with lines of a packet. Said to be poorly built, but really built of poor quality timber and broken up as rotten. Last privately built frigate in the sailing Navy.

Service record: Brazil Station 1828–31 (flagship). Receiving ship, New York, 1831–44. Sold and BU, 1844.

MACEDONIAN

Name	Builder	Laid down	L	Comm
Macedonian	Norfolk NYd	1832	1 Nov 1836	Oct 1837

Rate	36 guns; (as razee) 24 guns
Dimensions	164′ (bp) × 41′ × 21′8″, d18′
Tonnage	1,341 tons
Complement	380/489
Battery	(planned) 32–32pdr, 24–32pdr crde; (as built) 30–18pdr, 16–32pdr crde; (1850) 6–8″, 32–32pdr; (1853, as razee) 16–8″, 4–32pdr; (1861) 2–10″, 16–8″, 4–32pdr; (1862) 1–10″, 4–8″; (1863) 2–100pdr MLR, 8–8″, 4–32pdr

Notes: Frigate. Officially the original *Macedonian* rebuilt. Designed by Samuel Humphreys. Too small for intended armament and reduced to corvette in 1853. Clipper type and fast sailer. Figurehead: Alexander the Great, taken from the old ship.

Service record: West Indies and Africa, 1839–47. Carried food to Ireland, 1847. Razeed to 1st class sloop at Brooklyn NYd, 1852–53. Expedition to Japan, 1853. North Pacific 1853–56. Mediterranean 1857–61. Sold 31 Dec 1875.

PAUL JONES

Name	Builder	Laid down	L	Comm
Paul Jones	Portsmouth NYd	1835	never	never

Notes: Details unknown. Broken up on ways, 1843.

CONGRESS

Name	Builder	Laid down	L	Comm
Congress	Portsmouth NYd	1 Jun 1839	16 Aug 1841	7 May 1842

Rate	44 guns
Dimensions	179′ (bp) × 47′8″ × d22′8″
Tonnage	1,867 tons
Complement	480
Battery	4–8″, 48–32pdr; (1845) 4–8″, 46–32pdr; (1850) 8–8″ shell, 42–32pdr; (1855) 10–8″, 40–32pdr

Notes: Designed by Samuel Humphreys. Officially the rebuilt frigate of 1794. Best frigate built in U.S., and last frigate designed for USN.

Service record: Mediterranean 1842. Brazil Station 1843–45. Pacific Sqn 1845–48 (flagship). Occupation of San Pedro, Calif., 6 Aug 1846. Capture of Mazatlan, Mexico, 11 Nov 1847. Brazil Station, 1850–53 (flagship). Mediterranean Sqn 1855–57 (flagship). Brazil Station 1859–61 (flagship). Sunk by CSS *Virginia* in Hampton Roads, 8 Mar 1862.

SLOOPS

MARYLAND CLASS

Name	Builder	Laid down	L	Comm
Maryland	Baltimore (Price)	1799	3 Jun 1799	Aug 1799
Patapsco	Baltimore (De Rochbrune)	1799	20 Jun 1799	1799

ex-*Chesapeake* (10 Oct 1799)

Rate	20 guns
Dimensions	87′ (keel) × 29′ × 12′
Tonnage	380 tons
Complement	180
Battery	20–9pdr, 6–6pdr

Notes: Built by public subscription. Good sailers. Figureheads: *Maryland*, goddess of commerce and plenty; *Patapsco*, Neptune.

Service record:

Maryland: West Indies and Surinam, 1799–1800. Sold at Baltimore, 2 Oct 1801.

> Ships captured: Schr *Clarissa*, 4 Jan 1800; Portuguese brig *Gloria da Mar* from French, 26 Jul 1800.

Patapsco: West Indies 1799–1800. Ordered to carry Gen. Wilkinson to New Orleans and then join Talbot's Sqn in Mediterranean, 1799. Sold Jun 1801.

> Ships captured: *La Dorade*, 6 (LofM), 1800.

HORNET

Name	Builder	Built	Acquired	Comm
Hornet ex-*Traveller*	Amesbury, Mass.	1802	1804	1805

Rate	10 guns
Dimensions	(U)
Tonnage	440 tons
Complement	140
Battery	(U)

Notes: Purchased at Malta.

Service record: Attack on Derna, North Africa, 27 Apr 1805. Employed principally as transport in Mediterranean during war with Tripoli. Sold at Philadelphia, Sep 1806.

LOUISIANA

Name	Builder	Built	Acquired	Comm
Louisiana	New Orleans	1812	Sep 1812	Sep 1812

Rate	16 guns
Dimensions	99′6″ (bp) × 28′ × 14′ beam, d23′
Tonnage	341 tons
Complement	160
Battery	16–24pdr; also reported as 4–24pdr, 8–12pdr, 4–6pdr

Notes: Purchased. Not armed until 1814.

Service record: Flagship of Patterson at Battle of New Orleans, 8 Jan 1815; sustained cannonade of 7 hours, firing 800 rounds. Laid up 1815. BU 1821.

The sloop *Erie*, completed in 1814, as she appeared in 1824. Painting by Nicholas Cammilieri. (U.S. Naval Historical Center)

U.S. Sloop *Ontario*, 18, heaving to at Marseille to take on a pilot. (U.S. Naval Historical Center)

ONTARIO CLASS

Name	Builder	Laid down	L	Comm
Argus	Washington NYd	1813	29 Jan 1814	never
Erie	Baltimore (Thos. Kemp)	1813	3 Nov 1813	Mar 1814
Ontario	Baltimore (Thos. Kemp)	1813	1813	1814

Rate	18 guns
Dimensions	117'11″ (bp) × 31'6″ × d14'6″
	Erie: (1821) 121'11″ (bp) × 32'6″
Tonnage	509 tons
	Erie: (1821) 611 tons
Complement	150
Battery	2–18pdr, 20–32pdr crde
Erie:	(1821) 2–18pdr, 20–42pdr crde
Ontario:	(1850) 2–32pdr, 18–32pdr crde

Notes: Designed by William Doughty. Authorized 2 Jan 1813. Fast, but did not steer well. *Erie* rebuilt and lengthened at New York NYd, 1820–21; launched in late 1821.

Service records:

Argus: Burned incomplete at Washington, 24 Aug 1814.

Erie: Blockaded at Baltimore, 1814. Mediterranean 1815–19. Rebuilt at New York, 1820–21. Mediterranean 1823–26. Gulf of Mexico 1827–32. Laid up 1832–34. Brazil Station. BU at Boston, 1841. Rebuilt as storeship (q.v.).

    Ship captured: Privateer *Federal* at St. Barthélemy, Dec 1828.

Ontario: Mediterranean 1815–17. Action with ship *Mashouda*, 46, and brig *Esledio*, 22, off Cape de Gatt, Spain, 17–19 Jun 1815. Pacific 1817–19. Capt. James Biddle landed at Cape Disappointment and claimed Oregon for U.S., 19 Aug 1818. Mediterranean 1821–24, 1825–27, 1829–32, 1833–36. West Indies 1837–40. Gulf of Mexico 1842–43. Receiving ship, Baltimore, 1842–56. Sold 15 Jul 1856.

WASP CLASS

Name	Builder	Laid down	L	Comm
Frolic	Boston (Josiah Barker)	1813	11 Sep 1813	Feb 1814
Peacock	New York (A & N Brown)	9 Jul 1813	19 Sep 1813	Mar 1814
Wasp	Newburyport, Mass. (Cross & Merrill)	1813	21 Sep 1813	May 1814

Rate	18 guns
Dimensions	*Frolic:* 119'6″ (bp) × 32' × 14'2″
	Peacock: 119' (bp) × 31'6″ × 14'6″
	Wasp: 117'11″ (bp) × 31'6″ × 14'6″
Tonnage	509 tons
Complement	140
Battery	2–12pdr, 20–32pdr crde

Notes: Designed by William Doughty. *Peacock* was fast in heavy winds.

Service records:

Frolic: Captured by HMS *Orpheus*, 36, and *Shelburne*, 12, off Matanzas, Cuba, after chase of 60 miles during which *Frolic* threw all her lee guns overboard (171 captured), 20 Apr 1814.

    Ships captured: Brig *Little Fox* off St. Thomas (destroyed), 17 Mar 1814; one schr privateer (sunk), 3 Apr 1814.

    Later history: HMS *Florida*, 20, 6th rate. BU May 1819.

Peacock: Took HMS *Epervier*, 18,[7] in action off Cape Canaveral, Fla., 29 Apr 1814. Took brig HMS *Nautilus*, 14, in Straits of Sunda after end of war (later released), 30 Jun 1815. Mediterranean 1816–21. West Indies 1822–24 (flagship). Pacific 1824–27. Struck by a whale and damaged, 1827. BU at New York, 1828.

    Ships captured: Brig *Sea Flower* off Grand Banks (burned), 17 Jun 1814; brig *Stranger*, 4 (sunk), sloop *Fortitude* (sunk), brig *Venus*, 4 (sunk), brig *Adiona* in Irish Channel, 5 Jul 1814; sloop *Leith Packet*, sloop *William & Ann*, sloop *Peggy & Jane* (sunk) off Shannon River and Tory Island, 1–3 Aug 1814; bark *William* (burned), ship *Sir Edward Pellew*, 12, off northern Ireland, 14–15 Aug 1814; brig *Bellona*, brig *Triton* (sunk) off Cape Finisterre, 21–23 Aug; brig *Duck* (sunk), 2 Sep 1814; ship *Mary* off Barbuda (sunk), 12 Oct 1814; ships *Union* (burned), *Venus*, and *Brio de Mar* (burned) in Straits of Sunda, 13 Jun–29 Jun 1814. (With *Louisiana*) six pirate ships, Sep 1822. Pirate schr near Cuba, Apr 1823.

Wasp: Sank HMS *Reindeer*, 18, in action south of Ireland (5 killed), 28 Jun 1814. Sank HMS *Avon*, 18, in night action south of Ireland (2 killed), 1 Sep 1814. Lost at sea with all hands in South Atlantic (140 killed), Oct 1814.

[7] Later USS *Epervier*.

Ships captured: Brig *Hazard*, 6, Oct 1812; bark *Neptune* southwest of Ireland (burned), 2 Jun 1814; brig *William* (burned), 13 Jun 1814; brig *Pallas* off Land's End (scuttled), 18 Jun 1814; ship *Henrietta*, 23 Jun 1814; ship *Orange Boven* (scuttled), 26 Jun 1814; brig *Regulator* (burned), 4 Jul 1814; schr *Jenny* (scuttled), 6 Jul 1814; brig *Lettice* (or *Lulice*), brig *Bon Accord*, brig *Mary* (scuttled), 30 Aug–1 Sep 1814; brig *Three Brothers*, 2 (burned), 12 Sep 1814; brig *Bacchus*, 2 (burned), 14 Sep 1814; brig *Atlanta*, 8 (ex-U.S. privateer *Siro*), 21 Sep 1814.

LEXINGTON CLASS

Name	Builder	Laid down	L	Comm
Lexington	New York NYd	1825	9 Mar 1826	11 Jun 1826
Natchez	Norfolk NYd	1827	8 Mar 1827	Jul 1827
Warren	Boston NYd	1 Jun 1825	29 Nov 1826	14 Jan 1827

Rate	18 guns
Dimensions	127′ (bp) × 34′7″ × 16′6″, d15′3″
Tonnage	691 tons
Complement	190
Battery	24–24pdr
	Lexington: (1844) 4–9pdr, 2–32pdr crde; (1840, as storeship) 6–32pdr crde
	Warren: 2–32pdr, 18–32pdr crde

Notes: Designed by William Doughty. Poor sailers, not well built.
Service records:
Lexington: Mediterranean 1827–30. Brazil Station 1831–36. Landing party in Falkland Islands, 1 Jan 1832. Pacific 1837–40. Converted to storeship, 1840. Mediterranean 1843–45. West Coast 1846. Bombardment of San Blas, Mexico, 12 Jan 1848. East Coast 1850. Expedition to Japan, 1853. Decomm 16 Feb 1855. Sold 1860.
  Ships captured: Two schrs at San Blas, 12 Jan 1848.
Natchez: West Indies, 1827–28, 1829–31. Charleston, S.C., during Nullification Crisis, 1833. Brazil Station 1834–35, 1836–38. Caribbean 1839. BU at New York, 1840.
  Ship captured: Mexican brig *General Urrea* off Brazos Santiago, 16 Apr 1837.
Warren: Mediterranean 1827–30. Attack on pirates at Mykonos and Andros, 1–7 Nov 1827. Brazil Station 1831–33. West Indies 1836–42. Pacific Sqn 1843–46. Storeship, 1846–63. Sold at Panama, 1 Jan 1863.
  Ships captured: Two pirate vessels, off Carabusa (Mediterranean), 4 Oct 1827; pirate brig and her prize off Syros, 25 or 28 Oct 1827; Mexican brig *Malek Adhel*[8] off Mazatlan, 7 Sep 1846. (With *Columbus* and *Erie*) British schr *William* at Monterey, Calif., 22 Mar 1847.

BOSTON CLASS

Name	Builder	Laid down	L	Comm
Boston	Boston NYd	13 May 1825	15 Oct 1825	1826
Concord	Portsmouth NYd	19 Mar 1827	24 Sep 1828	7 May 1830
Fairfield	New York NYd	1826	28 Jun 1828	Aug 1828
John Adams	Norfolk NYd	1829	17 Nov 1830	May 1831
St. Louis	Washington NYd	12 Feb 1827	18 Aug 1828	20 Dec 1828
Vandalia	Philadelphia NYd	1825	26 Aug 1828	6 Nov 1828
Vincennes	New York NYd	1825	27 Apr 1826	27 Aug 1826

Rate	18 guns
Dimensions	127′ (bp) × 34′9″ × 16′6″

[8] Later USS *Malek Adhel*.

The U.S. sloop *Fairfield* was one of seven authorized in 1825. From the collection of Franklin D. Roosevelt. (U.S. Naval Historical Center)

	Boston: 127′ × 33′9″ × 16′
	Vandalia: (1850) 157′
Tonnage	700 tons; also reported as 614 tons
Complement	125/190
Battery	24–24pdr; (1846–48, most) 4–8″, 16–32pdr
	Boston: (1840) 2–24pdr, 20–42pdr crde; (1846) 4–8″, 16–32pdr
	Fairfield: (1850) 4–8″, 16–32pdr
	John Adams: (1842) 2–18pdr, 22–32pdr crde; (1846) 22–24pdr; (1850) 4–8″, 14–32pdr; (1862) 2–8″, 4–32pdr, 2–30pdr MLR, 2–20pdr MLR
	St. Louis: (1848) 4–8″, 16–32pdr; (1850) 4–8″, 14–32pdr; (1862) 4–8″, 12–32pdr, 2–20pdr MLR
	Vincennes: (1838) 8–24pdr, 2–9pdr; (1842) 24–24pdr; (1845) 4–8″, 16–32pdr; (1861) 4–8″, 14–32pdr; (1861) 2–9″, 4–8″
	Vandalia: (1850) 4–8″, 16–32pdr; (1863) 4–8″, 16–32pdr, 1–30pdr MLR

Notes: Authorized 3 Mar 1825. Designed by Samuel Humphreys. Original armament too heavy for hulls. Not fast but well built; good sea boats. *John Adams* was officially the old frigate rebuilt. *St. Louis* lengthened 13′ at Norfolk NYd, 1845. *Vandalia* rebuilt at Norfolk NYd and also lengthened 13′, 1848.
Service records:
Boston: Brazil Station 1826–29. Mediterranean 1830–32. West Indies 1836–39. East Indies, 1841–43. Brazil Station 1843–46. Wrecked in squall on Eleuthera en route to blockading duty off Mexico (all saved), 15 Nov 1846.
Concord: Mediterranean 1830–32. West Indies 1836–37. Brazil Station 1841–43. Ran aground in mouth of Loango River, Mozambique (3 killed, including captain, Cdr. William Boerum), 2 Oct 1842; acting captain chartered Portuguese brig *Union* to bring home survivors and the following year the brig *Chipola* was chartered to bring home guns and equipment.
Fairfield: Mediterranean 1828–31. West Indies 1831–32 (flagship). Pacific Sqn 1833–35. Brazil Station 1837–40. Mediterranean 1841–45. Decomm 3 Feb 1845. Sold 11 Jun 1852 and BU.
John Adams: Mediterranean 1831–33. Second attack on Kuala Batu, Sumatra, 1–2 Jan 1839. Africa 1848–53. Destroyed towns in Fiji as retaliation, 28–31 Oct 1855. Sold 5 Oct 1867.
St. Louis: Pacific Sqn 1829–31. West Indies Sqn 1832–38. Pacific Sqn

The sloop *Levant*, riding out a storm at anchor in Naples harbor during the 1850s. Painting by Francisco de Simone. (U.S. Naval Historical Center)

1839–42. East Indies Sqn 1843–45 (flagship). South American Sqn 1848–51. Mediterranean 1852–55. Africa Sqn 1855–58. Home Sqn 1858–61. Receiving ship, Philadelphia, 1866–94. Sold 5 Jun 1907.

Vandalia: Brazil Station 1828–31. West Indies 1832–34, 1835–38. Laid up 1839–42. Home Sqn 1842–45. Pacific Sqn 1849–52. East Indies 1853–56. Expedition to Japan, 1853. Pacific Sqn 1857–60. BU 1870–72.

Vincennes: Pacific Sqn 1826–30. First U.S. naval vessel to circumnavigate the world, 1829–30. West Indies 1831–32. Pacific Sqn 1834–36. Wilkes survey expedition to South Seas, Aug 1838–Jul 1842. West Indies 1842–44. Far East 1845–47. First visit to Japan, 20 Jul 1846. Pacific Sqn 1850–52. Ringgold's Far East expedition, 1853–56. Africa Sqn 1857–60. Sold 5 Oct 1867.

FALMOUTH

Name	Builder	Laid down	L	Comm
Falmouth	Boston NYd	5 Dec 1826	3 Nov 1827	19 Jan 1828

Rate	18 guns
Dimensions	127′6″ (bp) × 33′9″ × 16′6″, d15′6″
Tonnage	703 tons
Complement	190
Battery	24–24pdr; (1850) 4–8″, 16–32pdr

Notes: Designed by Josiah Barker. Good sailer, steered well.

Service record: West Indies, Mexico, and Pacific, 1828–40. Home Sqn 1841–46. Expedition against Alvarado, Mexico, 7 Aug 1846. Pacific Sqn 1849–52. West Indies 1854–55. Brazil Station 1857–59. Paraguay Expedition, 1858. Stationary storeship, Aspinwall, Panama, 1860. Sold at Aspinwall, 7 Nov 1863.

PEACOCK

Name	Builder	Laid down	L	Comm
Peacock	New York NYd	1828–30	Sep 1828	Aug 1829

Rate	18 guns
Dimensions	118′9″ (bp) × 31′6″ × 15′6″, d14′10″
Tonnage	559 tons
Complement	190
Battery	6–18pdr; (1831) 2–12pdr, 20–32pdr crde; (1840) 2–9″, 8–24pdr crde

Notes: Officially the old sloop *Peacock* rebuilt; similar size but new lines. Designed by Samuel Humphreys. Too small for her armament, later reduced for exploration.

Service record: West Indies 1829–31. Brazil Station 1832–34. East Indies 1835–37. Almost lost on coral reef at mouth of Persian Gulf; after lying 61 hours, was extricated by lightening ship, throwing guns overboard, etc.; 1837. Wilkes survey expedition to South Seas, Aug

1838–Jul 1842. Cruise to Antarctic, 1838–41. Landing in Samoa, Feb 1841. Wrecked off Columbia River, Ore. (all saved), 18 Jul 1841.

CYANE CLASS

Name	Builder	Laid down	L	Comm
Cyane	Boston NYd	1837	2 Dec 1837	May 1838
Levant	New York NYd	1837	28 Dec 1837	17 Mar 1838

Rate	22 guns
Dimensions	132'3" (bp) × 36'3" × 16'6"
Tonnage	792 tons
Complement	200
Battery	4–24pdr, 18–32pdr crde; (1840) 20–32pdr
	Cyane: (1850) 4–8", 16–32pdr; (1856) 4–8", 14–32pdr; (1863) 1–8", 1–32pdr
	Levant: (1843) 4–8", 18–32pdr; (1850) 4–8", 16–32pdr; (1856) 4–8", 14–32pdr

Notes: Designed by Samuel Humphreys. *Cyane* officially the old ship rebuilt. Corvettes, good sailers, satisfactory ships.

Service records:

Cyane: Mediterranean 1838–41. Pacific Sqn 1841–44, 1845–48. Seizure of Monterey, Calif., 7 Jul 1846. Occupation of San Diego, 29 Jul 1846. Capture of Mazatlan, 11 Nov 1847. Home Sqn 1851–52. Bombarded Greytown, Nicaragua, as retaliation, 13 Jul 1854. Pacific 1858–71. Decomm 20 Sep 1871. Sold 30 Jul 1887.

    Ships captured: Mexican brigantine *Juanita*, brig *Prima Vera* at San Diego, 9–10 Aug 1846; Mexican sloop *Solita*, brigantine *Susana* off San Blas, Calif., 2–3 Sep 1846; Mexican sloop *San Jose*, schr *Adelaide*, schr *Victoria*, schr *Eliza*, schr *Mazolea*, schr *Julia*, brigantine *La Paz*, brigantine *Manuela*, brigantine *Correo* at La Paz, Baja Calif., 14 Sep 1846; Mexican schr *Libertad*,[9] schr *Fortuna*, schr *Rosita*, sloop *Chapita*, sloop *Alerto*, brig *Condor* at Loreta, Baja Calif., 1–7 Oct 1846.

Levant: West Indies 1838–42. Pacific 1843–45. Laid up 1847. Mediterranean 1852–55. Seizure of Monterey, Calif., 7 Jul 1846. East India Sqn 1856–58. Bombardment of forts at Canton, China (22 shot holes, 1 killed), 20–22 Nov 1856. Left Hilo, Hawaii, for Panama, 18 Sep 1860, and disappeared.

DALE CLASS

Name	Builder	Laid down	L	Comm
Dale	Philadelphia NYd	1839	8 Nov 1839	11 Dec 1840
Decatur	New York NYd	1838	9 Apr 1839	Mar 1840
Marion	Boston NYd	1838	24 Apr 1839	4 Oct 1839
Preble	Portsmouth NYd	Apr 1838	13 Jun 1839	Jun 1840
Yorktown	Norfolk NYd	1838	17 Jun 1839	15 Nov 1840

Rate	16 guns
Dimensions	117'7" (bp) × 33'10" × 15'
	Dale: 117' × 32' × 15'6"
Tonnage	566 tons
Complement	150
Battery	14–32pdr, 2–12pdr
	Dale: (1846) 16–32pdr; (1853) 14–32pdr; (1863) 2–32pdr, 1–30pdr MLR
	Decatur: (1846) 16–32pdr; (1853) 14–32pdr; (1863) 4–8", 4–32pdr
	Marion: (1845) 16–32pdr; (1855) 14–32pdr; (1862) 10–32pdr, 1–20pdr MLR

[9] Later USS *Libertad*.

A *Dale*-class sloop in dry dock at Charlestown Navy Yard, Boston, during the 1850s. One of the earliest known photographs of an American naval vessel. (Peabody Museum of Salem)

	Preble: (1846) 16–32pdr; (1851) 10–32pdr; (1853) 8–32pdr; (1858) 10–32pdr; (1861) 2–8", 7–32pdr
	Yorktown: (1844) 2–32pdr, 2–18pdr, 12–32pdr crde; (1846) 16–32pdr

Notes: Designed by John Lenthall as duplicates of *Peacock*. Very successful. Stiff, sailed well.

Service records:

Dale: Pacific Sqn 1840–43, 1846–49. Took Muleje, Baja Calif., 1 Oct 1847. African Sqn 1850–59. Decomm May 1859. Renamed ***Oriole*** 30 Nov 1904. Trfd to USRCS, 27 Feb 1906.

    Ships captured: Schr *Magdalena* at Muleje, Mexico (burned), 30 Sep 1847; several vessels on Mexican Pacific coast, Feb–Apr 1848.

Decatur: Brazil Station 1840–43. Africa Sqn 1845–46. Mexico 1847–48. Africa Sqn 1848–49. Protection of North Atlantic fisheries, 1853. Pacific Sqn 1854–59. Defended Seattle against Indians, 26 Jan 1856. Decomm 20 Jun 1859. Sold at San Francisco, 27 Aug 1865.

Marion: Brazil Station 1839–42. West Indies 1842–43. Sunk when heaved down at Rio de Janeiro, early 1842; raised. Laid up at Boston. East Indies 1850–52. Africa Sqn 1853–55, 1858–60. BU 1871–72.

    Ships captured: Slaver ketch *Brothers* off southeast coast of Africa, 8 Sep 1858; slaver bark *Orion* near Congo River, 21 Apr 1859; slaver bark *Ardennes* near Congo River, 27 Apr 1859.

USS *Dale* as Naval Academy practice vessel during the late 19th century. (National Archives)

Preble: Labrador 1840. Mediterranean 1841–43. Africa 1844–45. Pacific 1847–48. East Indies 1848–50. Paraguay Expedition, 1858. Burned at Pensacola, 27 Apr 1863.

Yorktown: Pacific Sqn 1841–43. Africa Sqn 1844–46, 1848–50. Wrecked in Cape Verde Islands (all saved), 6 Sep 1850.

  Ship captured: Slaver bark *Pons* off Cabinda, Africa, 30 Nov 1845.

SARATOGA

Name	Builder	Laid down	L	Comm
Saratoga	Portsmouth N Yd	Aug 1841	26 Jul 1842	4 Jan 1843

Rate	20 guns
Dimensions	146′4″ (bp) × 35′3″ × 16′3″
Tonnage	882 tons
Complement	275/210
Battery	4–8″, 16–32pdr; (1846) 4–8″, 18–32pdr; (1855) 6–8″, 12–32pdr; (1856) 6–8″, 14–32pdr; (1857) 6–8″, 12–32pdr; (1863) 6–8″, 12–32pdr, 10–30pdr MLR

Notes: Designed by Samuel Pook and Samuel Humphreys. Improved *Cyane.* Weatherly and fast.

Service record: Dismasted on first day of first cruise, 17 Mar 1843. Africa Sqn 1843–44. Mexico 1845–47. West Indies 1848–49. East Indies Sqn 1850–54. Expedition to Japan, 1853. Africa Sqn 1860–61. Sold 14 Aug 1907.

Ships captured: Mexican rebel steamers *General Miramon* and *Marques de la Habana*[10] in Gulf of Mexico, intervening in Mexican Civil War on government side, 7 Mar 1860; schr *Express* off Africa, 25 Feb 1861; ship *Nightingale*[11] off Cabinda, Africa, 21 Apr 1861.

ALBANY

Name	Builder	Laid down	L	Comm
Albany	New York N Yd	1843	27 Jun 1846	6 Nov 1846

[10] Later CSS *McRae.*
[11] Later USS *Nightingale.*

The sloop *Portsmouth,* built in 1843, as she appeared later in the 19th century, drying sails and laundry at Portsmouth Navy Yard.

Rate	20 guns
Dimensions	147′11″ (bp) × 38′6″ × 17′9″ (maximum)
Tonnage	1,042 tons
Complement	210
Battery	4–8″, 18–32pdr; (1853) 6–8″, 16–32pdr

Notes: Designed by Francis Grice. Well-built, handsome vessel on Baltimore clipper model.

Service record: Home Sqn 1846–47; Mexican War. Landings at Veracruz, 9 Mar 1847, and siege. Capture of Tuxpan, 17 Apr 1847. Departed Aspinwall, Colombia, 29 Sep 1854, and was never heard from again (193 lost).

PORTSMOUTH

Name	Builder	Laid down	L	Comm
Portsmouth	Portsmouth N Yd	15 Jun 1843	23 Oct 1843	10 Nov 1844

Rate	20 guns
Dimensions	153′1″ (bp) × 38′1″ × 17′6″
Tonnage	1,022 tons
Complement	210
Battery	4–8″, 18–32pdr; (1852) 6–8″, 16–32pdr; (1856) 16–8″; (1861) 16–8″, 1–20pdr MLR

The sloop *Portsmouth* of 1844 was considered the best of her class. (U.S. Naval Historical Center)

USS *Jamestown*, a sloop built in 1844, remained in service until 1892.

Notes: Designed by Josiah Barker. Best of the 1841 sloops.
Service record: Mexico 1845–46. Africa 1848–51. Took possession of San Francisco Bay, 9 Jul 1846. Took San Jose, Baja Calif., 30 Mar 1847. Far East 1856–58. Fired on by forts at Canton, China, 16 Nov 1856. Bombardment of Canton forts (3 killed), 20–22 Nov 1856. Sold 1915.
Ships captured: Schr *Jose Eliza* near Mazatlan, 11 Mar 1847; ship *Admittance* near San Jose, Baja Calif., 7 Apr 1847; Chilean brig *Argo* in Gulf of Mexico, 10 Oct 1847; schr *Caroline* in Gulf of Mexico, 29 Oct 1847; slaver sloop *Emily* off Loango, Africa, 21 Nov 1859; slaver brigantine *Virginian* off Congo River, 6 Feb 1860; slaver brig *Falmouth*, off Port Praya, Africa, 6 May 1860.

PLYMOUTH

Name	Builder	Laid down	L	Comm
Plymouth	Boston NYd	1843	11 Nov 1843	Apr 1844

Rate	20 guns
Dimensions	147'6" (bp) × 38'1" × 17'2"
Tonnage	989 tons
Complement	210
Battery	(1857) 1–11", 4–9"; (1859) 2–8", 6–32pdr; (1862) 4–8", 18–32pdr

Notes: Designed by Samuel Pook. Stiff, dry, and fast.
Service record: Mediterranean 1844–46. Far East 1848–51. Expedition to Japan, 1853. Training ship, 1855–56, 1859–60. Burned at Norfolk NYd, 20 Apr 1861.

JAMESTOWN

Name	Builder	Laid down	L	Comm
Jamestown	Norfolk NYd	1843	16 Sep 1844	12 Dec 1844

Rate	20 guns
Dimensions	163'6" × 32'2" × 17'3"
Tonnage	985 tons; 1,150 tons D
Complement	210
Battery	4–8", 18–32pdr; (1851) 6–8", 16–32pdr; (1861) 6–8", 14–32pdr

Notes: Designed by Foster Rhodes. Fast, difficult to trim.
Service record: Africa Sqn 1845–47 (flagship). Mediterranean 1849–50. Brazil Station 1851–54. Africa Sqn 1855–57 (flagship). West Indies 1857–60. To Marine Hospital Service, 9 Sep 1892. Quarantine ship, 1892–1912. Sold 7 Oct 1912. Destroyed by burning, 3 Jan 1913.

ST. MARY'S

Name	Builder	Laid down	L	Comm
St. Mary's	Washington NYd	1843	24 Nov 1844	13 Dec 1844

Rate	20 guns
Dimensions	150' (bp) × 37'4" × d16'8"
Tonnage	958 tons
Complement	210
Battery	4–8", 18–32pdr; (1850) 6–8", 16–32pdr

Notes: Designed by Charles B. Brodie. Fast and weatherly.
Service record: Pacific Sqn 1848–53, 1854–58. Bombarded Tampico, 8–15 Jun 1856. School ship, 1875–1908. Public Marine School. Stricken 14 Jun 1908 and sold.

GERMANTOWN

Name	Builder	Laid down	L	Comm
Germantown	Philadelphia NYd	7 Sep 1843	21 Aug 1846	9 Mar 1847

Rate	20 guns
Dimensions	150' (bp) × 36' × 17'3"
Tonnage	939 tons
Complement	210
Battery	4–8", 18–32pdr; (1853) 6–8", 14–32pdr; (1855) 6–8", 16–32pdr

Notes: Designed by John Lenthall. Good sailer. Completed at Norfolk NYd.
Service record: Mexico 1847–48. West Indies 1848–49. Africa Sqn 1851–53 (flagship). Brazil Station 1853–57. Landed Marines at Montevideo, 27 Nov 1855. East India Sqn 1857–60. Burned at Norfolk NYd, 20 Apr 1861.
Ship captured: Slaver schr *Rachel P. Brown*, 1 Feb 1853.

Austin, see chapter 5

CONSTELLATION

Name	Builder	Laid down	L	Comm
Constellation	Norfolk NYd	1853	26 Aug 1854	28 Jul 1855

Rate	24 guns
Dimensions	176' (bp) × 42' × 19'3"
Tonnage	1,265 tons
Complement	227
Battery	2–10", 16–8", 4–32pdr; (1856) 16–8", 4–32pdr; (1862) 16–8", 4–32pdr, 1–30pdr MLR, 1–20pdr MLR

Notes: Corvette. Officially the old frigate rebuilt. Sailed and steered well.
Service record: Mediterranean Sqn 1855–58. Cuba 1858. Africa Sqn 1859–61 (flagship). Mediterranean Sqn 1861–64. Receiving ship, 1865–1933. Renamed **Old Constellation**, 1917–20. Trfd for museum at Baltimore, 15 Aug 1955.

The sloop *Constellation*, built in 1854, still in service in 1905 as a training ship.

Ships captured: Slaver brig *Delicia* off Cabinda, Africa, 21 Dec 1859; slaver bark *Cora* off Congo River, 25 Sep 1860; slaver brig *Triton* off West Africa, 21 May 1861.

BRIGS

In addition to those ships listed below, two brigs not to exceed 360 tons, with armament of 18–9pdr, which had been ordered to be built at Newburyport and Conway, were canceled in 1799. A larger clipper brig, *Burrows*, 14 guns, was proposed in 1845 but not built; she was to have been 126′ (bp) × 30′ × 14′.

For details on the brigs *Archer* and *Wharton*, see chapter 5.

Name	Builder	L	Comm
Norfolk	Norfolk (Nash & Herbert)	1798	Sep 1798
Richmond ex-*Augusta*	Norfolk	1798	(U)

Rate	*Norfolk:* 18 guns
	Richmond: 14 guns
Dimensions	(U)
Tonnage	200 tons
Complement	140
Battery	18–6pdr
	Richmond: 10–6pdr, 4–4pdr

Service records:

Norfolk: West Indies with Murray's Sqn, then with Truxtun, 1798 and 1800. Sold 1801.

Ships captured: (With *Boston* and *General Greene*) schr *Flying Fish*, 1 Dec 1799. (With *Boston*): *La Gourde, Le Pelican,* 1800.

Richmond: Purchased while building. West Indies with Truxtun's Sqn, then with Talbot; later on coast under C. Talbot, 1799–1800. Sold Apr 1801.

Ships captured: Recaptured American schr *Chance*, 22 May 1800; *Thomas Chalkley*, 28 May 1800.

Name	Builder	Laid down	L	Comm
Pinckney	Charleston, S.C. (Pritchard)	1798	22 Sep 1798	1798

Rate	18 guns
Dimensions	62′ (keel) × 23′ × 10′6″
Tonnage	195 tons
Complement	140
Battery	(U)

Notes: Trfd from USRCS while under construction. Converted to galley, 11 Dec 1798. Sold 1801.
Service record: West Indies 1798–99 with Tingey's and Bainbridge's sqns.

Name	Builder	Built	Acquired	Comm
Augusta	Norfolk	(U)	30 Jun 1799	late 1799

Rate	14 guns
Dimensions	(U)
Tonnage	(U)
Complement	100
Battery	10–6pdr, 4–4pdr

Notes: Purchased merchantman.
Service record: West Indies in Talbot's Sqn, 1799. Sold, spring 1801.
Ships captured: (With *Herald*) French privateer *La Mutiné*, 21 Jan 1800. *Le Républicain*, 1800; French schr *La Jeanne*, schr *La Victoire* off Jacmel, Haiti, Jun 1800. (With *Boston*) ship *L'Espoir*, 24 Jun 1800. (With Haitian schr) two brigs at Aux Cayes, Haiti, 28 Jul 1800.

Name	Builder	Laid down	L	Comm
Argus	Boston (Edmund Hartt)	12 May 1803	21 Aug 1803	Sep 1803
ex-*Merrimack* (4 Jun 1803)				

Rate	16 guns
Dimensions	94′6″ (bp), 80′ (keel) × 28′2″ × d12′8″
Tonnage	298 tons
Complement	120 or 142
Battery	2–12pdr, 16–24pdr crde; (1811) 2–12pdr, 18–24pdr crde **or** (1804) 1–long 12pdr, 12–24pdr crde

Notes: Designed by Joseph Hartt for use on North African coast. Authorized 28 Feb 1803.
Service record: Mediterranean 1803–06; War with Tripoli under Decatur and Hull. Attacks on forts at Tripoli (12 killed), Aug–Sep 1804. Attack on and capture of Derna, Libya, 27 Apr 1805. Laid up, Jul 1805–1807. Captured by HMS *Pelican*, 18, in English Channel after severe action of 45 minutes and loss of commander, W. H. Allen (10 killed), 14 Aug 1813.
Ships captured: Ship *Ariadne* in North Atlantic, 16 Oct 1812; brig *Fly*, 28 Oct 1812; brig *Recovery*, 2 Dec 1812; schr *Dorothy*, 6 Dec 1812; schr *Vancise*, 17 Dec 1812; schr *Salamanca* (burned), May 1813; brig *Susannah*, schr *Matilda* (later recaptured), brig *Richard*, brig *Fowey*, sloop *Lady Francis*, ship *Barbadoes*, brig *Alliance*, schr *Cordelia* (later recaptured), ship *Betsey*, ship *Mariner*, sloop *John & Thomas*, brig *Helen*, brig *Ann*, sloop *Diana & Betsey*, ship *Defiance*, brig *Baltic*, brig *Bedford* (all except *Matilda* and *Cordelia* burned), 14 Jul–14 Aug 1813.

USS *Wasp*, 18, built in 1806, was captured by HMS *Frolic* in 1812. (National Archives)

Name	Builder	Laid down	L	Comm
Syren	Philadelphia (Nathaniel Hutton)	1803	6 Aug 1803	Sep 1803

Rate	16 guns
Dimensions	93′4″ (bp) × 27′9″ × 12′6″
Tonnage	240 tons
Complement	137
Battery	(1813) 2–12pdr, 16–24pdr crde; (1814) 2–9pdr, 2–42pdr crde, 12–24pdr crde

Notes: Built for North African service. Light weather vessel; qualities spoiled by overloading. Designed by Benjamin Hutton, Jr.
Service record: Mediterranean 1803–06; War with Tripoli under Stewart and Smith. Attacks on forts at Tripoli, Aug–Sep 1804. Returned home in 1806. Renamed *Siren* 1810. Captured at sea off Africa under Nicholson by HMS *Medway*, 74, after an 11-hour chase during which guns, anchors, cables, boats, and spars were thrown overboard, 12 Jul 1814.
Ships captured: Brig *Transfer*,[12] 21 Mar 1804; polacre *Madonna de Catapalliari* off Tripoli, 22 Mar 1804; ship *Barton* (destroyed) off Africa, May 1814; brig *Adventurer* (destroyed) off Africa, 12 Jul 1814.
Later history: Hospital hulk until 1815.

[12] Later USS *Scourge*.

Name	Builder	Built	Acquired	Comm
Scourge ex-*Transfer*, ex–*Quatre Freres*	(U)	1804	(U)	17 Apr 1804

Rate	16 guns
Dimensions	80′ × 23′6″ × (U)
Tonnage	181 tons
Complement	36/80
Battery	16–6pdr

Notes: Captured by USS *Syren* as a Tripolitanian blockade runner off Tripoli, 21 Mar 1804. Former French privateer *Quatre Frères*, captured by British in 1797. Built in America or Bermuda.
Service record: Attacks on forts at Tripoli, Aug–Sep 1804. Laid up in U.S., 1805. Sold 1812.

Name	Builder	Laid down	L	Comm
Wasp	Washington NYd	1805	21 Apr 1806	May 1807

Rate	18 guns
Dimensions	105′7″ (bp) × 30′11″ × 14′1″
Tonnage	440 tons
Complement	140
Battery	(1813) 2–12pdr, 18–32pdr crde

Notes: Authorized 26 Mar 1804. Designed by Joseph Fox; altered to ship rig while under construction. Fast, steady, and weatherly.
Service record: Cruised off U.S. coast, 1809, 1810. Under Jacob Jones, captured and manned HMS *Frolic*, 18 Oct 1812, then was taken at sea by *Poictiers*, 74 (5 killed).
Later history: HMS *Peacock*, 18. Foundered off southern U.S. coast, Aug 1814.

Name	Builder	Laid down	L	Comm
Hornet	Baltimore (Wm. Price)	(U)	28 Jul 1805	18 Oct 1805

Rate	18 guns
Dimensions	106′9″ (bp) × 31′5″ × 14′11″; (1811) beam 39′; (1812) d14′
Tonnage	441 tons
Complement	140
Battery	16–9pdr; (1811) 2–12pdr, 18–32pdr crde; (1813) 1–18pdr, 18–32pdr crde

Notes: Designed by Josiah Fox. Authorized 26 Mar 1804. Rebuilt as ship-rigged sloop of war at Washington NYd, Nov 1810–Sep 1811.
Service record: Mediterranean 1806–07. Europe 1812. Captured HMS *Peacock*, 18, which later sank, in action off Demerara (4 killed), 24 Feb 1813. Sank HMS *Penguin*, 18, in action off Tristan da Cunha, unaware war was over (1 killed), 23 Mar 1815. Mediterranean 1819. West Indies 1822. Foundered in gale off Tampico with all hands (140 killed), 29 Sep 1829.
Ships captured: Privateer brig *Dolphin*, 14 (later recaptured), 9 Jul 1812; schr *Ellen* off Brazil, 6 Jan 1813; brig *Resolution* (burned) off Pernambuco, 4 Feb 1813; ship *William*, 1814; slaver brigantine *Alexander*, 1820; pirate schr *Moscow* off Santo Domingo, West Indies, 29 Oct 1821.

Name	Builder	Built	Acquired	Comm
Rattlesnake ex-*Rambler*	Medford, Mass. (Turner)	(U)	1813	Jan 1814

Rate	14 guns
Dimensions	(U)
Tonnage	278 tons
Complement	(U)
Battery	(U)

Notes: Purchased privateer.
Service record: West Indies 1814. Captured at sea by HMS *Leander*, 50, off Cape Sable, N.S., after a long chase during which all but two guns were thrown overboard, 22 Jun 1814.
Ships captured: (With *Enterprise*) brig *Isabella* (prize), 18 Jan 1814; ship *Sincerity*, 20 Jan 1814; brig *Rambler* (burned) south of Azores, 7 Feb 1814; schr *Eliza*, schr *Mars* (LofM), 23 Feb 1814. Brig *John* (burned), 9 Jun 1814; brig *Crown Prince* (burned), sloop *Fanny*, 22 Jun 1814.

Name	Builder	Built	Acquired	Comm
Vixen	Savannah	1813	1813	(U)

Rate	14 guns
Dimensions	(U)
Tonnage	(U)
Complement	(U)
Battery	never armed

Notes: Purchased.
Service record: Captured at sea by HMS *Belvidera* on passage from Wilmington, N.C., to Newcastle, Del., without armament or stores, 23 Dec 1813.

Name	Builder	L	Acquired	Comm
Epervier ex-HMS *Epervier*	Rochester (Mary Ross)	2 Dec 1812	1814	1814

Rate	18 guns
Dimensions	100′ (deck), 77′3″ (keel) × 30′6″ × d12′9″ (English measure)
Tonnage	477 tons (in RN, 382 tons)
Complement	128
Battery	18–32pdr crde

Notes: British brig-sloop, 18 guns. Captured by USS *Peacock* off Indian River Inlet, Fla., 29 Apr 1814.
Service record: Action with ship *Mashouda*, 46, and brig *Esledio*, 22, off Cape de Gatt, Spain, 17–19 Jun 1815. Passed Strait of Gibraltar, 14 Jul 1815, and disappeared at sea in North Atlantic (all lost).

Name	Builder	Built	Acquired	Comm
Flambeau ex-*Leader*	(U)	(U)	3 Dec 1814	May 1815

Rate	14 guns
Dimensions	107′ (bp), 100′ (keel) × 26′ × 11′9″
Tonnage	300 tons
Complement	90/100
Battery	2- or 4–18pdr, 10–18pdr crde

Notes: Purchased.
Service record: One cruise to Mediterranean, 1815. Sold 3 Apr 1816.

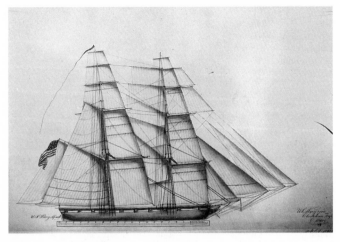

Spar and sail plan of the brig *Spark*, built in 1813 and purchased at New York. (U.S. Naval Historical Center)

Name	Builder	Built	Acquired	Comm
Firefly ex-*Volent*	(U)	(U)	8 Dec 1814	1815

Rate	14 guns
Dimensions	109′ (bp), 100′ (keel) × 29′4″ × 12′10″, d11′
Tonnage	330 tons
Complement	100
Battery	4–18pdr, 10–18pdr crde; (1816) 4–12pdr, 12–18pdr crde

Notes: Purchased at New York.
Service record: One cruise to Mediterranean, 1815. Sold 3 Apr 1816.

Name	Builder	Built	Acquired	Comm
Spark	Sag Harbor, N.Y.	1813	1814	8 Dec 1814

Rate	14 guns; (later) 12 guns
Dimensions	103′3″ (bp) × 25′4″ × 12′8″
Tonnage	287 tons
Complement	90
Battery	2–18pdr, 10–18pdr crde

Notes: Purchased at New York.

The brig *Porpoise*, built in 1836, disappeared in the Pacific in 1854. (U.S. Naval Historical Center)

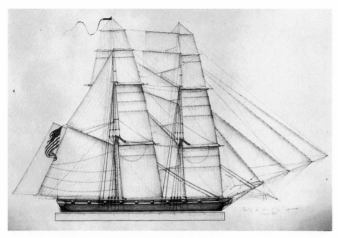

Spar and sail plan of the brig *Chippewa*, built in 1815 and wrecked in 1816. (U.S. Naval Historical Center)

Service record: Mediterranean 1815, 1816–21. Action with ship *Mashouda*, 46, and brig *Esledio*, 22, off Cape de Gatt, Spain, 17–19 Jun 1815. West Indies 1822–25. Sold 1826.
Ship captured: Dutch sloop (prize), 7 Jan 1822.

Name	Builder	Laid down	L	Comm
Chippewa	Warren, R.I.	1814	Apr 1815	Jul 1815

Rate	14 guns
Dimensions	107′ (bp) × 29′11″ × 16′9″
Tonnage	390 tons
Complement	90
Battery	2–18pdr, 14–32pdr crde

Notes: Designed by William Doughty.
Service record: Mediterranean 1815. Wrecked in Caicos Islands (crew saved), 12 Dec 1816.

Name	Builder	Laid down	L	Comm
Saranac	Middletown, Conn. (Beldin & Churchill)	1814	1815	Dec 1815

Rate	14 guns
Dimensions	94′ (keel) × 28′7″ × 14′
Tonnage	360 tons
Complement	90
Battery	2–12pdr, 14–32pdr crde

Notes: Designed by William Doughty.
Service record: Mediterranean 1815–16. West Indies 1816–18. Sold Dec 1818.

Name	Builder	Laid down	L	Comm
Boxer	Middletown, Conn. (Beldin & Churchill)	1814	May 1815	1815

Rate	14 guns
Dimensions	114′11″ × 28′7″ × 14′2″
Tonnage	370 tons

Complement	90
Battery	2–9pdr, 14–24pdr crde

Notes: Designed by William Doughty.
Service record: Mediterranean 1815. Gulf of Mexico 1816–17. Foundered off Belize (crew saved), 25 Oct 1817.

Name	Builder	Laid down	L	Comm
Dolphin	New York NYd	1836	17 Jun 1836	6 Sep 1836
Porpoise	Boston NYd	1836	31 May 1836	25 Aug 1836

Rate	10 guns
Dimensions	88′ (bp) × 25′ × 13′, d11′
Tonnage	224 tons
Complement	80
Battery	2–9pdr, 8–24pdr crde
	Dolphin: (1850) 6–32pdr; (1858) 4–32pdr; (1859) 3–11″, 1–9″
	Porpoise: (1846) 2–9pdr, 9–24pdr crde; (1850) 2–32pdr, 6–24pdr crde

Notes: Improved versions of *Boxer* class, designed by Samuel Humphreys. Very fast. *Dolphin* rigged as a brig; *Porpoise* originally rigged as a brigantine, then rerigged as a brig about 1840.
Service records:
Dolphin: Brazil Station 1836–39. Africa Sqn 1839–41. Home Sqn 1841–43. Africa Sqn 1845–47. East India Sqn 1848–51. Survey expedition under Maury, 1852–53. Africa Sqn 1855–57. Paraguay Expedition, 1858. Burned at Norfolk NYd, 20 Apr 1861.
   Ships captured: Slaver bark *Chancellor* off Cape Mount, Africa, 1846; slaver brig *The Echo*, north of Cuba, 21 Aug 1858.
Porpoise: Wilkes survey expedition to South Seas, Aug 1838–Jul 1842. Africa Sqn 1843–44. Gulf of Mexico 1845–47. Africa Sqn 1848–50. Ringgold exploring expedition in Pacific, 1853. Disappeared in China Sea, probably foundered in typhoon, Feb 1854.
   Ship captured: Schr *Nonata*[13] off Lagunas, Mexico, 21 Aug 1846.

Name	Builder	Laid down	L	Comm
Bainbridge	Boston NYd	1842	26 Apr 1842	16 Dec 1842
Somers	New York NYd	1842	16 Apr 1842	12 May 1842

Rate	12 guns
Dimensions	100′ (bp) × 25′ × 13′6″, d14′
Tonnage	259 tons
Complement	80
Battery	12– or 10–32pdr crde; (1850) 6–32pdr

Notes: Designed by Samuel Humphreys. Fast and weatherly.
Service records:
Bainbridge: Home Sqn 1843–44. Brazil Station 1844–47. Africa Sqn 1848–50. Brazil Station and Africa Sqn 1850–56. Paraguay Expedition, 1859. Capsized off Cape Hatteras (1 survivor), 21 Aug 1863.
Somers: Attempted mutiny on board foiled, 1 Dec 1842—the only case of mutiny on a USN ship; three hanged, including the son of Secretary of War Spencer. West Indies 1843–46. Attack on Alvarado, Mexico, 7 Aug 1846. Capsized in squall off Tampico (32 killed), 8 Dec 1846.

---

[13] Later USS *Nonata*.

Name	Builder	Laid down	L	Comm
Truxtun	Norfolk NYd	Dec 1841	16 Apr 1842	18 Feb 1843

Rate	10 guns
Dimensions	102′6″ (bp) × 28′2″ × 12′3″
Tonnage	331 tons
Complement	80
Battery	10–32pdr crde

Notes: Designed by Francis Grice. Fast and weatherly.
Service record: Mediterranean 1843. Africa Sqn 1844–45. Stranded on Tuxpan bar, 15 Aug 1846; crew taken prisoner by Mexicans and wreck burned by U.S. sqn.
Ship captured: (With HMS *Ardent*) slaver *Spitfire* taken by boats in Rio Pongas, West Africa, 29 Mar 1845.

Name	Builder	Laid down	L	Comm
Perry	Norfolk NYd	18 Feb 1843	9 May 1843	13 Oct 1843

Rate	10 guns
Dimensions	105′ (bp) × 25′6″ × 12′3″, 13′6″ (maximum)
Tonnage	280 tons
Complement	80
Battery	10–32pdr crde; (1846) 2–32pdr, 6–32pdr crde

Notes: Designed by Francis Grice. Reputedly the fastest vessel in the Navy when built.
Service record: Far East 1843–44. Dismasted in hurricane, Nov 1846. Mexico 1846. Brazil Station 1847. Africa Sqn 1849–54. Paraguay Expedition, 1858. Sold 10 Aug 1865.
Ships captured: Slaver bark *Ann D. Richardson* off Rio de Janeiro, slaver brig *Independence*, 1847; slaver ship *Martha* off Loanda, Africa, 6 Jun 1850; slaver brig *Glamorgan* off West Africa, 10 Mar 1854.

Name	Builder	Laid down	L	Comm
Lawrence	Baltimore (L. B. Culley)	1843	1 Aug 1843	19 Sep 1843

Rate	10 guns
Dimensions	109′9″ (bp) × 26′2″ × 13′3″
Tonnage	364 tons
Complement	80
Battery	2–32pdr, 8–32pdr crde

Notes: Drew too much water. Not too successful, but good sailer. Armed at Norfolk NYd.
Service record: South Atlantic 1843–44. Home Sqn 1846. Decomm 12 Sep 1846. Sold after three years' service, condemned as unseaworthy, Oct 1846.

SCHOONERS

Name	Builder	Built	Acquired	Comm
Retaliation ex–*Le Croyable*	(U)	(U)	30 Jul 1798	1798

Rate	14 guns
Dimensions	(U)

USS *Enterprise*, a schooner built in 1799, depicted by Baugean in France in 1806. (U.S. Naval Historical Center)

Tonnage	107 tons
Complement	87
Battery	4–6pdr, 10–4pdr

Notes: French privateer. Captured by USS *Constitution* and *Delaware* off Delaware Capes, 7 Jul 1798.
Service record: Recaptured by French frigates *La Volontaire* and *L'Insurgente* off Guadeloupe, while under command of Bainbridge, 20 Nov 1798.
Later history: French *Magicienne*. Again recaptured by USS *Merrimack*, 29 Jun 1799. Sold 29 Nov 1799.

Name	Builder	L	Comm
Enterprise	Eastern Shore of Md. (Henry Spencer)	1799	Dec 1799
Experiment	Eastern Shore of Md. (Henry Spencer)	1799	Nov 1799

Rate	12 guns
Dimensions	84′7″ (deck), 60′ (keel) × 22′6″ × 10′
	Enterprise: (1805) 92′9″ (deck), 80′6″ (bp) × 23′9″ × 10′10″
Tonnage	135 tons
	Enterprise: (1811) 165 tons
Complement	70
Battery	12–6pdr
	Enterprise: (1803) 12–12pdr; (1811) 2–9pdr, 14–18pdr crde; (1821) 1–9pdr, 6–18pdr crde, 1–13″ M

Notes: Successful design; fast and handy vessels, but not after rebuilding. Owing to *Enterprise*'s gallant services during the French War, she was the only small cruiser retained afterward. *Enterprise* was rebuilt and converted to brig at Washington NYd, 1811–12.
Service records:
Enterprise: Caribbean 1799–1800. In action with a Spanish man-of-war (brig), 18, off Mona Passage, 1 Apr 1800. Action with French *Flambeau*, 14 (LofM), off Dominica (3 killed), 14 Dec 1800. Mediterranean 1801–07. Action with Tripolitanian corsair *Tripoli* in Mediterranean, 1 Aug 1801. Attacks on forts at Tripoli, Aug–Sep 1804. Rebuilt in Venice, 1804–05. U.S. East Coast, 1807–09. Took brig HMS *Boxer*, 14, off Portland, Maine (1 killed, captain Lt. Burrows), 5 Sep 1813. Mediterranean 1815. Caribbean 1817–23. Wrecked off Curaçao (crew saved), 9 Jul 1823.

Another view of the *Enterprise* by Baugean after she was rigged as a brigantine in 1812. (U.S. Naval Historical Center)

Ships captured: Recaptured 11 American ships, 1800; French *Le Citoyen*, 6 (LofM), off St. Kitts, 1800; privateer *Le Cygne*, 4, 17 Jun 1800; French privateer *L'Aigle*, 10, 4 Jul 1800; *Pauline*, 6, Guadeloupean, 7, 13 others, Dec 1800; privateer *Amour de la Patrie*, 6, 24 Dec 1800; Turkish ketch *Mastico*[14] off Tripoli, 23 Dec 1803; schr *Fly* off Portsmouth, N.H., 20 Aug 1813. (With *Rattlesnake*) brig *Isabella* (prize), 18 Jan 1814; ship *Sincerity*, 20 Jan 1814; brig *Rambler* (burned), 7 Feb 1814; schr *Eliza*, schr *Mars* (LofM), 23 Feb 1814. Four schrs, one sloop (pirates) at Cape Antonio, Cuba, 16 Oct 1821; pirate schr, 21 Dec 1814; three launches, four barges, 8 Mar 1822.

Experiment: Caribbean 1799–1800. Fought off 10 pirate barges (sank two) off Haiti, Jan 1800. Action with British *Louisa Bridger*, 8, in error off Barbuda, 16 Nov 1800. Sold Oct 1801.

Ships captured: *Les Deux Amis*, 8 (LofM), off Barbuda, 1 Sep 1800; schr *Diana*, 14, off Barbuda, 13 Sep 1800.

Name	Builder	Laid down	L	Comm
Vixen	Baltimore (Wm. Price)	1803	25 Jun 1803	Aug 1803

Rate	12 guns
Dimensions	83'6" (bp) × 23'7" × 9'6"
Tonnage	185 tons
Complement	111
Battery	2–9pdr, 12–18pdr crde; (1804) 12–6pdr

Notes: Authorized 28 Feb 1803. Designed by Benjamin Hutton, Jr.; similar to *Enterprise*. Rerigged as brig at Washington NYd, 1804. Slow, crank, and overcrowded after rerigging as brig.
Service record: Mediterranean 1801–03. Attacks on forts at Tripoli, Aug–Sep 1804. Fired upon by HMS *Moselle* off Berry Island, Wisc., 24 Jun 1810. Captured at sea in West Indies by HMS *Southampton*, 32, 22 Nov 1812; both vessels wrecked soon after in Bahamas, (crew saved). Captain, Lt. George W. Reed, died a prisoner in Jamaica.

[14] See USS *Intrepid*.

Name	Builder	Built	Acquired	Comm
Nautilus	Eastern Shore of Md. (Henry Spencer)	1799	May 1803	Apr 1805

Rate	12 guns
Dimensions	87'6" (deck) × 23'8" × 9'10"
Tonnage	185 tons
Complement	103
Battery	14–12pdr; (1804) 12–6pdr; (1810) 2–9pdr, 12–18pdr crde; (1810, as brig) 12–18pdr crde, 2 long guns

Notes: Purchased. Very fast. Rerigging in 1810 hurt her sailing qualities.
Service record: Mediterranean 1803–06. Attacks on forts at Tripoli, Aug–Sep 1804. Attack on Derna, Libya, 27 Apr 1805. Attached to Decatur's Sqn, 1811. Captured by British sqn of *Shannon*, *Africa*, and *Aeolus* off New Jersey, having thrown overboard lee guns, 16 Jul 1812. First American man-of-war captured in 1812.
Later history: HMS *Emulous*, 14. Sold Aug 1817.

Name	Builder	Laid down	L	Comm
Ferret	Norfolk NYd	(U)	1806	18 Apr 1809

Rate	10 guns
Dimensions	73' (deck) × 23'8" × 7'6"
Tonnage	143 tons
Complement	64
Battery	(U)

Notes: Built as cutter *Ferret*, designed by Josiah Fox. Rerigged as brig and renamed *Viper*, 1809–10.
Service record: Captured by HMS *Narcissus*, 38, off Belize, 17 Jan 1813.

Name	Builder	Built	Acquired	Comm
Revenge	(U)	(U)	Dec 1806	1807

Rate	12 guns
Dimensions	about 70' × (U)
Tonnage	(U)
Complement	43
Battery	12–6pdr

Notes: Purchased at New Orleans. Fore topsail schr, very sharp.
Service record: Recaptured American ship *Diana* at Amelia Island, Spanish Florida, Jul 1810. Wrecked under O. H. Perry off Newport, R.I., through carelessness of pilot, 9 Jan 1811.

Name	Builder	Built	Acquired	Comm
Carolina	Charleston, S.C. (James Marsh)	1812	10 Nov 1812	4 Jun 1813

Rate	14 guns
Dimensions	89'6" (bp), 78' (keel) × 24'4" × 11'4"
Tonnage	230 tons
Complement	100
Battery	3–9pdr, 12–12pdr crde

Notes: Purchased before completion.
Service record: Captured schr HMS *Shark* in Gulf of Mexico, 1813. Expedition against pirates in Barataria Bay, La., 16 Sep 1814. Blew up from hot shot fired by enemy at New Orleans, having just been aban-

doned by her captain, J. D. Henley (7 killed or wounded), 27 Dec 1814.

Name	Builder	Built	Acquired	Comm
Nonsuch	Baltimore	1812	1812	Dec 1812

Rate	14 guns; (later) 6 guns
Dimensions	86' (bp) × 21' × 9'
Tonnage	148 tons
Complement	61
Battery	1–6pdr, 12–12pdr crde; (1815) 1–12pdr, 5–12pdr crde

Notes: Purchased privateer.
Service record: Active cruiser on Southern coast during war. Threw 11 guns overboard when closely pursued by enemy, 13 Jun 1814. West Indies 1815–19. Capt. Oliver Hazard Perry died of fever on board, 23 Aug 1819. BU 1826.
Ships captured: Schr *Sancho Panza*, Apr 1813; schr *Caledonia* (privateer), 9 Apr 1813.

Name	Builder	Built	Acquired	Comm
Spitfire ex-*Grampus*	Baltimore	1812	Dec 1814	1814

Rate	12 or 10 guns
Dimensions	106' (bp) × 25'6" × 11'8"
Tonnage	278 tons
Complement	60
Battery	2–32pdr, 4–9pdr, 6–32pdr crde; (1816) 1–32pdr, 4–9pdr, 4–18pdr crde

Notes: Purchased LofM.
Service record: Mediterranean 1815–16. Action with ship *Mashouda*, 46, and brig *Esledio*, 22, off Cape de Gatt, Spain, 17–19 Jun 1815. Sold 3 Apr 1816.

Name	Builder	Acquired	Comm
Eagle	New Orleans	1814	(U)

Rate	12 guns
Dimensions	(U)
Tonnage	270 tons
Complement	(U)
Battery	(U)

Notes: Purchased at New Orleans. Sold 1820.

Name	Builder	Built	Acquired	Comm
Torch	Baltimore	(U)	1814	1814

Rate	12 guns
Dimensions	106' (bp) × 26' × 11'9"
Tonnage	252 tons
Complement	60
Battery	1–18pdr, 1–4pdr, 10–18pdr crde

Notes: Purchased privateer.
Service record: Mediterranean 1815. Action with ship *Mashouda*, 46, and brig *Esledio*, 22, off Cape de Gatt, Spain, 17–19 Jun 1815. Sold 3 Apr 1816.

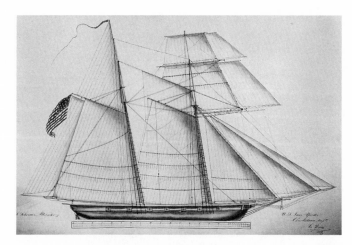

Spar and sail plan of the schooner *Alligator*, built by the Boston Navy Yard in 1820. (U.S. Naval Historical Center)

Name	Builder	Built	Acquired	Comm
Firebrand	New Orleans	(U)	Apr 1815	Aug 1815

Rate	12 guns
Dimensions	70' × 21' × 10'6"
Tonnage	(U)
Complement	52
Battery	6–12pdr, 1–6pdr

Notes: Purchased.
Service record: Gulf of Mexico 1815–19. Operations against pirates. Lost her anchors boats and one gun in heavy gale, Oct 1817. Wrecked in heavy gale in Bay St. Louis, La. (or, according to other reports, Square Handkerchief Shoal, Miss.) (36 lost), 28 Jul 1819.

Name	Builder	Laid down	L	Comm
Alligator	Boston NYd	26 Jun 1820	2 Nov 1820	26 Mar 1821
Dolphin	Philadelphia NYd	1820	23 Jun 1821	7 Oct 1821
Porpoise	Portsmouth NYd	16 Aug 1820	2 Dec 1820	30 Mar 1821
Shark	Washington NYd	1820	17 May 1821	2 Jun 1821

Rate	12 guns
Dimensions	86' (bp) × 24'7" × 10'4", 12'4" (maximum)
	Dolphin: 88' × 23'6" × 12'4"
Tonnage	198 tons
Complement	70/100
Battery	*Alligator, Dolphin*: 12–6pdr; (1825) 2–18pdr, 10–6pdr
	Porpoise: 1–18pdr, 10–6pdr
	Shark: (1840) 2–9pdr, 8–24pdr crde; (1842) 2–9pdr, 10–24pdr crde

Notes: Known as the *Porpoise* class. Designed by William Doughty. Fast and handy. *Porpoise* and *Shark* had regulation man-of-war bows. Fitted with high pivot gun, which was later removed and replaced with two 18 pdr on carriages. Figurehead: *Alligator*: alligator.
Service records:
Alligator: Africa Sqn, where Stockton negotiated first settlement leading to establishment of Liberia, 1821. Engaged Portuguese ship *Marianna Flora*, 12 (or LofM *Mariana Faliero*), south of Azores, 5

The schooner *Shark*, built in 1821, was wrecked in the Columbia River in 1846. (U.S. Naval Historical Center)

A sketch of the schooner *Experiment*, 10, built in 1831. (U.S. Naval Historical Center)

Nov 1821; rtnd by prize court. Lt. W. H. Allen and three others killed in action with pirates, 8 Nov 1822. Wrecked on Carysfort Reef, Fla., and destroyed by crew, 19 Nov 1823.

Ships captured: Slaver schrs *Jeune Eugenie, Elize, La Daphne, Matilda* off west coast of Africa, 17–25 May 1821; pirate schr *Cienega* (*Cincqua*) off Nuevitas, Cuba, 29 Apr 1822. (With *Grampus*) four pirate schrs, 1 May 1822. Three pirate schrs off Cuba, 9 Nov 1822.

Dolphin: Completed at New York NYd. Pacific Sqn 1821–35; cruised Columbia River. Unsafe to bring her home around the Capes owing to her decayed state. Sold in Pacific 2 Dec 1835.

Porpoise: West Indies 1821–23. Africa 1824–25. Mediterranean 1826–30. West Indies 1830–33. Wrecked on reef off Port Lizardo, West Indies, or on Sacrificios Island, Mexico, near Veracruz, 2 Nov 1833.

Ships captured: Six pirate vessels off Cuba, 7 Jan 1822; one schr, 3 boats, 20 Oct 1824; five pirate boats and prize brig off Andros Island in Aegean, 16 Oct 1827.

Shark: Africa 1821–22. Captain, Lt. M. C. Perry, raised U.S. flag over Key West, 25 Mar 1822. Africa 1826–27. West Indies 1828. Africa 1830–32. Mediterranean 1833–35. West Indies 1835–38. Pacific Sqn 1839–46. Wrecked at mouth of Columbia River (all saved), 10 Sep 1846; crew reached San Francisco on chartered schr *Cadboro*, 16 Nov 1846.

Ship captured: (With *Grampus*) schr *Bandara d'Saugare*, West Indies, Jun 1822.

Name	Builder	Laid down	L	Comm
Grampus	Washington NYd	1820	2 Aug 1821	1821

Rate	12 guns
Dimensions	97′ (oa), 92′6″ (bp) × 24′6″ × 11′6″, d9′6″
Tonnage	171 tons
Complement	64
Battery	1–18pdr, 10–12pdr crde; (1825) 2–9pdr, 10–12pdr crde; (1840) 2–9pdr, 8–24pdr crde

Notes: Designed by Henry Eckford. One of the fastest schooners of her day. Designed with pivot without gunports amidships.

Service record: First cruise West Indies, 1822–23. Attack on pirates at Foxardo, P.R., captured a noted pirate, 14 Nov 1824. West Indies 1825–26, 1828–39. Northeast coast of Africa, 1840–41. Left Charleston, 14 Mar 1843, and was never seen again.

Ships captured: (With *Alligator*) four pirate schrs, 1 May 1822. (With *Shark*) schr *Bandara d'Saugare* in West Indies, Jun 1822. Pirate brig *Palmyra* (released), 16 Aug 1822; two pirate vessels off Yucatan, 22 May 1823: one pirate ship, 4 Mar 1825; slaver *Fenix* off Haiti, 5 Jun 1830.

Name	Builder	Laid down	L	Comm
Boxer	Boston NYd	1831	22 Nov 1831	1832
Enterprise	New York NYd	1831	26 Oct 1831	15 Dec 1831
Experiment	Washington NYd	1831	1831	Apr 1832

Rate	10 guns
Dimensions	88′ (bp) × 23′6″ × 12′, d10′6″ *Experiment:* 90′ × 21′6″ × 6′1″
Tonnage	194 tons
	Experiment: 209 tons
Complement	72
Battery	*Boxer:* 2–9pdr, 8–24pdr crde

Notes: Known as the *Boxer* class. Designed by Samuel Humphreys. *Experiment* probably built to a different design. Fast sailers. *Boxer* converted to brig, 1840.

Service records:

Boxer: Brazil Station 1832–33. West Indies 1834. Pacific Sqn 1835–40. Home Sqn 1842–44. Africa Sqn 1846–48. Sold 7 Aug 1848. (Also reported as sunk in a mine experiment in 1842.)

Enterprise: Brazil Station 1832–34. Cruise to Africa, Far East, and west coast of South America, 1835–39. Brazil Station 1840–44. Sold 28 Oct 1844.

Ship captured: Pirate brig *Malek Adhel*, 4, off Bahia, Brazil, Sep 1840.

Experiment: East Coast 1832–33. West Indies 1833–35. Lost rudder at sea in gale, 26 Apr 1835. Surveying, 1836–39. Receiving ship, Philadelphia, 1839–48. Sold 1848.

Name	Builder	Built	Acquired	Comm
Ariel	Baltimore (Dorgin & Baily)	(U)	19 May 1831	1832
ex–*Fourth of July* (9 Jun 1831)				
Spark	(U)	(U)	1831	19 May 1832
Sylph	Baltimore (Dorgin & Baily)	1831	Apr 1831	19 May 1831
ex–*Sarah Ann*				

Rate	1 gun
Dimensions	(U)
Tonnage	*Ariel:* 48 tons
	Spark: 50 tons
Complement	14
	Ariel: 13
Battery	varied

Notes: Purchased for protection of timber on Southern coast.
Service records:
Ariel: Guarded oak forest on Gulf coast of Florida. Sold 3 Jan 1833.
Spark: Florida coast 1832. Sold 1832.
Sylph: Lost in storm in West Indies after leaving Pensacola, Aug 1831.

Name	Builder	Built	Acquired	Comm
Bonita	New York (Brown & Bell)	1846	May 1846	30 May 1846
Falcon	New York (Brown & Bell)	1845	Nov 1846	Mar 1847
ex–*Isabel*				
Petrel	New York (Brown & Bell)	1846	9 Jun 1846	Jun 1846
Reefer	New York (Brown & Bell)	(U)	25 May 1846	19 Jun 1846
Tampico	New York (Brown & Bell)	1845	Nov 1846	(U)
ex–*Pueblano*				
Union	New York (Brown & Bell)	1845	Nov 1846	(U)
ex–*Union*				

Rate	1 gun, except *Petrel:* 2 guns
Dimensions	68′6″ × 19 × 6′
	Reefer: 59′ × 19′ × 6′
Tonnage	76 tons
Complement	30
Battery	*Bonita, Reefer:* 1–18pdr
	Falcon, Tampico, Union: 1–24pdr
	Petrel: 1–32pdr

Notes: Former Mexican gunboats. *Bonita*, *Petrel*, and *Reefer* were under construction for the Mexican Navy and were purchased by the USN. The others were captured and placed in service.
Service records:
Bonita: Attack on Alvarado, Mexico, 7 Aug 1846. Attacks on Frontera and Tampico, Mexico, Oct–Nov 1846. Landings at and siege of Veracruz, 9–29 Mar 1847. Capture of Tuxpan, Mexico, 18 Apr 1847. Sold 15 Oct 1848.
  Ships captured: Schr *Yucateca* near Tabasco, Mexico, 22 or 30 Apr 1847; steamer *Montezuma* near Tabasco, 22 Jun 1847; schr *Gavitan* in Rio Los Brocas, 9 Nov 1847; schr *Guadalupe*, schr *Jacinta* near Frontera, Mar 1848.
Falcon: Captured at Tampico, 14 Nov 1846. Siege of Veracruz, Mar 1847. Decomm 4 Sep 1848. Sold 18 Oct 1848.
Petrel: Expedition against Alvarado, 7 Aug 1846. Siege of Veracruz, 9–29 Mar 1847. Attack on Tuxpan, 18 Apr 1847. Trfd to Coast Survey, 1851.
Reefer: Expedition against Alvarado, 7 Aug 1846. Siege of Veracruz, 9–29 Mar 1847. Sold 1848.
Tampico: Captured at Tampico, 14 Nov 1846. Siege of Veracruz, Mar 1847. Sold at Norfolk, 1849.

Union: Captured by *Princeton* at Tampico, 14 Nov 1846. Wrecked off Veracruz, 16 Dec 1846.

MISCELLANEOUS SMALLER SHIPS

MISCELLANEOUS SHIPS

Name	Builder	Built	Acquired	Comm
Troup	(U)	(U)	1812	1812

Rate	16 guns
Dimensions	(U)
Tonnage	(U)
Complement	(U)
Battery	4–18pdr crde, 4–12pdr crde, 4–6pdr crde

Notes: Guardship and receiving ship at Savannah. Sold 1815.

Name	Builder	Built	Acquired	Comm
Essex Junior	(U)	(U)	28 May 1813	Jun 1813
ex–*Atlantic*				

Rate	16 guns
Dimensions	(U)
Tonnage	355 tons
Complement	60
Battery	10–6pdr, 10–18pdr crde

Notes: British whaler (LofM), captured by USS *Essex* off Galapagos Islands, 29 May 1813. Converted to cruiser and comm.
Service record: Captured by British ships off Valparaiso; used to transport prisoners to New York, 28 Mar 1814. Seized at New York and sold, 26 Aug 1814.

Name	Builder	Built	Acquired	Comm
Georgiana	(U)	(U)	29 Apr 1813	8 May 1813

Rate	16 guns
Dimensions	(U)
Tonnage	280 tons
Complement	42
Battery	10–6pdr, 6–18pdr crde

Notes: Captured British whaler, taken by USS *Essex* off Galapagos Islands, 29 Apr 1813.
Service record: Recaptured off U.S. coast by frigate HMS *Barrosa* on return from Pacific with cargo of oil, early 1814. Made three captures while a cruiser in Pacific under J. Downes.
Ships captured: *Catherine, Rose, Hector,* 28 May 1813. (With *Greenwich*) *Seringapatam,* 13 Jul 1813.

Name	Builder	Laid down	L	Comm
Tchifonta	New Orleans (M. Pechon)	late 1813	never	never

Rate	22 guns
Dimensions	152′9″ (gun deck) × 43′ × 8′2″
Tonnage	1,500 tons
Complement	(U)
Battery	26–32pdr, 16–42pdr crde

Notes: Corvette. Ship rig, broad beam, and flat bottom. Designed as blockship for defense of New Orleans. Construction suspended, Mar 1814; sold on stocks, 1825.

Name	Builder	Built	Acquired	Comm
Prometheus ex-*Escape*	Philadelphia (Wm. Seguin)	(U)	1814	1815

Rate	12 guns
Dimensions	99'9" (bp), 82' (keel) × 27' × 11'4"
Tonnage	273 tons; also reported as 290 tons
Complement	60
Battery	2–32pdr, 4–9pdr, 6–32pdr crde; (1816) 1–32pdr, 4–9pdr, 4–18pdr crde

Notes: Purchased privateer.
Service record: West Indies 1815. Surveying, 1817–18. Sold 1819.

Name	Builder	L	Comm
Alligator ex–Gunboat No. 166 (1812)	Wilmington, N.C. (Ames Perry)	1809	mid-1809

Rate	4 guns
Dimensions	60' (bp) × 16' × d5'11"
Tonnage	80 tons
Complement	40
Battery	(U)

Notes: Converted gunboat.
Service record: Fought off attack by armed boats from British frigate in Stono River, S.C. (2 killed), 29 Jan 1814. Capsized and sank in violent storm in Port Royal Sound (21 killed), Jul 1814. Raised 1815 and sold 12 Jun 1815.

Name	Builder	Acquired	Comm
Lynx	Georgetown, D.C. (James Owner)	1814	early 1815

Rate	6 guns
Dimensions	80' × (U)
Tonnage	150 tons
Complement	50
Battery	(U)

Notes: Purchased.
Service record: Accompanied *Independence*, 74, to Mediterranean, 1815. Surveyed northeast U.S. coast with Bainbridge and Swift on board, 1817. Gulf of Mexico 1817–19. Departed St. Marys, Ga., for Kingston, Jamaica, Jan 1820, and was not heard from again (50 lost).
Ships captured: Two schrs, three boats (pirates) in Gulf of Mexico, 24 Oct–5 Nov 1819.

Name	Rate	Type	Builder	Built	Acquired	Dimensions	Battery
Alligator	1	sloop			1813		1–4pdr
Asp ex-*Adeline*	3	sloop			17 Feb 1813		1–12pdr, 2–12pdr crde
Bull Dog	2	felucca			1814		
Buffalo	5	sloop	Philadelphia		Apr 1813		4–18pdr, 1–6pdr
Camel	5	sloop 2–24pdr crde	Philadelphia		Apr 1813		2–18pdr, 1–4pdr,
Comet		schr	Baltimore		1813		
Corporation	2	schr			1814		
Despatch	2	schr			1814		
Ferret	8	schr	Charleston, S.C.		Nov 1812		
Helen	4	schr	Philadelphia		Sep 1813		4–4pdr
Hornet	5	schr	Georgetown, D.C.		1813		1–18pdr, 4–18pdr crde
Norwich		schr			1812		
Patapsco		schr			1813	101' × 25' × 11'5"	
Ranger	1	schr			Mar 1814		1–18pdr
Revenge	16	schr	Baltimore	1810/12	1813	102' × 23' × 10'	
Revenge—see Gunboat No. 158							
Roanoke	7	schr			1814		
Scorpion	2	block sloop			1812	48'8" × 18'2" × 4'6"	1–24pdr, 1–18pdr, 2–12pdr crde
Sea Horse	1	schr	New Orleans		1812		
Surprise	12	ketch			1815		6–12pdr crde
Tickler		sloop			Aug 1812		
Torpedo		schr	New York		1814		

Notes: Small vessels acquired during the War of 1812.

Service records:

Alligator: Captured off Malheureux Islands in Lake Borgne near New Orleans by boats of British Sqn, 14 Dec 1814.

Asp: Captured, set on fire, and abandoned by enemy in 1813 after a gallant resistance during which her commander Sigourney and others were killed. Second in command McCormick recovered her again upon retreat of the enemy. Employed on Southern coast until 1815, then tender to *Java* and receiving ship at Baltimore. Sold 1826.

Bull Dog: Purchased for suppression of piracy, 1814. Sold 1821.

Buffalo: Delaware Flotilla 1813. Sold 12 Aug 1816.

Camel: Delaware Flotilla 1813. Sold 12 Aug 1816.

Comet: Hired privateer. Loaned to the Navy, Apr–Sep 1813. Took 35 prizes as privateer.

Corporation: Purchased at Philadelphia. Receiving ship. Sold Sep 1820.

Despatch: Employed on detached survey of coast. Sold 1820.

Ferret: Went aground in Stono Inlet, S.C. (all saved), 22 Feb 1814.

Helen: Purchased as inland dispatch vessel. Lost in Delaware Bay, 1815.

Hornet: Purchased as inland dispatch boat. Comm 15 Mar 1814. BU 1820.

Norwich: Hired 1812–14.

Patapsco: Hired privateer, 1813–14.

Ranger: Purchased at Baltimore. Sold 1816.

Revenge: Hired privateer, Chesapeake Bay. Probably returned to owners in 1813.

Roanoke: Trfd from State Dept. Sold 1816.

Scorpion: Sloop-rigged floating battery. Potomac Flotilla to protect Washington. Burned in Chesapeake Bay, 21 Aug 1814.

Sea Horse: Purchased for service on Lake Borgne, La. Expedition against pirates in Barataria Bay, La., Sep 1814. Burned at New Orleans to prevent capture, after resisting two attacks by enemy boats (several killed), 13 Dec 1814.

Surprise: Employed on New Orleans station. Condemned 1820.

Ships captured: Schr *Merino*, schr *Louisa*, 18 Jun 1818; pirate schr, fall 1818.

Tickler: Purchased as despatch vessel at New Orleans. Sold 1818.

Torpedo: Purchased. Special design by Fulton for towing torpedoes. Never completed. Sold 1818?

Name	Builder	Laid down	L	Comm
Fox	(U)	(U)	1817	(U)

Rate	4 guns
Dimensions	(U)
Tonnage	130 tons
Complement	(U)
Battery	(U)

Notes: Receiving ship, Baltimore. Sold 1821. No official information.

Name	Builder	Laid down	L	Comm
Active ex-*Clara*	Baltimore	(U)	Sep 1837	(U)
Pilot	New York NYd	(U)	Sep 1836	(U)

Rate	2 guns
Dimensions	*Pilot:* 65′ (bp) × 21′6″ × 9′
Tonnage	122 tons
Complement	50
Battery	(U)

Notes: Built for Wilkes Expedition but were too slow and unsuitable.

Service records:

Active: Sold, summer 1838.

Pilot: Sold 1838.

Name	Builder	Laid down	L	Comm
Consort	Boston NYd	(U)	25 Oct 1836	(U)
Pioneer	Norfolk NYd	(U)	29 Oct 1836	(U)

Rate	6 guns
Dimensions	78′9″ (bp) × 25′4″ × (U)
Tonnage	230 tons
Complement	75
Battery	(U)

Notes: Designed by Samuel Humphreys. Could be rigged as brig or bark. Built for Wilkes exploring expedition but was too slow; used for salvage work.

Service records:

Consort: Government packet to West Indies, 1838. Surveying Southern harbors, 1840–41. Receiving vessel, Portland, Maine, 1842. Africa 1843–44. U.S. coast, 1844. Sold 25 May 1844.

Pioneer: Carried General Santa Anna to Veracruz in 1837 after he had been taken prisoner by Sam Houston in Texas. Almost lost in Long Island Sound, Mar 1838. Receiving vessel, Baltimore, 1838–44. Converted to store vessel, sent to Brazil. Sold 1844.

Name	Builder	Built	Acquired	Comm
Flying Fish ex-*Independence*	New York	(U)	3 Aug 1838	12 Aug 1838

Rate	2 guns
Dimensions	85′6″ (oa) × 22′6″ × (U)
Tonnage	96 tons
Complement	15
Battery	(U)

Notes: Purchased. Former New York pilot boat.

Service record: Wilkes survey expedition to South Seas and Antarctica, Aug 1838–Jul 1842. Sold at Singapore, 26 Feb 1842.

Later history: Merchant *Spec* (opium smuggler).

Name	Builder	Built	Acquired	Comm
Sea Gull ex-pilot *New Jersey*	(U)	1838	1838	1838

Rate	2 guns
Dimensions	(U)
Tonnage	100 tons
Complement	15

Notes: Purchased at New York.

Service record: Tender to Wilkes expedition. Sailed on 25 Feb 1839 and was last seen in severe gale off Cape Horn (15 lost).

Name	Builder	Built	Acquired	Comm
Otsego	(U)	(U)	1840	(U)

Rate	2 guns
Dimensions	(U)

Tonnage	(U)
Complement	(U)
Battery	(U)

Notes: Loaned from War Dept. for Seminole Campaign. Returned to War Dept., 1844.

Name	Builder	Built	Acquired	Comm
Oregon Fort Vancouver, B.C. ex–*Thomas H. Perkins*		(U)	Aug 1841	1841

Rate	2 guns
Dimensions	(U)
Tonnage	250 tons
Complement	(U)
Battery	(U)

Notes: Brig purchased to accommodate crew of wrecked *Peacock*.
Service record: Purchased by commander of Exploring Expedition at Fort Vancouver. Brought home, 1842. Employed in survey of Tampa Bay, 1842–43. Sold Apr 1845.

Name	Builder	Built	Acquired	Comm
On-ka-hy-e	Williamsburg, N.Y. (Capes)	1840	1843	11 Jul 1843

Rate	2 guns
Dimensions	96' × 22' × 12'
Tonnage	250 tons
Complement	(U)
Battery	(U)

Notes: Yacht with two keels, designed by R. L. Stevens. Purchased. Very fast and stiff.
Service record: Caribbean 1845. Laid up 1846–47. Went aground and lost on Caicos Reef in West Indies (all saved), 21 Jun 1848.
Ship captured: Slaver bark *Laurens* (*Lawrence*) off Rio de Janeiro, 24 Jan 1848.

Name	Builder	Built	Acquired	Comm
Malek Adhel	New York (Webb)	1840	7 Sep 1846	1846

Rate	2 guns
Dimensions	80' (deck) × 27'7" × 7'9"
Tonnage	114 tons
Complement	(U)
Battery	2–9pdr, 10–6pdr

Notes: Brig. Former Mexican merchant ship, one-time slaver; name retained. Captured off Mazatlan by USS *Warren*, 6 Sep 1846.
Service record: Cruised off California. Sold 1848.

Name	Acquired	Type	Battery
Libertad	1847	schr	1–9pdr
Mahonese	1846	schr	(U)
Morris ex–*Laura Virginia*	1846	schr	(U)
Nonata	1846	schr	4–42pdr

Notes: Prizes taken during Mexican War and taken into service.

Service records:
Libertad: Taken by *Cyane* off Baja California, 1 Oct 1846. Sold Feb 1848.
Mahonese: Taken 14 Nov 1846. Dispatch boat. Sold at Norfolk, 1847.
Morris: Mexican prize taken in Tabasco River, Oct 1846. Sold 1848.
Nonata: Captured by USS *Porpoise* off Tabasco, 21 Aug 1846. Dispatch boat, 1847. Damaged in storm, Mar 1847. Sold 1848.

GALLEYS

Name	Builder	Launched
Beaufort	Beaufort, S.C.	1798
Charleston ex-*Mars*	Charleston, S.C.	1798
Governor Davie	Wilmington, N.C.	1798
Governor Williams	Wilmington, N.C.	1799
St. Mary's	St. Marys, Ga.	1799
Savannah	Savannah, Ga.	1799
South Carolina ex-*Protector*	Charleston, S.C.	1799

Rate	1 gun
Dimensions	52' × 15' × 5'8" *Savannah:* 51'9" × 15'3" × 5'1"
Tonnage	(U)
Complement	28
Battery	1–24pdr, 6–3pdr swivels

Notes: Of little value but for harbor defense. Built by Act of May 4, 1798, as a type of naval militia.
Service records:
Beaufort: Patrolled off South Carolina, 1799–1801. Sold 1 Feb 1802.
Charleston: Defense of Charleston, 1798–99. Sold 1 Feb 1802.
Governor Davie: Sold Feb 1802.
Governor Williams: Trfd to USRCS, 1802.
St. Marys: Trfd to USRCS, 1802.
Savannah: Sold Feb 1802.
South Carolina: Sold at Charleston, 1 Feb 1802.

Name	Builder	Launched
Senator Ross	Pittsburgh, Pa. (John Taylor)	1798

Rate	1 gun
Dimensions	50'6" × 13'6"

Notes: Built to protect commerce on Mississippi River.

In addition to the above, the U.S. Navy operated a galley named *Marietta* and others that were unnamed.

GUNBOATS

GUNBOATS OBTAINED ABROAD

Nos. 1, 2: Bomb ketches ("bombards") of 90' length.
Nos. 3–6: Obtained by Preble from the government of the Kingdom of the Two Sicilies at Messina for use against Tripoli, Mar 1804. Returned to Naples later in the year. No. 1 damaged in action, 24 Aug 1804.

Several types of the gunboats built under President Jefferson to protect the coast. (U.S. Naval Historical Center)

Nos. 7, 8, 9: Very small boats captured from Tripoli; (No. 9) 31'1" × 14' × 5'. No. 9 blew up in action with batteries at Tripoli (9 killed), 7 Aug 1804; the others were sold in Sicily, fall 1804.

Four gunboats and two bomb vessels (*trabacolos*) were purchased at Ancona, spring 1805.

GUNBOATS BUILT IN THE UNITED STATES

Under the policy of President Jefferson to provide for coast defense, Congress authorized the first 15 gunboats in 1803. One experimental

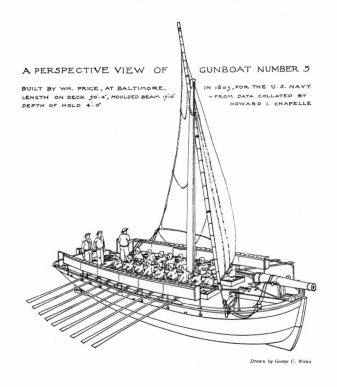

A PERSPECTIVE VIEW OF GUNBOAT NUMBER 5

BUILT BY WM. PRICE, AT BALTIMORE, LENGTH ON DECK 50'·4", MOULDED BEAM 17'·0" DEPTH OF HOLD 4'·0'

IN 1803, FOR THE U.S. NAVY. —FROM DATA COLLATED BY HOWARD I. CHAPELLE

Drawn by George C. Wales

A sketch of Gunboat No. 5 by George C. Wales.

boat had been built in Washington. Additional authorizations included 50 on 21 Apr 1806 and 188 more on 18 Dec 1807. They were built in groups in various sections of the country. Being locally built and manned, they were similar to naval militia. Altogether some 278 gunboats were authorized, but of these the last 88 were not built and a number on the ways were never finished. A total of 166 were completed, but by Dec 1809, 148 of these had been laid up. In chronological order, the gunboats were:

Two experimental boats.

No. 1: Built at Washington NYd. Comm Jul 1804. Battery: 1–long 32pdr, 2–6pdr swivels.

No. 2: Built at Hampton, Va. (Geo. Hope). Launched Aug 1804. Battery: 1–long 32pdr. Service record: Mediterranean 1805–06. Wrecked off St. Marys, Ga. (28 killed), Oct 1811.

No. 3: Built at Philadelphia (Nathaniel Hutton). Launched Dec 1804. Battery: 2–long 24pdr. Service record: Mediterranean 1805–06.

No. 4: Built at Washington NYd. Launched 5 Mar 1804. Battery: 2–long 32pdr. Service record: Mediterranean 1805.

No. 5: Built at Baltimore (Price). Launched 1 Mar 1805. Service record: Mediterranean 1805. Stopped by British fleet off Cadiz, three men impressed, 12 Jun 1805. Captured by British on Lake Borgne, La., 14 Dec 1814. Ship captured: One unarmed pirate brig at sea, 23 Sep 1814.

No. 6: Built at New York. Launched 4 Feb 1805. Service record: Mediterranean 1805.

No. 7: Built at New York. Launched 6 Feb 1805. Service record: Sailed from New York to Mediterranean, 20 Jun 1805; lost at sea with all hands.

No. 8: Built at Boston. Launched 24 Apr 1805. Service record: Mediterranean 1805.

No. 9: Built at Charleston, S.C. (Pritchard). Launched Mar 1805. Dimensions: 71' (bp) × 21' × 6'2". Service record: Mediterranean 1805.

No. 10: Built at Washington NYd. Launched 30 Apr 1805. Service record: Mediterranean 1805. Ships captured: Brig *Maria*, schr *Trimmer*, 1813.

No. 11: Built for Preble at Portland, Maine (N. Dyer). Rate: 2 guns. Dimensions: 73'10" × 18'11" × 5'3". Schr rig. Service record: Sent to New Orleans. Condemned by 1812.

No. 12: Built for Preble at Newburyport, Mass. (J. Coffin). Dimensions: 67'8" × 18'11" × 5'4". Schr rig. Service record: Sent to New Orleans. Condemned by 1812.

Nos. 13–16: Built on Western rivers, 1805–06; Nos. 13 and 14 at Cincinnati (John Smith), Nos. 15 and 16 at Eddyville, Ky. (Matthew Lyon). Dimensions: 60' × 18'6" × 5'. Battery: 2–24pdr. Sloop-rigged.

Nos. 17–27: Built on Western rivers, all completed 1807–08; Nos. 17 and 18 at Cincinnati (John Smith), Nos. 19 and 20 at Lexington (or Louisville), Ky. (J. Jordan & James Morrison), Nos. 21 and 22 at Marietta, Ohio (Edw. Tapper & Thomas Vail), No. 23 at Charleston, Va. (John Connell & Peter Mills), No. 24 at Cincinnati (Thomas Reagan), Nos. 25–27 at Eddyville, Ky. (Matthew Lyon). Similar to No. 13. Battery: 2–24pdr.

No. 23: Captured by British on Lake Borgne, La., 14 Dec 1814. Ship captured: One unarmed pirate felucca, Southwest Pass, Miss., 24 Sep 1814.

No. 28: Built at Washington NYd, 1808.

No. 7 (II): Built at Havre de Grace, Md. (Bennett Barnes). Dimensions: 59'6" × 16'6" × 6'1".

Nos. 29–33: Built at Portland, Maine (three by Wm. Moulton, two by E. Higgins).

Nos. 34–37: Built at Brunswick, Maine (Ephraim Hunt & Robert Giveen).

Nos. 38–41: Built at Middletown, Conn. (Wm. Van Deusen & J. & T. Childs).

Nos. 42, 43: Built at Newport, R.I. (Benj. Marble).

Nos. 44, 45: Built at Greenwich, R.I. (John Glozier).

Nos. 46–57: Built in New York (Nos. 46–49 by A & N Brown, Nos. 50–53 by Eckford & Beebe, Nos. 54–57 by Chr. Berghe), 1806. Dimensions: 47′4″ (keel) × 18′ × 5′6″. Battery: 1–24pdr or 32pdr, 2–12pdr crde. Nos. 50–57 built to a different design, with "Periagua" rig, in which masts did not have the same rake.

No. 46: Wrecked off Newport, R.I. (10 killed), 29 Oct 1812.

No. 54: Captured schr *Favorite* off New Bedford, Mass., Jun 1814.

Nos. 58–78: Built in Virginia; Nos. 58 and 59 at Hampton (Hope), Nos. 60 and 61 at Hampton (Pool & Servant), Nos. 62–65 at Mathews City (J. Patterson & H. Gayle), Nos. 66–69 at Portsmouth (Forster), Nos. 70–78 at Washington NYd. No. 73 differed in design.

No. 62: Lost in gale off St. Marys, Ga., 16 Sep 1812.

Nos. 79–88: Built at Portland, Maine (D. Green). Battery: 1–32pdr or 24pdr.

No. 81: Captured one launch, Nov 1814.

No. 88: Captured schr *Chebacque* off New England coast, 14 Jul 1814.

Nos. 89–92: Built at Norwich, Conn. (E. Tracy), and Westerly, R.I. (A. Cross).

Nos. 93–115: Built to two designs at New York (five by Eckford & Beebe, five by C. Bergh, five by A & N Brown, five by Chas. Browne, two by R. Jenkins, and one by T. Bell).

Nos. 116–135: Built at Philadelphia NYd and seven other shipyards.

No. 121: Captured by boats from HMS *Junon*, 29 Jun 1813.

Nos. 136–145: Built at Baltimore (some by Price). Dimensions: 60′ × 16′6″ × 6′6″.

No. 140: Blew up by accident in Ocracoke Inlet, N.C. (9 killed), 23 Oct 1814.

Nos. 146–155: Built at Norfolk, Va. (T. Armistead).

No. 151: (With No. 160) Captured privateer schr *Fortune of War*, 3, at Sapelo Bar, S.C., 9 Sep 1814.

No. 152: Struck by lightning and blew up in Mississippi River (27 casualties), 14 Jul 1815.

Nos. 156–165: Built at Charleston and Beaufort, S.C. (most by J. Marsh & F. Saltus, No. 158 by James Ingraham).

No. 156: Captured by British on Lake Borgne, La., 14 Dec 1814.

No. 158 (**Revenge**): Built in 1808. Laid up 1817–22. Mosquito Fleet 1822–24. Captured one pirate barge, 7 Mar 1822.

No. 159: Lost in gale off St. Marys, Ga. (no survivors), Oct 1810.

No. 160: (With No. 151) Captured privateer schr *Fortune of War*, 3, at Sapelo Bar, S.C., 9 Sep 1814.

No. 161: Lost in gale off St. Marys, Ga., 16 Sep 1812.

No. 162: Captured by British on Lake Borgne, La., 14 Dec 1814. Captured schrs *La Franchise*, 5, *Santa Maria*, 4, *La Sophie*, *La Vengeance*, *La Divina Pastora*, 14, off Pensacola and Mobile, Aug–Sep 1811.

No. 163: Captured by British on Lake Borgne, La., 14 Dec 1814.

No. 164: Lost in gale off St. Marys, Ga., 16 Sep 1812.

No. 166–168: Built at Wilmington, N.C. (A. Perry).

No. 166: Renamed USS **Alligator** in 1812 (q.v.).

No. 169–176: No information available.

BOMB KETCHES

Name	Builder	Built	Acquired	Comm
Intrepid ex-*Mastico*	France	1798	early 1804	1804

Rate	4 guns
Dimensions	(in USN) 60′ × 12′
Tonnage	(U)
Complement	70
Battery	4–24pdr crde

Notes: Built for Napoleon's Egyptian expedition. Captured by *Enterprise* and *Constitution*, 23 Dec 1803, and purchased.
Service record: Used by Decatur to destroy captured frigate *Philadelphia* in Tripoli harbor, 16 Feb 1804. Blew up prematurely as fire ship under Somers in Tripoli harbor (13 killed), 4 Sep 1804.

Name	Builder	Laid down	L	Comm
Etna	Portland, Maine (Wm. Moulton)	(U)	18 Jun 1806	19 Jul 1806
Vesuvius	Newburyport, Mass. (Jacob Coffin)	(U)	31 May 1806	Sep 1806

Rate	4 guns
Dimensions	*Etna:* 83′6″ (deck) × 24′ × 8′
	Vesuvius: 82′5″ (bp) × 25′5″ × 8′4″
Tonnage	*Etna:* 139 tons
	Vesuvius: 145 tons
Complement	30
Battery	*Etna:* 1–13″ M, 2–8″ H, 8–8pdr
	Vesuvius: 2–24pdr, 8–9pdr; (later) 10–6pdr

Notes: Navy-built. Designed by Jacob Coffin. Near-sisters.
Service records:
Etna: Passage to New Orleans in 1806 and 1809. Sunk in a hurricane at New Orleans, 19 Aug 1812. Also reported to have disappeared off New Orleans (30 killed), 22 Nov 1812.
Vesuvius: In passage to New Orleans on 19 Oct 1806, went ashore in Gulf of Abaco and was obliged to throw guns overboard; returned to New York, 1807. Receiving ship, New York, 1816. Was a decayed hulk alongside steamship *Fulton* when she blew up at Brooklyn, 1829; BU.
Ships captured: Pirate schr *Duc de Montebello*, 5, pirate schr *Diomede*, 1, slaver *Alexandria*, 4, off Mississippi River, Feb 1810.

Name	Builder	Built	Acquired	Comm
Spitfire	Conn.	1803	25 Apr 1805	25 Apr 1805

Rate	3 guns
Dimensions	(U)
Tonnage	92 tons
Complement	30
Battery	1–13″ M, 2–9pdr; (later) 7 guns

Notes: Ex-merchant sloop. Purchased at Boston and converted at Boston NYd.
Service record: Sailed for Tripoli, 22 Jun 1805. Laid up 1807. BU 1820.

A contemporary sketch of the USS *Intrepid*, which was used by Decatur to destroy the captured frigate *Philadelphia* in February 1804. Later in the year, all on board were killed when she blew up while attempting to enter Tripoli harbor. (U.S. Naval Historical Center)

Name	Builder	Built	Acquired	Comm
Vengeance	(U)	1804	Apr 1805	Apr 1805

Rate	3 guns; (later) 7 guns
Dimensions	(U)
Tonnage	92 tons
Complement	30
Battery	(U)

Notes: Ex-merchant schr. Purchased and converted at Boston NYd.
Service record: Sailed for Tripoli, 19 Jun 1805. Mediterranean 1805–06. BU 1818.

Name	Builder	Built	Acquired	Comm
Etna	(U)	(U)	1813	(U)

Rate	11 guns
Dimensions	(U)
Tonnage	220 tons
Complement	(U)
Battery	2–6pdr, 2–7.5″ H

Notes: Officially a brig. Purchased to replace lost *Etna* at New Orleans. Unfit for service, 1814. BU 1817.
Ship captured: Spanish schr *Terrible*, Mar 1814.

BOMB BRIGS

Name	Builder	Built	Acquired	Comm
Etna	(U)	(U)	Feb 1847	Mar 1847
Hecla	(U)	(U)	1846	9 Mar 1847
Stromboli ex-*Howard* (brig)	(U)	(U)	1846	18 Mar 1847

Rate	1 gun
Dimensions	*Etna:* 84′3″ × 26′5″ × 9′10″
	Stromboli: 80′ (bp) × 22′8″ × 10′
Tonnage	182 tons
	Hecla: 194 tons
Complement	44
Battery	1 H/M
	Stromboli: 1–10″ columbiad

Service records:
Etna: Converted at Boston NYd. Sold Oct 1848.
Hecla: Purchased in New York, 1846. Mexican War; Veracruz, Tuxpan. Decomm 9 Sep 1848 and sold.
Stromboli: Mexican War. Decomm 6 Sep 1848 and sold.

Name	Builder	L	Acquired	Comm
Vesuvius ex–*Saint Mary*	Williamsburg, N.Y.	1845	1846	1846

Dimensions	97′ × 26′ × 9′8″, d10′
Tonnage	239 tons
Complement	(U)
Battery	1–10″ M; also reported as 10–6pdr

Notes: Acquired at New York.
Service record: Attack on Tuxpan, Mexico, 1847. Capture of Tabasco, Mexico, Jun 1847. Sold Oct 1848.
Ship captured: Schr *Wasp*, 10 Oct 1847.

MOSQUITO FLEET

Name	Builder	Acquired	Comm
Beagle	(U)	20 Dec 1822	1823
Ferret	(U)	20 Dec 1822	1823
Fox	Baltimore	20 Dec 1822	1823
Greyhound	(U)	1822	(U)
Jackall	(U)	Jan 1823	(U)
Terrier	(U)	1822	early 1823
Weasel	(U)	1822	(U)
Wild Cat	(U)	1822	(U)

Rate	3 guns, except *Wild Cat:* 2 guns
Dimensions	*Greyhound:* 65′ × (U); others: (U)
Tonnage	47 to 65 tons
	Beagle: 52 tons
	Fox: 51 tons
	Wild Cat: 48 tons
Complement	31
Battery	varied

Notes: Purchased for David Porter's "Mosquito Fleet" to suppress West Indian pirates. Particulars varied.
Service records:
Beagle: Piracy suppression in West Indies, 1823–25. Attack on pirates at Cape Cruz, Cuba, 21–22 Jul 1823. Attack on pirates at Foxardo, P.R., 14 Nov 1824. Sold Apr 1825.
Ferret: West Indies 1823–25. Capsized in gale off Canasi, Cuba (9 killed), 4 Feb 1825.
　　Ships captured: Five pirate launches at Matanzas, Cuba, Jun–Jul 1823.
Fox: Gulf of Mexico 1823–26. Receiving ship, Baltimore, 1826. Sold 8 Dec 1837.
Greyhound: Attack on pirates at Cape Cruz, Cuba, 21–22 Jul 1823. Sold at Baltimore, 1824.
Jackall: Suppression of pirates in West Indies. Sold 1825.
Terrier: West Indies 1823–25. Sold 1825.
　　Ships captured: One schr, one launch (pirates) off Havana, 17–26 Aug 1824.
Weasel: Sold 1825.
　　Ships captured: Schr *Gallago Segunda*, at Colorados, Cuba, 3 Aug 1823.
Wild Cat: Lost with all hands in storm in West Indies (14 killed), Oct 1824.

Name	Builder	Acquired
Gallinipper		1823
Gnat		1823
Mosquito	Washington NYd	1823
Midge		1823
Sandfly		1823

Several gunboats used as part of the Mosquito Fleet, as depicted by Fred S. Cozzens. (U.S. Naval Historical Center)

Notes: Perhaps old gunboat barges of the War of 1812 refitted and renamed. Fitted to row and to sail.
Large crews, one or two guns, useful for attacking pirates in shallow water. All sold by 1824.
Service records:
Gallinipper: Armed boat in West Indies. FFU after 1825.
　　Ships captured: (With *Mosquito*) pirate schr, 8 Apr 1823; schr *Catalina* Jul 1823.
Gnat: FFU.
Mosquito: Employed in West Indies under Porter. Sold, summer 1825.
　　Ships captured: (With *Gallinipper*) pirate schr, 8 Apr 1823; schr *Catalina* Jul 1823.
Midge: Armed boat in West Indies, 1823–24.
Sandfly: Armed boat employed in West Indies.

Name	Builder	Built	Acquired	Comm
Flirt	Baltimore	1839	Nov 1839	Dec 1839
Phoenix	Baltimore	(U)	1841	1841
Taney	New York (Webb & Morgan)	1833	1847	(U)
Wave	New York (Brown & Bell)	1832	1836	(U)

Rate	2 guns
Dimensions	*Taney:* 74′6″ (bp) × 20′8″ × d7′6″
Tonnage	*Flirt:* 150 tons
	Phoenix: 90 tons
Complement	89
Battery	*Flirt:* 2–18pdr crde; also reported as 2–9pdr, 6–24pdr crde
	Taney: 4–9pdr

Notes:
Flirt: Built for War Dept. Pilot boat, purchased as survey vessel. Receiving ship, Charleston, 1842–43. Despatch vessel, 1843–47. Gulf of Mexico 1847–50. Decomm 29 Nov 1850 and sold.
Phoenix: Seminole War, 1842. Sold 1853.
Taney: Trfd from Revenue Service, 1846. Mediterranean 1847–49. Trfd to USCS, Aug 1850. Capsized at New York, 3 Aug 1852; salved. Damaged by lightning off Tybee Island, Ga., 30 Aug 1857. Sold 5 Jan 1858.
Wave: Seminole War, 1836–40. Surveying. Sold 1846.

SUPPORT VESSELS

STORESHIPS

Name	Builder	Built	Acquired	Comm
Franklin	Philadelphia	1795	27 Apr 1805	Jun 1805

Rate	8 guns
Dimensions	72′4″ (deck) × 22′4″ × (U)

Notes: Brig transport, captured by Tripolitanian corsairs, 1802. Purchased at Trieste as a supply ship, Apr 1805. Sold at New Orleans, 21 Mar 1807.

Name	Builder	Built	Acquired	Comm
Alert	Howdenpoint, England	1803	13 Aug 1812	1812
ex-HMS *Alert*, ex-*Oxford*				

Rate	2 guns
Dimensions	105′ (bp) × 29′ × 11′
Tonnage	393 bm, 325 tons
Complement	100
Battery	2–12pdr, 18–32pdr crde

Notes: Former collier, acquired by Royal Navy, May 1804. Captured by USS *Essex* off East Coast, 13 Aug 1812. Converted to storeship, receiving ship at Norfolk, 1818. BU at Norfolk, 1829.

Name	Builder	Built	Acquired	Comm
Greenwich	(U)	(U)	28 May 1813	May 1813

Rate	2 guns
Dimensions	(U)
Tonnage	338 tons
Complement	25
Battery	(U)

Notes: British whaler (LofM), captured by USS *Essex* off Galapagos Islands, 28 May 1813. Armed storeship.
Service record: Burned to prevent capture in Marquesa Islands by her captain, Lt. J. M. Gamble, not having enough men to man her, 1814.
Ship captured: (With *Georgiana*) *Seringapatam*, 13 Jul 1813.

Name	Builder	Built	Acquired	Comm
Tom Bowline	(U)	(U)	1814	late 1814

Rate	12 guns
Dimensions	(U)
Tonnage	260 tons
Complement	90
Battery	(U)

Notes: Brig or schr. Purchased at Portsmouth, N.H. Store vessel in 1814. Raiding in South Atlantic, 1815. Sold 1818.

Name	Builder	Built	Acquired	Comm
Decoy	New York	(U)	27 Dec 1822	1822
ex-*Zodiac*				

Rate	2 guns
Dimensions	(U)
Tonnage	(U)
Complement	(U)
Battery	(U)

Notes: Purchased. Storeship for "Mosquito Fleet." Sold Jan 1826.

Name	Builder	Laid down	L	Comm
Relief	Philadelphia NYd	1835	14 Sep 1836	1836

Rate	6 guns
Dimensions	109′ (bp) × 30′ × 12′
Tonnage	468 tons
Complement	(U)
Battery	4–18pdr, 2–12pdr

Notes: Ship rig. Slow sailer.
Service record: Survey expedition to South Seas, Aug 1838–Jul 1842. Sold 27 Sep 1883.

Name	Builder	Laid down	L	Comm
Erie	Boston NYd	1840	1842	1843

Rate	4 guns
Dimensions	117′11″ (bp) × 32′4″ × 17′10″, d14′6″
Tonnage	(U)
Complement	(U)
Battery	4–9pdr

Notes: Sloop of war, officially rebuilt, 1840–43. Considered too small.
Service record: Pacific, 1843–44, 1845–48. Capture of Mazatlan, 11 Nov 1847. Sold 26 Nov 1850.
Ship captured: (With *Columbus* and *Warren*) British schr *William* at Monterey, Calif., 22 Mar 1847.
Later history: Bark-rigged merchant ship.

Name	Builder	Laid down	L	Comm
Southampton	Norfolk NYd	Oct 1841	1845	27 May 1845

Rate	2 guns
Dimensions	156′ × 27′10″ × 17′, d13′6″
Tonnage	567 tons
Complement	(U)
Battery	2–42pdr crde

Notes: Laid down as sidewheel steamer but converted to sail. Two sisters not begun. Fast but tender.
Service record: Africa Sqn 1845–46. Pacific Sqn, 1847–50, 1850–52. Expedition to Japan, 1853.
Decomm 6 Apr 1855.
Later history: Merchant ship.

Name	Builder	Built	Acquired	Comm
Fredonia	Newburyport, Mass.	1845	14 Nov 1846	5 Jan 1847

Rate	4 guns
Dimensions	160′ × 32′11″ × 16′6″
Tonnage	800 tons
Complement	37
Battery	4–24pdr crde

Notes: Bark rig.
Service record: Mexican War, 1847–48. Made several trips to California, 1848–53. Storeship at Valparaiso, 1853–62, and at Callao, 1862–68. Wrecked in tidal wave at Arica, Chile (27 killed), 13 Aug 1868.

Name	Builder	Built	Acquired	Comm
Supply	Medford, Mass. (Ewell)	1846	8 Dec 1846	19 Dec 1846

Rate	4 guns
Dimensions	(U)
Tonnage	547 tons
Complement	40
Battery	4–24pdr crde

Notes: Ship rig.
Service record: Mediterranean 1847. Sailed on expedition to explore the Dead Sea under William Lynch, Dec 1847. Expedition to Japan, 1853. Transported cargo of camels from the Levant, 1855. Paraguay Expedition, 1858. Sold 3 May 1884.

Name	Builder	Built	Acquired	Comm
Electra ex-*Rolla*	Philadelphia	1843	15 Jan 1847	19 Mar 1847

Rate	2 guns
Dimensions	100′ × 25′ × 11′
Tonnage	248 tons
Complement	21
Battery	2 guns

Notes: Bark. Purchased and fitted out at New York NYd.
Service record: Storeship for Mexican War. Decomm 27 Oct 1848. Sold Nov 1848.

Name	Builder	Built	Acquired	Comm
Release ex-*Eringol*	Boston (Brown & Lovell)	1853	3 Apr 1855	3 Apr 1855

Rate	2 guns
Dimensions	113′9″ × 27′2″ × 11′9″
Tonnage	327
Complement	85
Battery	2–32pdr

Notes: Bark.
Service record: Arctic expedition, 1855. Paraguay Expedition, 1859. Sold 25 Oct 1865.

TENDERS

Name	Builder	Built	Acquired
Advance	New Kent Co., Va.	1847	7 May 1850

Dimensions	88′ × 21′9″ × 8′5″
Tonnage	144 tons
Complement	17

Notes: Brigantine. Loaned to Navy by Henry Grinnell for Arctic search and manned by volunteers.
Service record: Search for Franklin expedition north of Baffin Bay, May 1850–Aug 1851. Second search for Franklin Expedition started, Jun 1853. Imprisoned in ice, Sep 1853, and eventually crushed. Crew finally reached open water, July 1855.

Name	Builder	Acquired	Comm
Rescue	(U)	1850	May 1850

Dimensions	(U)
Tonnage	91 tons
Complement	16

Notes: Brig. Loaned to Navy by Henry Grinnell for Arctic search and manned by volunteers.
Service record: Search for Franklin expedition, May 1850–Aug 1851. Returned to New York and to Grinnell, Sep 1851.

Name	Builder	Built	Acquired	Comm
Fenimore Cooper ex-*Skiddy*	(U)	1852	1852	1852

Rate	3 guns
Dimensions	(U)
Tonnage	95 tons
Complement	16
Battery	(U)

Notes: Schooner, former New York pilot.
Service record: Tender for Ringgold's exploring expedition to North Pacific and China Seas. Went aground in typhoon in Kanagawa Bay off Yokohama, 13 Aug 1859.

Name	Builder	Built	Acquired	Comm
John P. Kennedy ex-*Sea Nymph*	(U)	1853	1853	1853

Rate	3 guns
Dimensions	(U)
Tonnage	350 tons
Complement	45
Battery	1–24pdr H, 2–12pdr H

Service record: Purchased in 1853 for Ringgold's exploring expedition to North Pacific and China Seas. Decomm 31 Oct 1855. Sold at Hong Kong, Nov 1855.

GREAT LAKES

The Great Lakes were not only a barrier between the United States and British Canada but also a highway for commerce and trade. Many Americans thought Canada would be easy to capture, and as in 1776 an expedition was mounted to do that. The American plan was two-pronged, crossing over at either end of Lake Erie—Detroit and Niagara. But the only American naval presence was a single brig, *Oneida*, on Lake Ontario. In 1812 the British captured Detroit, which made clear the necessity of naval ships on Lake Erie. Captain Isaac Chauncey had been given overall command of the Navy on the lakes.

Conflicting opinions resulted in ships being built at both Presque Isle (now Erie), Pa., and Black Rock, N.Y. (near Niagara). In addition, a yard was erected at Sackets Harbor, N.Y., on Lake Ontario. On 8

October 1812, two British ships, *Detroit* and *Caledonia*, were captured near Black Rock, and their loss gave an advantage to the Americans.

Chauncey considered Lake Ontario more important than Lake Erie and the fighting there was more frequent. He held command of the lake. In November 1812 his squadron attacked Kingston, Ontario. In April 1813 he attacked and captured Fort York (now Toronto), which was burned. But the British reaction led to the burning of the yard at Sackets Harbor and an evening of the balance of power. Later the British forced the Americans out of the Niagara positions, while the two fleets had occasional engagements. The relative balance of power, combined with the reluctance of the two commanders, meant stalemate on the lake.

On Lake Erie, an aggressive American commander made a difference. The arrival of Oliver Hazard Perry in March 1813 helped speed the progress of shipbuilding there. Six ships were under construction, together with a naval yard at Presque Isle. The American squadron was superior in weight of metal and number of ships when the two squadrons met in battle at Put-in-Bay in the southwest corner of the lake on 10 September 1813.[15] The battle ended in a decisive victory for the Americans. As the enemy concentrated their fire on his flagship *Lawrence*, the ship became unmanageable and Perry transferred his flag to the virtually untouched *Niagara*. The British squadron surrendered. American casualties were 123 dead and wounded. Perry's message became legend: "We have met the enemy and they are ours."

During the summer of 1814, an American joint Army-Navy expedition to Lakes Superior and Huron captured enemy forts, although three ships were lost to capture.

On Lake Ontario in October 1814, the British launched the 102-gun *St. Lawrence* and Chauncey laid down two 74-gun ships, *Chippewa* and *New Orleans*. The last of these remained on the stocks until her decaying hulk was sold in 1883.

The steam warship *Michigan* was commissioned on Lake Erie in 1844 and remained there until the 1920s.

LAKE ERIE SQUADRON

SLOOPS

Name	Builder	Built	Acquired	Comm
Trippe ex-*Contractor*	(U)	(U)	1812	1812

Rate	1 gun
Dimensions	(U)
Tonnage	60 tons
Complement	35
Battery	1–32pdr

Notes: Purchased on Niagara River.
Service record: Battle of Lake Erie, 10 Sep 1813. Captured by British and burned after running aground near Buffalo Creek, Oct 1814.

Name	Builder	Built	Acquired	Comm
Queen Charlotte	Amherstburg, Ont.	1809	Sep 1813	never

Rate	16 guns
Dimensions	116′ × 26′ × 11′; also reported as 96′ (dk) × 25′ × 12′
Tonnage	400 tons
Complement	126
Battery	2–9pdr, 14–24pdr crde; also reported as 14–24pdr, 3–12pdr

Notes: Canadian Provincial Marine. Captured at Battle of Lake Erie, 10 Sep 1813. Not put in service. Sold 1825.

Name	Builder	Built	Acquired	Comm
Detroit	Amherstburg, Ont.	1813	Sep 1813	never

Rate	12 guns
Dimensions	(U)
Tonnage	305 tons
Complement	150
Battery	2–24pdr, 1–18pdr, 6–12pdr, 8–9pdr, 1–24pdr crde, 1–18pdr crde

Notes: British sloop, captured in sinking condition at Battle of Lake Erie, 10 Sep 1813. Laid up. Sold 1825.
Later history: Fitted as trading bark, 1825. Reportedly sent over Niagara Falls with a cargo of wild animals as a spectacle, 1841.

BRIGS

Name	Builder	Laid down	L	Comm
Lawrence	Presque Isle, Pa. (Brown)	Mar 1813	24 May 1813	5 Aug 1813
Niagara	Presque Isle, Pa. (Brown)	Mar 1813	May 1813	4 Aug 1813

Rate	4 guns
Dimensions	109′9″ × 29′ × 9′
Tonnage	493 tons
Complement	134
Battery	2–12pdr, 18–32pdr crde

Notes: Designed by Noah Brown. Built of green wood. Ready by 23 Jun 1813 but lacked crews. Both sunk in Misery Bay to preserve hulls, 1818–20.
Service records:
Lawrence: Battle of Lake Erie (22 killed), 10 Sep 1813; severely damaged, and Commodore Perry trfd flag to *Niagara*. Sold 12 Jul 1825. Raised and exhibited at Centennial Exhibition, 1876. Later destroyed by fire.
Niagara: Battle of Lake Erie (2 killed), 10 Sep 1813. Landings at Detroit River, Sep 1813. Receiving ship, Erie, 1814–20. Sold 12 Jul 1825. Hulk raised in 1913. Restored, now a museum at Erie, Pa.
Ships captured: Schr *Mink*, schr *Perserverance*, schr *Nancy* in Lake Superior, Jul–Sep 1814.

Name	Builder	Built	Acquired	Comm
Adams	(U)	1812	1812	never

Rate	14 guns
Dimensions	(U)
Tonnage	200 tons
Complement	(U)
Battery	6–6pdr (as British?)

[15] British: *Detroit*, 19, *Queen Charlotte*, 17, *Lady Prevost*, 13, *Hunter*, 10, *Little Belt*, 3, and *Chippewa*, 1.

Notes: Purchased at Detroit.
Service record: Surrendered with Detroit to British, not yet armed, 16 Aug 1812. Armed and commissioned as HMS *Detroit*. Recaptured by American boat expedition at Fort Erie but abandoned and burned, 9 Oct 1813.

Name	Builder	Built	Acquired	Comm
Caledonia	Amherstburg, Ont.	1807	6 Feb 1813	1813

Rate	3 guns
Dimensions	(U)
Tonnage	85 tons
Complement	53
Battery	2–24pdr, 1–32pdr crde

Notes: Northwest Fur Co. trading vessel in Canadian Provincial Marine. British vessel captured by boarding off Fort Erie, Ont., 8 Oct 1812.
Service record: Battle of Lake Erie, 10 Sep 1813. Sold May 1815.
Later history: Merchant *General Wayne*.

Name	Builder	Built	Acquired	Comm
Hunter ex–*General Hunter*	Amherstburg, Ont.	1806	10 Sep 1813	(U)

Rate	10 guns
Dimensions	(U)
Tonnage	180 tons
Complement	45
Battery	4–6pdr, 2–4pdr, 2–2pdr, 2–12pdr crde

Notes: Canadian Provincial Marine ship captured at Battle of Lake Erie, 10 Sep 1813. Sold.

SCHOONERS

Name	Builder	Built	Acquired	Comm
Somers ex-*Catherine*	(U)	(U)	1812	(U)

Rate	2 guns
Dimensions	58′6″ × 19′ × (U)
Tonnage	98 tons
Complement	30
Battery	1–32pdr on pivots, 1–24pdr

Notes: Purchased merchant schr.
Service record: Battle of Lake Erie, 10 Sep 1813. Captured by British, 12 Aug 1814.
Later history: HMS *Sauk*. RR 1831.

Name	Builder	L	Comm
Ariel	Presque Isle, Pa. (A & N Brown)	Apr 1813	summer 1813

Rate	4 guns
Dimensions	(U)
Tonnage	75 tons
Complement	36
Battery	4–12pdr

Service record: Battle of Lake Erie (1 killed), 10 Sep 1813. FFU.

Name	Builder	Built	Acquired	Comm
Lady Prevost	Amherstburg, Ont.	13 Jul 1812	11 Sep 1813	Sep 1813

Rate	10 guns
Dimensions	83′ × 21′ × 9′
Tonnage	230 tons
Complement	86
Battery	10–12pdr, 1–9pdr, 2–6pdr

Notes: Captured by U.S. sqn, 11 Sep 1813.
Service record: Burned and sunk at Erie, Pa., 1815, then raised and sold.

Name	Builder	Built	Acquired	Comm
Little Belt	Canada	1812	Sep 1813	23 Oct 1813

Rate	3 guns
Dimensions	59′ × 16′ × 7′
Tonnage	96 tons
Complement	18
Battery	1–12pdr, 2–6pdr

Notes: British schr. Captured by USS *Scorpion* and *Chippewa* off Put-in-Bay, Lake Erie, 12 Sep 1813.
Service record: Driven ashore in storm at Black Rock, N.Y., 8 Dec 1813. Burned by British, 29 Dec 1813.

Name	Builder	Built	Acquired	Comm
Ohio	Cleveland	1812	1813	Jun 1813

Rate	1 gun
Dimensions	54′ × 17′6″ × (U)
Tonnage	62 tons
Complement	35
Battery	1–24pdr

Notes: Purchased merchant ship. Captured by British near Fort Erie, 12 Aug 1814.
Later history: HMS *Huron*, 2. RR 1817.

Name	Builder	Built	Acquired	Comm
Porcupine	Presque Isle, Pa. (A & N Brown)	1813	1813	spring 1813

Rate	3 guns
Dimensions	(U)
Tonnage	60 tons
Complement	25
Battery	1–32pdr on pivot, 2–12pdr crde

Service record: Battle of Lake Erie, 10 Sep 1813. Trfd to Collector of Revenue, Detroit, 2 Jun 1819.
Later history: Sold 1821, merchant ship. Beached near Grand Haven, Mich., 1873.

Name	Builder	Laid down	L	Comm
Scorpion	Presque Isle, Pa.	1812	spring 1813	1813

Rate	2 guns
Dimensions	62′ × 17′ × 5′
Tonnage	86 tons
Complement	35
Battery	1–32pdr, 1–24pdr crde

Service record: Battle of Lake Erie (2 killed), 10 Sep 1813. Captured by newly taken schr *Tigress* in Lake Huron, 6 Sep 1814.
Later history: HMS *Confiance*. RR 1831.

Name	Builder	Built	Acquired	Comm
Tigress ex-*Amelia*	Erie, Pa. (Brown)	1813	26 Dec 1812	1813

Rate	1 gun
Dimensions	50′ × 17′6″ × 5′
	(in British service) 57′ × 17′6″ × (U)
Tonnage	52 tons
Complement	27
Battery	1–32pdr

Notes: Another schr *Amelia* was purchased on 26 Dec 1812, found unfit for service, and sold in May 1815.
Service record: Battle of Lake Erie, 10 Sep 1813. Captured by British on Lake Huron near Mackinaw, 3 Sep 1814.
Later history: HMS *Surprise*. RR 1831.

Name	Builder	Built	Acquired	Comm
Ghent	Presque Isle, Pa. (Thos. Eyre)	(U)	1815	1815

Rate	1 gun
Dimensions	55′x 16′ × 6′
Tonnage	50 tons
Complement	(U)
Battery	1–12pdr

Service record: Sold 20 Mar 1826.

Name	Builder	Built	Acquired	Comm
Chippewa	Maumee, Ohio	1810	1813	(U)

Rate	1 gun
Dimensions	59′ × 16′ × 7′
Tonnage	70 tons
Complement	15
Battery	1–18pdr, 2 swivels

Notes: Captured from British, 10 Sep 1813.
Service record: Driven ashore in violent squall in Black Rock, N.Y., Oct 1813. Burned by British landing party, 29 Dec 1813.

LAKE ONTARIO SQUADRON

SHIPS-OF-THE-LINE

Name	Builder	Built	Acquired	Comm
Chippewa	Sackets Harbor, N.Y. (A & N Brown)	1815	never	never
New Orleans	Sackets Harbor, N.Y. (A & N Brown)	Jan 1815	never	never

Rate	74 guns
Dimensions	212′ (bp), 204′ (keel) × 56′ × 26′6″
Tonnage	2,805 tons
Complement	(U)
Battery	63–32pdr, 24–32pdr crde

Notes: Construction ceased at end of the war.
Service records:
Chippewa: Sold on stocks, 1 Nov 1823. Nearly completed in one month, never launched.
New Orleans: Sold on stocks, 24 Sep 1883.

FRIGATES

Name	Builder	Laid down	L	Comm
Superior	Sackets Harbor, N.Y. (Eckford)	11 Feb 1814	1 May 1814	1814

Rate	44 guns
Dimensions	180′ (bp) × 43′ × (U)
Tonnage	1,580 tons
Complement	500
Battery	30–32pdr, 2–24pdr, 26–42pdr crde

Notes: Designed by Henry Eckford. Lengthened 20′ during construction. Largest U.S. vessel on the lake.
Service record: Flag of Commodore Chauncey. Sold 1824.

Name	Builder	Laid down	L	Comm
Mohawk	Sackets Harbor, N.Y. (Eckford)	7 Apr 1814	11 Jun 1814	Jul 1814

Rate	32 guns
Dimensions	155′ (bp) × 37′6″ × 15′6″
Tonnage	1,350 tons
Complement	350
Battery	26–24pdr, 16–32pdr crde

Notes: Designed by Henry Eckford. Completed and launched in 34 days.
Service record: Sold 1822 and BU.

Name	Builder	Laid down	L	Comm
Plattsburg	Sackets Harbor, N.Y. (A & N Brown)	1814	never	never

Rate	44 guns
Dimensions	185′ (keel) × 46′ × (U)

The incomplete ship-of-the-line *New Orleans*, laid down in 1815 at Sackets Harbor, N.Y., to serve on Lake Ontario, was still incomplete in 1882.

Tonnage	1,749 tons
Complement	(U)
Battery	32–24pdr, 20–42pdr crde

Notes: Sold on stocks, 30 Apr 1825.

SLOOPS (CORVETTES)

Name	Builder	Laid down	L	Comm
General Pike	Sackets Harbor, N.Y.	9 Apr 1813	12 Jun 1813	Jul 1813

Rate	24 guns
Dimensions	145′ (bp) × 37′ × 15′
Tonnage	875 tons
Complement	300
Battery	26–24pdr

Notes: Designed by Henry Eckford. Completed in 63 days.
Service record: Battle of Lake Ontario, 10 Aug 1813. Action off York, Ont., 28 Sep 1813; burst one of her guns and sustained considerable injury (3 killed). Action off False Ducks, Ont., 5 Oct 1813. Sold 1825.
Ships captured: (With *Governor Tompkins, Lady of the Lake, Sylph*) sloop *Elizabeth*, sloop *Mary Ann*, 5 Oct 1813.

Name	Builder	Laid down	L	Comm
Madison	Sackets Harbor, N.Y. (Eckford)	11 Sep 1812	26 Nov 1812	Apr 1813

Rate	20 guns
Dimensions	112′ × 32′6″ × 11′6″
Tonnage	593 tons
Complement	200
Battery	24–32pdr crde; (1814) 14–18pdr, 8–32pdr crde

Notes: Ship. Completed in 63 days.
Service record: Capture of Fort York, 27 Apr 1813. Capture of Fort George, 27 May 1813. Action off York, Ont., 28 Sep 1813. Sold 30 Apr 1825.

BRIGS

Name	Builder	Laid down	L	Comm
Oneida	Oswego, N.Y. (C. Bergh & H. Eckford)	1808	31 Mar 1809	1809

Rate	14 guns
Dimensions	85′6″ (bp) × 22′6″ × 8′
Tonnage	242 tons
Complement	115
Battery	1–32pdr, 16–24pdr crde; (1814) 2–12pdr, 14–24pdr crde

Spar and sail plan of the sloop *General Pike*, which served on Lake Ontario. (U.S. Naval Historical Center)

Notes: Designed by Christian Bergh. First vessel of war built on the Lakes. Stoutly built, but a dull sailer.
Service record: Action with British sqn at Sackets Harbor, N.Y., 19 Jul 1812. Attack on Kingston, Ont. (1 killed), 9 Nov 1812. Capture of Fort York, 27 Apr 1813. Action off York, Ont., 28 Sep 1813. Sold 15 May 1815 but repurchased. Sold 1825.

Name	Builder	Laid down	L	Comm
Jefferson	Sackets Harbor, N.Y. (Eckford)	Feb 1814	7 Apr 1814	1814
Jones	Sackets Harbor, N.Y. (Eckford)	Feb 1814	10 Apr 1814	Jul 1814

Rate	18 guns
Dimensions	121′6″ (bp) × 31′6″ × (U)
Tonnage	509 tons
Complement	160
Battery	*Jefferson:* 4–long 24pdr, 16–42pdr crde
	Jones: 2–12pdr, 20–32pdr crde; (1815) 2–24pdr, 18–42pdr crde

Notes: Designed by Henry Eckford.
Service records:
Jefferson: Nearly lost in gale and obliged to throw overboard 10 guns on her first cruise. Sold 30 Apr 1825.
Jones: Receiving ship several years after war. Sold 1821 and BU.

SCHOONERS

Name	Builder	Built	Acquired	Comm
Conquest ex–*Genesee Packet*	(U)	(U)	8 Oct 1812	Nov 1812

Rate	3 guns
Dimensions	(U)
Tonnage	82 tons
Complement	(U)
Battery	3–18pdr

Notes: Purchased merchant ship.

Service record: Attack on Kingston, Ont., 8 Nov 1812. Capture of Fort York, 27 Apr 1813. Capture of Fort George, 27 May 1813. Action off York, Ont., 28 Sep 1813. Sold 15 May 1815.

Name	Builder	Built	Acquired	Comm
Fair American	(U)	(U)	10 Nov 1812	1812

Rate	2 guns
Dimensions	(U)
Tonnage	82 tons
Complement	52
Battery	1–32pdr, 1–12pdr

Service record: Capture of Fort York, 27 Apr 1813. Action off York, Ont., 28 Sep 1813. Converted to transport, 1814. Sold 15 May 1815.

Name	Builder	Built	Acquired	Comm
Governor Tompkins ex–*Charles & Ann*	(U)	(U)	4 Oct 1812	Oct 1812

Rate	6 guns
Dimensions	(U)
Tonnage	96 tons
Complement	40
Battery	(U)

Notes: Name also spelled *Governor Tomkins*.
Service record: Attack on Kingston, Ont., 8 Nov 1813. Capture of Fort York, 27 Apr 1813. Capture of Fort George, 27 May 1813. Action off York, Ont., 28 Sep 1813. Action off False Ducks, Ont., 5 Oct 1813. Sold 15 May 1815.
Ships captured: (With *General Pike, Lady of the Lake, Sylph*) sloop *Elizabeth*, sloop *Mary Ann*, 5 Oct 1813.

Name	Builder	Built	Acquired	Comm
Growler ex–*Experiment*	(U)	(U)	1812	1812

Rate	2 guns
Dimensions	(U)
Tonnage	53 tons
Complement	40
Battery	(U)

Notes: Schooner or sloop.
Service record: Attack on Kingston, Ont., 8 Nov 1812. Capture of Fort York, 27 Apr 1813. Capture of Fort George, 27 May 1813. Captured by British at Battle of Lake Ontario, 10 Aug 1813; renamed HMS *Hamilton*. Recaptured, 5 Oct 1813. Reported recaptured by British at Oswego, 5 May 1814.
Later history: HMS *Hamilton*?

Name	Builder	Built	Acquired	Comm
Hamilton ex-*Diana*	(U)	(U)	1812	1812

Rate	9 guns
Dimensions	(U)
Tonnage	112 tons
Complement	50
Battery	1–32pdr, 1–24pdr, 8–6pdr

Service record: Attack on Kingston, Ont., 8 Nov 1812. Capture of Fort York, 27 Apr 1813. Capture of Fort George, 27 May 1813. Capsized in squall and lost with all hands, 8 Aug 1813.

Name	Builder	Built	Acquired	Comm
Julia	Oswego, N.Y.	1812	Sep 1812	1812

Rate	2 guns
Dimensions	(U)
Tonnage	53 tons
Complement	40
Battery	(U)

Service record: Attack on Kingston, Ont., 8 Nov 1812. Capture of Fort York, 27 Apr 1813. Capture of Fort George, 27 May 1813. Captured by British, 10 Aug 1813; renamed *Confiance*. Recaptured and renamed, 5 Oct 1813. Sold.

Name	Builder	Built	Acquired	Comm
Ontario	(U)	(U)	Oct 1812	1813

Rate	2 guns
Dimensions	(U)
Tonnage	81 tons
Complement	(U)
Battery	(U)

Notes: Purchased merchant ship.
Service record: Capture of Fort York, 27 Apr 1813. Capture of Fort George, 27 May 1813. Action off York, Ont., 28 Sep 1813. Sold 15 May 1815.

Name	Builder	Built	Acquired	Comm
Pert ex-*Collector*	(U)	(U)	1812	1812

Rate	3 guns
Dimensions	(U)
Tonnage	50 tons
Complement	(U)
Battery	(U)

Notes: Purchased.
Service record: Attack on Kingston, Ont., 8 Nov 1812; burst a gun, which wounded her captain, who later drowned. Action off York, Ont., 28 Sep 1813. Sold May 1815.

Name	Builder	Built	Acquired	Comm
Asp(U) ex-*Elizabeth*	(U)	1812	6 Feb 1813	

Rate	2 guns
Dimensions	(U)
Tonnage	57 tons
Complement	45
Battery	1–32pdr, 2–6pdr

Notes: British merchant ship captured in 1812 by *Growler*.
Service record: Capture of Fort York, 27 Apr 1813. Capture of Fort George, 27 May 1813. Action off York, Ont., 28 Sep 1813. Sold 15 May 1815.

Name	Builder	L	Comm
Lady of the Lake	Sackets Harbor, N.Y. (Eckford)	6 Apr 1813	19 Apr 1813

Rate	5 guns
Dimensions	(U)
Tonnage	89 tons
Complement	40
Battery	1–9pdr

Service record: Capture of Fort York, 27 Apr 1813. Action off York, Ont., 28 Sep 1813. Action off False Ducks, Ont., 5 Oct 1813. Sold 2 Feb 1826.
Ships captured: (With *General Pike, Governor Tompkins, Sylph*) sloop *Elizabeth*, sloop *Mary Ann*, 5 Oct 1813. Schr *Lady Murray*, 16 Jun 1813.

Name	Builder	Built	Acquired	Comm
Raven ex-*Mary*	(U)	(U)	6 Feb 1813	1813

Rate	1 gun
Dimensions	(U)
Tonnage	50 tons
Complement	(U)
Battery	1 mortar

Notes: Bomb schr. Served as transport and supply ship. Sold 15 May 1815.

Name	Builder	Built	Acquired	Comm
Scourge ex-*Lord Nelson*	(U)	(U)	May 1812	1812

Rate	12 guns
Dimensions	(U)
Tonnage	110 tons
Complement	(U)
Battery	1–32pdr, 8–12pdr crde

Notes: British schr, captured by USS *Oneida*, May 1812.
Service record: Capture of Fort York, 27 Apr 1813. Capture of Fort George, 27 May 1813. Capsized and sank in squall (all but 16 killed), 8 Aug 1813.

Name	Builder	Laid down	L	Comm
Sylph	Sackets Harbor, N.Y. (Eckford)	26 Jul 1813	18 Aug 1813	Aug 1813

Rate	16 guns
Dimensions	(U)
Tonnage	300 tons
Complement	70
Battery	4–32pdr, 12–6pdr; (1814) 2–9pdr, 16–24pdr crde

Notes: Rerigged as 18-gun brig, 1814; ready for service in 33 days.
Service record: Action off York, Ont., 28 Sep 1813. Action off False Ducks, Ont., 5 Oct 1813. Sold 1825.
Ships captured: (With *General Pike, Governor Tompkins, Lady of the Lake*) sloop *Elizabeth*, sloop *Mary Ann*, 5 Oct 1813. Schr *Lady Gore*, 6 Oct 1813; brig *Charwell* (chased ashore and burned), 5 Aug 1814.

Name	Builder	Built	Acquired	Comm
Ranger	(U)	(U)	1814	(U)

Rate	14 guns
Dimensions	(U)
Tonnage	(U)
Complement	(U)
Battery	(U)

Notes: Brigantine.
Service record: Transport/supply ship. Sold 15 May 1821.

LAKE CHAMPLAIN SQUADRON

During the War of 1812, both sides appreciated that Lake Champlain was strategically important, as it had been in 1776, and Lt. Thomas MacDonough arrived there to take charge in September 1812. By spring he had three ships: *Growler, Eagle,* and *President.* In June the first two were sent to engage the enemy and, in pursuing, ended up in enemy territory and were captured.

A yard was set up at Vergennes, Vt., while the British were building at Ile aux Noix at the north end of the lake. In the summer of 1814 the British prepared to invade New York but their fleet was no match for MacDonough's four ships, six gunboats, and four galleys. By September their two largest ships were ready and on 11 September the second Battle of Lake Champlain took place, resulting in a decisive American victory. The Americans had 52 killed and 58 wounded. The ships were built of green wood, which decayed rapidly. After the war there was no further need for warships on Lake Champlain.

SLOOPS (CORVETTES)

Name	Builder	Laid down	L	Comm
Saratoga	Vergennes, Vt. (A & N Brown)	7 Mar 1814	11 Apr 1814	1814

Rate	26 guns
Dimensions	143′ (bp) × 36′6″ × 12′6″
Tonnage	734 tons
Complement	212
Battery	8–24pdr, 6–42pdr crde, 12–32pdr crde

Notes: Designed by Noah Brown. A successful ship.
Service record: Flagship of MacDonough. Battle of Lake Champlain (28 killed), 11 Sep 1814. Sold 1825.

BRIGS

Name	Builder	Laid down	L	Comm
Eagle	Vergennes, Vt. (A & N Brown)	29 Jul 1814	11 Aug 1814	6 Sep 1814
ex-*Surprise* (6 Sep 1814)				

[16] British: ship *Confiance*, 37; brig *Linnet*, 16; sloops *Chub*, 11, and *Finch*, 11; and seven gunboats, 2 or 1.

Rate	20 guns
Dimensions	128′ × 32′ × (U)
Tonnage	500 tons
Complement	150
Battery	8–18pdr, 12–32pdr crde

Service record: Battle of Lake Champlain, holed 39 times (13 killed), 11 Sep 1814. Sold 1825.

SCHOONERS

Name	Builder	Built	Acquired	Comm
Ticonderoga	Vergennes, Vt. (Sherman)	1814	1814	1815

Rate	14 guns
Dimensions	120′ × (U)
Tonnage	350 tons
Complement	112
Battery	4–18pdr, 8–12pdr, 5–32pdr crde

Notes: Built as a steamer but converted to sail and relaunched on 12 May 1814.
Service record: Battle of Lake Champlain (6 killed), 11 Sep 1814. Sold 19 Jul 1825.

SLOOPS

Name	Builder	Built	Acquired	Comm
Eagle ex–HMS *Bull Dog*	(U)	(U)	1812	1812

Rate	18 guns
Dimensions	64′ × 20′4″ × 5′8″
Tonnage	110 tons
Complement	50
Battery	1–6pdr, 10–18pdr crde

Notes: Purchased. American sources give British name as *Finch*.
Service record: Captured by British near Ile aux Noix, 3 Jun 1813; comm as HMS *Chubb*. Recaptured at Battle of Lake Champlain after running aground, 11 Sep 1814. Sold Jul 1815.

Name	Builder	Built	Acquired	Comm
Growler ex-*Hunter*	(U)	(U)	1812	(U)

Rate	10 guns
Dimensions	60′ (bp) × 19′ × 5′8″
Tonnage	112 tons
Complement	(U)
Battery	1–6pdr, 10–18pdr crde

Notes: American sources report British name as *Chub*.
Service record: Captured by British near Ile aux Noix, 3 Jun 1813; renamed HMS *Finch*. Recaptured at Battle of Lake Champlain, 11 Sep 1814. Sold Jul 1815.

A depiction of the Battle of Lake Champlain in 1814. Left to right are the USS *Ticonderoga*, USS *Eagle*, HMS *Confiance* (sails holed), USS *Saratoga* (flags flying), and HMS *Linnet*. (U.S. Naval Historical Center)

Name	Builder	Built	Acquired	Comm
Frances	(U)	(U)	1813	(U)

Rate	5 guns
Dimensions	(U)
Tonnage	(U)
Complement	(U)
Battery	4–12pdr, 1–18pdr columbiad

Notes: Hired. Returned to owner, 1814.

Name	Builder	Built	Acquired	Comm
Montgomery	(U)	1813	6 Aug 1813	(U)

Rate	6 guns
Dimensions	(U)
Tonnage	(U)
Complement	(U)
Battery	9–9pdr, 1–28pdr columbiad; (later) 7–9pdr, 4–18pdr crde

Service record: Sold 1815.

Name	Builder	Built	Acquired	Comm
Preble	(U)	1813	6 Aug 1813	Aug 1813

Rate	9 guns
Dimensions	(U)
Tonnage	(U)
Complement	30
Battery	7–12pdr, 2–18pdr columbiad

Notes: Sometimes called ***Commodore Preble***.
Service record: Battle of Lake Champlain (2 killed), 11 Sep 1814. Sold Jul 1815.

Name	Builder	Built	Acquired	Comm
President	(U)	(U)	1812	6 Aug 1813

Rate	12 guns
Dimensions	65′ × (U)
Tonnage	(U)
Complement	(U)
Battery	(U)

Notes: Purchased by War Dept. and trfd to Navy.

Service record: Captured by British, 1813; renamed HMS *Icicle*. Sold 28 May 1815.

Name	Builder	Built	Acquired	Comm
Wasp	(U)	U	1813	(U)

Rate	5 guns
Dimensions	(U)
Tonnage	(U)
Complement	(U)
Battery	4–12pdr, 1–18pdr columbiad

Service record: Returned to owners, 1814.

GALLEY GUNBOATS

Name	Builder	Built	Comm
Allen	Vergennes, Vt. (A & N Brown)	1814	1814
Borer	Vergennes, Vt. (A & N Brown)	1814	summer 1814
Burrows	Vergennes, Vt. (A & N Brown)	Jun 1814	1814
Centipede	Vergennes, Vt. (A & N Brown)	Jun 1814	1814
Nettle	Vergennes, Vt. (A & N Brown)	Jun 1814	1814
Viper	Vergennes, Vt. (A & N Brown)	1814	1814

Rate	2 guns
Dimensions	75′ (bp) × 15′ × 4′
Tonnage	70 tons
Complement	40
	Nettle: 41
Battery	1–24pdr, 1–18pdr columbiad

Notes: *Borer* was also known as **Boxer**.
Service records:
Allen: Battle of Lake Champlain, 11 Sep 1814. Sold 1824.
Borer: Battle of Lake Champlain (3 killed), 11 Sep 1814. Sold 1825.
Burrows: Battle of Lake Champlain, 11 Sep 1814. Sold 1825.
Centipede: Battle of Lake Champlain, 11 Sep 1814. Laid up 1815. Sold 1825.
Nettle: Battle of Lake Champlain, 11 Sep 1814. Sold 1825.
Viper: Battle of Lake Champlain, 11 Sep 1814. Sold 1825.

Name	Builder	Built	Comm
Aylwin	Vergennes, Vt. (A & N Brown)	1813	(U)
Ballard	Vergennes, Vt. (A & N Brown)	1813	(U)

Rate	1 gun
Dimensions	(U)
Tonnage	40 tons
Complement	26
Battery	1–12pdr

Service records:
Aylwin: Battle of Lake Champlain, 11 Sep 1814. Sold Jul 1815.
Ballard: Battle of Lake Champlain, 11 Sep 1814. Sold Jul 1815.

Name	Builder	Built	Acquired	Comm
Ludlow	(U)	1808	1812	(U)

Rate	1 gun
Dimensions	(U)
Tonnage	40 tons
Complement	(U)
Battery	1–12pdr

Service record: Battle of Lake Champlain, 11 Sep 1814. Sold Jul 1815.

Name	Builder	Built	Comm
Wilmer	(U)	1808	(U)

Rate	(U)
Dimensions	(U)
Tonnage	(U)
Complement	(U)
Battery	1–12pdr

Service record: Battle of Lake Champlain, 11 Sep 1814. Sold July 1815.

EX-BRITISH

Name	Builder	L	Acquired	Comm
Confiance ex-HMS *Confiance*	Ile aux Noix, Canada	25 Aug 1814	11 Sep 1814	never

Rate	36 guns
Dimensions	147′5″ (deck) × 37′2″ × d7′
Tonnage	1,200 tons, 831 bm
Complement	300
Battery	27–24pdr, 2–18pdr, 4–32pdr crde, 6–24pdr crde

Notes: British 5th rate frigate, captured in sinking condition, 11 Sep 1814. Not used by the United States Navy. Sold 1825.

Name	Builder	L	Acquired	Comm
Linnet ex-HMS *Linnet*, ex-*Growler* (1813)	Ile aux Noix, Canada	1814	Sep 1814	1815

Rate	16 guns
Dimensions	82′6″ (deck) × 27′ × 6′8″
Tonnage	350 tons
Complement	125
Battery	12–12pdr

Notes: Brig. British ship, captured on 11 Sep 1814. Not used by the United States Navy. Sold 1825.

STEAMERS

COMBATANT PADDLE STEAMERS

A steamer designed by Uriah Brown was begun in Baltimore in 1815 but work stopped after the end of the War of 1812. It was to have iron-sheathed shot-proof inclined wooden sides. Although the Navy ordered machinery for a steam frigate in 1818, no ship was built.

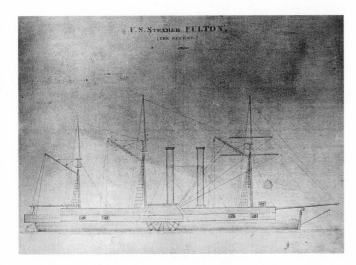

The steamer *Fulton* built in 1837 was the second of the name. She had two pairs of funnels side by side. She was too small for her guns and too weak for ocean operation. (Smithsonian Institution)

FULTON

Name	Builder	Laid down	L	Completed
Fulton	New York (Brown)	20 Jun 1814	29 Oct 1814	1 Jun 1815

Dimensions	153'2" (bp) × 58' × 10'4"
Tonnage	2,475 tons, 1,450 tons D
Machinery	Center wheel (48" × 5'), 2 boilers, HP 120, 6 knots
Complement	200
Battery	24–32pdr crde

Notes: The first steam warship. Designed by Robert Fulton, with divided hull and two-mast lateen rig. Four funnels in two pairs. Engines were reversible, had two sets of rudders. Originally intended to throw hot water, as well as shot. Four 100pdr columbiads not mounted. Sides 58" thick. Intended for defense of New York but never placed in service. Sometimes called ***Demologos***.
Service record: Housed over as receiving ship at Brooklyn N Yd, 1821. Blew up when magazine exploded (24 killed), 4 Jun 1829.

FULTON

Name	Builder	Laid down	L	Comm
Fulton	New York N Yd	1835	18 May 1837	13 Dec 1837

Dimensions	181'6" (bp) × 34'8" × 13'
Tonnage	720 tons, 1,011 tons D
Machinery	Side wheels, 2-cyl. horizontal condensing engine (50" × 9'), 4 boilers, NHP 221, 12 knots (West Point)
Complement	130
Battery	8–42pdr, 1–24pdr; (1840) 4–8", 2–32pdr

Notes: Wood hull designed by Samuel Humphreys. Schooner rig, four funnels in pairs. Engines designed by Charles H. Haswell. Too weak for ocean work, too small for original armament. Used as gunnery practice ship.
Service record: Bested British steamer *Great Western* in speed contest, 23 Nov 1838. Decomm 23 Nov 1842 and rebuilt.

MISSISSIPPI CLASS

Name	Builder	Laid down	L	Comm
Mississippi	Philadelphia N Yd	10 Aug 1839	5 May 1841	22 Dec 1841
Missouri	New York N Yd	1839	7 Jan 1841	early 1842

Dimensions:	220' (bp) × 39', 66'6" (oa) × 21'9"
Tonnage	1,732 tons; 3,220 tons D
Machinery	Side wheels
	Mississippi: 2-cyl. side lever engine (75" × 7'), IHP 650 (Merrick & Towne)
	Missouri: 2-cyl. inclined direct-acting condensing engine (62½" × 10'), NHP 515, 11 knots (West Point)
Complement	257
Battery	2–10", 8–8"; (1857) 1–10", 10–8"; (1861) 1–9", 10–8"

Notes: Hulls designed by Samuel Humphreys, Samuel Hartt, and John Lenthall and machinery by Charles W. Copeland. Successful powerful steamers. Bark rig, carried 19,000 sq. ft. of sail. Had watertight bulkheads. The largest naval vessels yet built.
Service records:
Mississippi: Flagship of Commo. M. C. Perry, H. A. Adams, and A. S. Mackenzie during Mexican War. Attack on Alvarado, Mexico, 7 Aug 1846. Mediterranean 1849–51. Brought the Hungarian patriot Kossuth to safety, Sep 1851. Expedition to Japan (flagship of M. C. Perry), 1852–54. Far East 1857–60. Sunk by Confederate batteries at Port Hudson, La., 14 Mar 1863.
Missouri: Burned at Gibraltar after turpentine ignited and later blew up (crew saved), 26 Aug 1843.

UNION

Name	Builder	Laid down	L	Comm
Union	Norfolk N Yd	1841	12 May 1842	early 1843

Dimensions	184'6" × 33'6" × 12'6"
Tonnage	1,040 tons; 956 tons D
Machinery	2 Hunter wheels; 2-cyl. horizontal non-condensing engine (28" × 4'), 3 boilers, HP 300, 5 knots (Washington)
Complement	120
Battery	4–8" SB

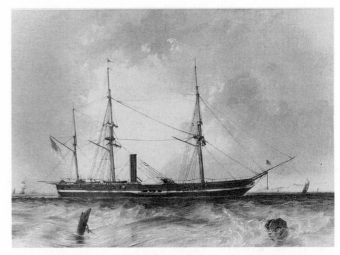

The paddle frigate *Mississippi*, the first successful steam warship in the U.S. Navy. From an engraving in *Naval and Mail Steamers of the U.S.* by Charles B. Stewart. (U.S. Naval Historical Center, Norman Polmar Collection)

Notes: Three-mast schr. Hull designed by Francis Grice and William W. Hunter, machinery by Hunter and William M. Ellis. Completed at Washington NYd. The hull was narrower below waterline to accommodate the Hunter wheels while docking. Funnel forward of mainmast. Made experimental cruise in 1843, repeated in 1844–45; Hunter wheels were a total failure. New boilers, 1844. Re-engined in 1846 with greater power but this did not increase efficiency of the Hunter wheels. Engines removed, 1848. Receiving ship, Philadelphia. Sold 1858.

WATER WITCH

Name	Builder	Laid down	L	Comm
Water Witch	Washington NYd	1843	1844	(U)

Dimensions	100′6″ × 21′4″ × 7′6″; (1845) 130′ length
Tonnage	190 tons
Machinery	Hunter wheel, 2-cyl. inclined engine (22″ × 4′), AHP 100, 6 knots; (1845) 2 screws, 2-cyl. inclined engine (20″ × 2′); (1846) side wheels, 1 inclined engine (37.6″ × 6′), 5 knots
Complement	25
Battery	(as built) none; (1845) 1–8″, 2–32pdr

Notes: Designed by John Porter. Fitted with Hunter propeller. Intended for harbor duty as tug and tender. Iron hull. Cut in two at Philadelphia NYd, lengthened, and re-engined with twin Loper propellers, 1845. Altered to sidewheel steamer, 1846.
Service record: West Indies 1847–50. Broke down, used as gunnery target. Decomm 25 Apr 1851.

EX-MEXICAN VESSELS

Name	Builder	Built	Acquired	Comm
Spitfire	New York (Brown & Bell)	1846	25 May 1846	21 Aug 1846
Vixen	New York (Brown & Bell)	1846	1846	1846

Dimensions	118′ × 22′6″ × 9′6″
Tonnage	240 tons
Machinery	Side wheels, horizontal beam engine (36″ × 6′), 2 boilers, AHP 90, 6 knots
Complement	55
Battery	1–8″, 2–32pdr crde; (later) 1–long 32pdr

Notes: Built for Mexican Navy, acquired on declaration of war.
Service records:
Spitfire: Siege of Veracruz, 9–29 Mar 1847. Sold 1848.
    Later history: Destroyed by fire at New York, 12 Oct 1849.
Vixen: West Indies during war and until 1851. Attack on Alvarado, Mexico, 16 Oct 1846. Capture of Tabasco, Mexico, 23–27 Oct 1846. Siege of Veracruz, Mar 1847. Sold 1855. Reacquired 26 Aug 1861.

SARANAC

Name	Builder	Laid down	L	Comm
Saranac	Portsmouth NYd	May 1847	14 Nov 1848	12 Oct 1850

Dimensions	216′ (oa), 210′ (bp) × 37′9″, 60′ (oa beam) × 16′6″
Tonnage	1,446 tons; 2,100 tons D
Machinery	Side wheels, 2-cyl. inclined direct-acting condensing engine (60″ × 9′), 3 boilers, HP 1,700, 12 knots (Coney)
Complement	228
Battery	6–8″ SB; (1854) 9–8″; (1862) 9–8″, 2–20pdr R

Notes: Bark rig. Hull designed by Samuel Hartt, engines by Charles W. Copeland. A successful design. Reboilered 1857.
Service record: Home Sqn 1850–52. Brazil Station 1852–53. Mediterranean 1853–56. Pacific Coast 1857–75. Wrecked in Seymour Narrows off Vancouver Island, 18 Jun 1875.

SUSQUEHANNA

Name	Builder	Laid down	L	Comm
Susquehanna	Philadelphia NYd	8 Sep 1847	5 Apr 1850	24 Dec 1850

Dimensions	257′ (bp) × 45′, 69′ (oa beam) × 19′6″, d26′6″
Tonnage	2,450 tons; 3,824 tons D
Machinery	Side wheels, 2-cyl. inclined direct-acting condensing engine (70″ × 10′), 4 boilers, IHP 1,450, 12 knots (Murray)
Complement	300
Battery	3–8″ SB, 6–32pdr R; (1851) 9–8″; (1856) 15–8″; (1861) 15–8″ SB, 1–24pdr H, 2–12pdr H

Notes: Hull designed by Lenthall, engines by Copeland. Engine was very reliable, but machinery was removed after Civil War; conversion to screw propulsion never completed. Bark rig.
Service record: East India Sqn 1851–55. Expedition to Japan, 1853–54. Mediterranean Sqn 1856–58, 1860–61. Decomm 14 Jan 1868. Sold 27 Sep 1883 and BU.

POWHATAN

Name	Builder	Laid down	L	Comm
Powhatan	Norfolk NYd	14 Jul 1847	14 Feb 1850	2 Sep 1852

Dimensions	276′6″ (oa), 250′ (bp) × 45′, 69′6″ (oa beam) × 20′9″
Tonnage	2,415 tons; 3,765 tons D
Machinery	Side wheels, 2-cyl. inclined direct-acting condensing engine (70″ × 10′), 4 boilers, IHP 1,500, 11 knots (Mehaffy)
Complement	300
Battery	3–8″ SB, 6–32pdr R; (1852) 9–8″; (1857) 1–11″, 10–9″; (1861) 1–100pdr R, 1–11″, 7–9″; (Nov 1861) 1–11″ SB, 10–9″ SB, 5–12pdr

Notes: Hull designed by Francis Grice, engines by Charles H. Haswell. Bark rig. Similar to *Susquehanna* but engines of a different design. Engines most reliable, a fast steamer even in old age.
Service record: East India Sqn 1853–56. Expedition to Japan, 1853–54. Aided British and French attack on forts in Peiho River, China, 25 Jun 1859. Ship's captain Tattnall is noted for his "Blood is thicker than water." Sold 30 Jul 1887 and BU.

PADDLE SLOOPS

ALLEGHENY

Name	Builder	Laid down	L	Comm
Allegheny	Pittsburgh, Pa. (Stackhouse)	1844	22 Feb 1847	22 Feb 1847

Dimensions	185′ (deck) × 33′4″ × 14′8″
Tonnage	989 tons; 1,020 tons D
Machinery	Hunter wheels, 2-cyl. horizontal condensing engine (60″ × 4′), NHP 243, 6 knots (Tomlinson); (1852) 1 screw
Complement	190

The paddle frigate *Fulton* was built in 1851, officially as the 1837 vessel rebuilt and third of the name. (U.S. Naval Historical Center)

The sidewheel gunboat *Michigan* was the first iron-hulled ship in the U.S. Navy. She served on the Great Lakes from 1844 to 1927. This shows her appearance during the 1870s.

Battery 4–8″ SB; (1847) 2–8″; (1852) 2–8″, 8–32pdr; (May 1863) 4–32pdr/33, 2–32pdr/27

Notes: Iron hull. Hull and machinery designed by Hunter, engines by Charles Haswell. Bark rig. Went downriver to Memphis and New Orleans. Rebuilt in 1852 by Mehaffy & Co. at Portsmouth, Va., as a screw steamer using original engines as converted by Isherwood, but was still a failure and was laid up.
Service record: Brazil Station and Mediterranean, 1848. Gulf of Mexico 1849. Receiving ship, Baltimore, 1856–68. Sold 15 May 1869.

FULTON

Name	Builder	Laid down	L	Comm
Fulton	Brooklyn NYd	1851	30 Aug 1851	25 Jan 1852

Dimensions	181′6″ (bp) × 34′10″ × 10′6″
Tonnage	750 tons; 1,200 tons D
Machinery	Side wheels, inclined condensing engine (50″ × 4′10″), HP 500, 11 knots (Dunham)
Complement	79
Battery	4–8″ SB, 4–32pdr SB; (1858) 2–9″ SB

Notes: Hull designed by Humphreys, engines by Charles B. Stuart. Officially the 1837 vessel rebuilt. Schooner rig, two masts.
Service record: Home Sqn 1852–58. Paraguay Expedition, 1859. Anti-slave trade patrol off Florida, 1859; stranded near Pensacola, 23 Aug 1859. While undergoing refit, captured by Confederates at Pensacola NYd, 12 Jan 1861, and destroyed by them, 10 May 1862.

WATER WITCH

Name	Builder	Laid down	L	Comm
Water Witch	Washington NYd	1852	1852	8 Feb 1853

Dimensions	150′ (bp) × 23′ × 9′
Tonnage	378 tons; 450 tons D
Machinery	Side wheels, inclined condensing engine (37.6″ × 3′), 2 boilers, HP 180, 11.5 knots (Ellis)
Complement	55
Battery	1–32pdr; (1862) 4–32pdr SB, 1–24pdr H

Notes: Hull designed by Lenthall, engine by Isherwood. Machinery taken from the previous *Water Witch* built in 1845. Schooner rig.
Service record: Surveyed rivers of South America, 1853–56. Fired on in Paraguay River while surveying, 1 Feb 1855. Paraguay Expedition, 1859. Captured by Confederate boarders in Ossabaw Sound, Ga., 3 Jun 1864, and taken into CSN service.

SIDEWHEEL GUNBOAT (LAKE)

MICHIGAN

Name	Builder	Laid down	L	Comm
Michigan	(Stackhouse)	1842	5 Dec 1843	29 Sep 1844

Dimensions	163′3″ (bp) × 27′, 45′10″ (oa beam) × 9′
Tonnage	582 tons; 685 tons D
Machinery	Side wheels, 2-cyl. inclined direct-acting condensing engine (36″ × 8′), 2 boilers, HP 365, 10.5 knots (bldr)
Complement	85
Battery	2–8″ SB, 4–32pdr SB; (1862) 1–30pdr, 5–20pdr, 6–24pdr SB

Notes: First iron-hulled vessel in the Navy. Built in Pittsburgh and reassembled at Erie, Pa.; remained on the Great Lakes during her entire service. Hull designed by Hartt, engines by Copeland. Barkentine rig. Pilothouse enlarged and rig reduced by 1890s.
Service record: Lake Erie. Renamed ***Wolverine*** 17 Jun 1905. Trfd to City of Erie, Pa., as a relic, 1927. BU 1949.

SCREW STEAMERS

SAN JACINTO

Name	Builder	Laid down	L	Comm
San Jacinto	Brooklyn, N.Y.	Aug 1847	16 Apr 1850	3 Mar 1852

Dimensions	237′ (oa), 210′ (bp) × 37′9″ × 17′3″
Tonnage	1,446 tons; 2,150 tons D
Machinery	1 screw, 2-cyl. horizontal condensing engine

(62½" × 4'2"), 3 boilers, HP 782, 9.9 knots (Merrick); (1854)

2-cyl. horizontal engine (70"x 4'), IHP 550, 8.5 knots

Complement	235
Battery	6–8" SB; (1862) 1–11" SB, 10–9" SB, 1–12pdr R

Notes: Frigate. Hull designed by Hartt, engines by Haswell. Competitive sister with paddle frigate *Saranac*. Propeller shaft was off-center. Engines were inadequate and unreliable. Re-engined and shaft centered, 1853–54.

Service record: Far East 1855–58. Bombardment of Canton, China, forts (4 killed), 20–22 Nov 1856. Africa Sqn 1859–60. Wrecked on Grand Abaco Island, Bahamas, 1 Jan 1865.

Ship captured: Brig *Storm King* with 619 slaves off Congo River, 8 Aug 1860.

PRINCETON   Ships in Scale May-June 2004

Name	Builder	Laid down	L	Comm
Princeton	Philadelphia NYd	20 Oct 1842	7 Sep 1843	9 Sep 1843

Dimensions	156'6" (bp) × 30'6 × 19'11"
Tonnage	672 tons; 1,046 D
Machinery	1 screw, 1 semi-cylinder engine, 3 boilers, NHP 204, 7 knots (Merrick & Towne)
Complement	166
Battery	2–12", 12–42pdr crde; (1844) 1–12", 12–42pdr crde; (1845) 1–8", 12–42pdr crde; (1847) 1–8", 8–42pdr crde

Notes: First screw warship and first screw propeller built for U.S. Navy. Machinery designed by John Ericsson, hull by Robert F. Stockton. Excellent sea boat and efficient cruiser. Also first ship with machinery (designed by Ericsson) entirely below the waterline and first with telescoping funnel. She carried two 12" guns, one of which—named "Peacemaker"—exploded on 29 Feb 1844, killing Secretary of State Abel P. Upshur, Secretary of the Navy Thomas Gilmer, and other officials, and missing President John Tyler. Ericsson propeller replaced by Stevens propeller, 1845. Boilers replaced, 1847.

Service record: Attack on Alvarado, Mexico, 7 Aug 1846. Home Sqn 1846–47. Mediterranean 1848–49. Condemned 17 Jul 1849 and BU.

The second USS *Princeton*, built in 1851 using the engines of the first *Princeton*. (National Archives)

PRINCETON

Name	Builder	Laid down	L	Comm
Princeton	Boston NYd	Jun 1851	29 Oct 1851	18 May 1852

Dimensions	184' (oa), 177'6" (wl) × 32'6" × d21'8"
Tonnage	900 tons; 1,370 tons D
Machinery	1 screw, 2 direct-acting half cylinder condensing engines, 3 boilers, IHP 490, 10 knots (Murray)
Complement	190
Battery	4–8" SB, 6–32pdr SB

Notes: Hull designed by Samuel Pook using engines of the previous gunboat *Princeton*.

Service record: Developed engine trouble and missed expedition to Japan, 1852. Eastern Sqn 1853–54. West Indies 1854–55. Receiving ship, Philadelphia, 1857–66. Sold 9 Oct 1866.

SUPPORT VESSELS

Name	Builder	L	Acquired	Comm
Sea Gull ex-*Enterprise*	Hartford, Conn.	Nov 1818	Nov 1822	(U)

Dimensions	(U)
Tonnage	105 tons
Machinery	Rotary engine, 1 boiler
Complement	(U)
Battery	3 guns

Notes: Steam galliot. Second steamer in USN.

Service record: Mosquito Fleet. West Indies 1823–24. Recaptured schr *Pacification*, Mar 1824. Receiving ship, Philadelphia, 1825. Sold 1840.

Name	Builder	L	Acquired	Comm
Engineer	Baltimore	(U)	1836	(U)

Dimensions	105' × 17'2" × 7'
Tonnage	142 tons
Machinery	Side wheels, beam engine (25" × 7'), 1 boiler, AHP 112, 7.5 knots
Complement	20
Battery	1 gun

Service record: Employed principally as tug and despatch boat at Norfolk NYd. Surveyed Southern coast, 1839. Sold Apr 1857.

Later history: Merchant *Albert Horn*, 1857. S/F 1860.

Name	Builder	Built	Comm
Germ	Norfolk NYd	1841	(U)

Dimensions	60' × 9' × 2'
Machinery	9 knots

Notes: Small experimental steamer, built to demonstrate Hunter's submerged horizontal paddle wheels.

Name	Builder	L	Acquired	Comm
Poinsett	New York	1840	1840	1840
ex–*New Brighton*				

Dimensions	(U)
Tonnage	250 tons
Machinery	Side wheels
Complement	(U)
Battery	1–32pdr pivot

Notes: Trfd from War Dept.
Service record: Employed against Florida Indians during Second Seminole War and for survey of Tampa Bay, 1840–45. Returned to War Dept. at Pensacola, 1845.
Later history: Merchant *Duncan C. Pell.* Abandoned 1850.

Name	Builder	L	Acquired	Comm
Colonel Harney	Baltimore	1840	1844	1844

Dimensions	133′ × 22′ × 9′
Tonnage	300 tons
Machinery	Side wheels
Complement	50
Battery	1–32pdr

Notes: Trfd from Army, 1844. Protected live oak industry. Returned to Army, 18 Mar 1846.

Name	Builder	L	Acquired	Comm
Edith	Boston (Samuel Hall)	14 Nov 1844	Mar 1849	1849

Dimensions:	120′ × 26′ × 14′
Tonnage	407 tons
Machinery	1 screw
Complement	25
Battery	2 guns

Notes: Three-mast steam bark trfd from War Dept., Mar 1849. Machinery built by Hogg & Delamater.

The steamer USS *Edith* served briefly with the Navy until wrecked in 1849. (U.S. Naval Historical Center)

Service record: West Coast. Ran aground in fog and wrecked off Point Conception, Calif., 24 Aug 1849.

Name	Builder	Built	Acquired	Comm
General Taylor	New York	(U)	1846	(U)

Dimensions	105′ × 17′6″ × 8′6″
Tonnage	150 tons
Machinery	Side wheels, square engine (25″ × 6′), 1 boiler, AHP 98, 8 knots
Complement	25
Battery	1 gun

Notes: Purchased by War Dept., 1840. Trfd to Navy, 1842.
Service record: Burned at Pensacola, 1846. Rebuilt and employed as tug at Pensacola until 1852, then sold.

Name	Builder	L	Acquired	Comm
Scourge	Wilmington, Del. (Harlan)	May 1844	30 Dec 1846	early 1847
ex–*Bangor*				

Dimensions	120′ × 23′ × 9′
Tonnage	231 tons
Machinery	2 screws, 2 horizontal engines (22″ × 2′), 1 boiler (bldr)
Complement	50
Battery	1–32pdr, 20–24pdr crde

Notes: First iron-hulled seagoing merchant ship in U.S. Two Loper propellers.
Service record: Attack on Alvarado, Mexico, 31 Mar 1847. Sold 7 Oct 1848.
Ships captured: Schr *Relampago*, 1 Apr 1847; schr *San Pablo* in Gulf of Mexico, Mar 1848.
Later history: Merchant *Scourge.* Seized as blockade runner by Venezuelan gunboat *Libertador* off Maracaibo, Oct 1848. FFU.

Name	Builder	L	Acquired	Comm
Petrita	U.S.	(U)	(U)	(U)

Dimensions	169′ × (U)
Tonnage	242 tons
Machinery	Side wheels
Complement	(U)
Battery	1 gun

Notes: Captured by a U.S. sqn at Frontera in Grijalva River, 23 Oct 1846. Had engine defects. Grounded off Alvarado (all saved), 21 Jun 1848.

Name	Builder	L	Acquired	Comm
Scorpion	New York (Bishop & Simonson)	1846	7 Jan 1847	23 Feb 1847
ex–*Aurora*				

Dimensions	160′9″ × 24′6″ × 8′
Tonnage	339 tons
Machinery	Side wheels, inclined direct-acting engine (40″ × 8′) (Hogg & Delamater), 7.5 knots
Complement	60
Battery	2–8″, 2–18pdr crde

Service record: Expedition against Tabasco, Mexico, Apr 1847. Sold Dec 1848.
Ship captured: Schr *Renaissance* in Gulf of Mexico, 6 Nov 1847.
Later history: Merchant *Isthmus* (also known as *Southerner*). Lost by stranding 60 miles south of Cape Flattery, Wash., 26 Dec 1854.

Name	Builder	Built	Acquired	Comm
Iris	New York (Bishop & Simonson)	1847	1847	25 Oct 1847
ex-*Osprey*				

Dimensions	145′ × 26′7″ × 9′9″
Tonnage	388 tons
Machinery	Side wheels, 1 steeple engine (59″ × 6′)
Complement	70
Battery	1–32pdr

Notes: Radial paddle wheels, wood hull. Purchased on completion.
Service record: Employed in Gulf of Mexico. Decomm and sold, 16 Dec 1848.
Later history: Merchant *Osprey*. Destroyed by fire at Kingston, Jamaica, 18 Apr 1856. May have been renamed *General Mosquera* in 1855.

Name	Builder	L	Acquired	Comm
Massachusetts	Boston (Samuel Hall)	23 Jul 1845	1 Aug 1849	1 Aug 1849

Dimensions	156′6″ (bp), 161′ (deck) × 32′2″ × 15′6″
Tonnage	750 tons; 1,168 tons D
Machinery	1 screw, 2-cyl. inclined engine (25″ × 3′), 2 boilers, HP 170, 8 knots (Hogg & Delamater), lifting screw
Complement	75
Battery	2–9pdr; (1854) 8–32pdr

Notes: Funnel aft. Designed by R. B. Forbes. Purchased by War Dept. for use as a transport, 16 Oct 1846. Trfd to the Navy at Mare Island, Calif., 1 Aug 1849.
Service record: Storeship, Mare Island. Rebuilt in 1857 at Norfolk NYd with new boilers; Ericsson lifting screw replaced. Returned to

War Dept., May 1859; laid up. Returned to Navy, 27 Jan 1862. Converted to storeship; engines removed. Renamed *Farralones* Jan 1863. Sold 15 May 1867.
Later history: Bark *Alaska*. Wrecked at Callao, Peru, 24 Jul 1871.

Name	Builder	Laid down	L	Comm
John Hancock	Boston NYd	1850	26 Oct 1850	19 Mar 1853

Dimensions	113′ (bp) × 22′ × 10′6″; (1853) 165′6″ × 22′ × 10′6″
Tonnage	230 tons; (1853) 382 tons
Machinery	1 screw, 2-cyl. oscillating HP engine (20″ × 1′9″), 9 knots (Washington); (1853) 2-cyl. oscillating LP engine (20″ × 2′)
Complement	20; (later) 61
Battery	1–6pdr SB

Notes: Designed by Pook with original machinery by Copeland. Brig rig. Rebuilt (cut in two), re-engined, and lengthened with bark rig, 1853; relaunched 24 Feb 1853.
Service record: Ringgold's North Pacific Survey Expedition, 1853–54. Decomm 23 Aug 1856. Receiving ship, San Francisco. Sold 17 Aug 1865.
Later history: Merchant *John Hancock*, 1865. Converted to schr, 1869.

Name	Builder	Laid down	L	Comm
Arctic	Philadelphia NYd	(U)	1855	1885

Dimensions	125′ × 25′ × (U)
Tonnage	125 tons
Machinery	1 screw, direct-acting engine
Complement	(U)
Battery	1–12pdr

Service record: Sailed with *Release* to rescue Kane Arctic Expedition, Jun 1855. Atlantic cable laying, 1856. Decomm 21 Oct 1856. Trfd to USCS, 1857–58. Machinery removed, converted to lightship, *Lightship No. 8*, 1859. Sold 16 Apr 1879.

4
UNITED STATES REVENUE CUTTER SERVICE

Introduction

The United States Revenue Cutter Service was the first armed service organized by the new government to deter smuggling and enforce customs laws and payment of tariffs. On 4 August 1790 Congress passed the bill authorizing the employment of forty officers and the construction of ten boats to collect revenue. The early operations were local ones with a collector of customs in various ports who was responsible for obtaining and operating the cutters—usually small schooners or sloops. This situation continued for decades with little attention to preserving records of either the ships or their activities. (A fire at the Treasury Department destroyed the few existing records in 1832.)

In times of war, cutters were taken into the Navy or operated with the Navy, and by the 1830s revenue cutters were engaged in safety at sea and attended to lighthouses. Secretary of the Treasury Walter Forward ordered two iron steamers in 1839, shortly followed by six more. Fitted with Hunter wheels, they were a disaster and were phased out of the Revenue Service within a few years, setting back the acquisition of steam vessels until the Civil War.

Name	Builder	L	Dimensions	Tonnage	Principal station
Massachusetts	Newburyport, Mass.	23 Jul 1791	60′ × 17′8″ × 7′8″	70	
Argus	New London, Conn.	1791	47′9″ × 16′3″ × 6′2″	48	New London
General Greene	Philadelphia	5 Aug 1791			Philadelphia
Scammel ex-*Ferret*	Portsmouth, N.H.	Aug 1791	57′10″ × 15′8″ × 6′6″	51	
Vigilant	New York	1791	47′ × 15′ × 4′6″	35	Newport
Virginia	Hampton, Va.	1791	40′ × 17′ × 6′6″	47	Norfolk
Active	Baltimore (David Stodder)	9 Apr 1791		50	Baltimore
Diligence	Washington, N.C.	1792		40	New Bern, N.C.
South Carolina	Charleston, S.C.	1793		35	Charleston
North Carolina		1792			
Eagle	Savannah, Ga.	1793		50	Savannah
Massachusetts	Cohasset, Mass. (Adna Bates)	1793		50	Boston
General Greene	Baltimore (Price)	1797		98	Delaware Bay
Virginia	Norfolk	1797	50′ × 18′10″ × 8′6″	187	Norfolk

Notes and service records:
Massachusetts: Sold 29 Sep 1792.
Argus: Rerigged as sloop, probably in 1802. Sold 1804.
General Greene: Sold Dec 1797.
   Ship captured: (With *Delaware*) schr *Le Marsouin*, 5 Mar 1799.
Scammel: Sold 16 Aug 1798.
Vigilant: Sold Sep 1798.
Virginia: Sold 1798.
Active: Sold 26 Feb 1800.
Diligence: Sold 5 Nov 1798.
South Carolina: Sold 1798.
North Carolina: Sold 1798.
Eagle: Sold 1799.
Massachusetts: Sold Jun 1804.
General Greene: Sloop. Rate: 10. USN 1798. In Decatur's sqn off Havana, 1798–1800. Sold 1802.
Virginia: Schooner. Rate: 14. Complement: 70. Battery: 6–6pdr, 8–4pdr. USN 1798. In Truxtun's sqn off St. Kitts, 1798–99. Returned to USRCS, Jun 1799.
   Ship captured: Schr *Louis*, 26 Apr 1799.

DILIGENCE CLASS

Name	Builder	L	Dimensions	Tonnage	Principal station
Diligence	Philadelphia (Humphreys)	1797	77′ (deck) × 23′8″ × 9′2″	135	North Carolina
Eagle	Philadelphia (Brown)	4 Aug 1798	77′ (deck) × 23′8″ × 9′2″	187	South Atlantic coast
Governor Gilman	Portsmouth, N.H. (Hackett)	1798	77′ (deck) × 23′8″ × 9′2″	135	Portsmouth, N.H.?
Governor Jay	New York	27 Jun 1798	58′ (keel) × 20′ × 9′	187	
Pickering	Newburyport, Mass. (O. Merrill)	Jul 1798	58′ (keel) × 20′ × 9′	187	
Scammel	Portsmouth, N.H. (Hackett)	11 Aug 1798	75′ (deck) × 21′2″ × 9′6″	131	

Notes and service records:

Diligence: Schooner. Rate: 12. USN 1798. In Barry's sqn off St. Kitts and Barbados, 1798–1800. Returned to USRCS, 1801. SE 1802.

Eagle: Brig. Rate: 14. Battery: 16–9pdr. USN 1798. Cruised in West Indies in sqn of Barry, Truxtun, and Decatur. Sold 17 Jun 1801.
   Ships captured: *Le Bon Père*,[1] 6, 1799. (With *Adams*) French schr *La Fougueuse*, 10 Jan 1800. *La Favorite, Dolphin, La Magdelen.*

Governor Gilman: Rate: 12. Sold 22 Feb 1802.

Governor Jay: Schooner. Rate: 14. USN 1798–1800. In Decatur's sqn off Havana, 1798–1800.

Pickering: Brig. Rate: 14. Complement: 90. USN 1798; cruised under Preble in Barry's sqn. Sailed from New Castle, Del., for Guadeloupe, 20 Aug 1800; lost at sea with all hands (90 lost).
   Ships captured: (With *Ganges* and *Merrimack*) recaptured schr *John*, 16 Aug 1799. Privateer *Le Conquereur d'Egypte*, 13 Nov 1799; *Atalanta, Fly, Voltigeur* (LofM), 10, *Active*, 12, 1800.

Scammel: Schooner. Rate: 14. USN 1798. In West Indies in sqn of Barry, Truxtun, and Decatur. Sold 20 Jun 1801.
   Ship captured: *Le Felix*, 1800.

[1] Later USRC *Bee*.

The revenue cutter *Pickering*, "jackass brig," built in 1798 and transferred to the Navy in 1800. (U.S. Naval Historical Center)

Name	Builder	L	Dimensions	Tonnage	Principal station
South Carolina (ii)	Charleston	27 Nov 1798			
Pinckney	Charleston (Pritchard)	17 Oct 1798	62′ × 23′ × 10′6″	195	
Bee		1799*			
ex–*Le Bon Père* (*Bon Pierre*)					
Patriot	Hampton, Va.	1800			Norfolk; Savannah
Massachusetts	Boston	1801	56′6″ × 17′9″ × 7′	62	Boston
St. Mary's	St. Mary's, Ga.	1801*	52′ × 15′ × 5′8″		Georgia
Governor Williams	Wilmington, N.C.	1802*			North Carolina
Collector	Philadelphia	1803			
ex-*Kitty*					
General Greene		1802			Charleston
Jefferson		1802			Norfolk
New Hampshire	Portsmouth, N.H.	1802			Portsmouth, N.H.
Vigilant		1802			New York
Diligence		1803			
Louisiana	Baltimore	1804	70′6″ × 22′4″ × 5′7″	74	New Orleans
Argus					
Dolly		1805*		172	Norfolk
Surveyor	Baltimore (Parsons)	1807	68′ × 19′6″ × 8′	75	Baltimore
Gallatin		1807*			Charleston
James Madison	Baltimore	1808	94′4″ × 24′2″ × 10′6″	252	Savannah
Mercury	Ocracoke, N.C.	1807			Ocracoke, N.C.; New Bern, N.C.
Virginia		1807			Baltimore
Hazard		1808			Ocracoke, N.C.

Notes and service records:

South Carolina: Schooner. Rate: 12. USN 1798. In Tingey's sqn off Cuba, 1798–1800. Returned to USRCS, 20 Aug 1799.

Pinckney: Brig. Rate: 16. Trfd to USN while under construction. Sold 1800.

Bee: Captured by *Eagle*, 5 Apr 1799, and purchased. Sold 1801.

Patriot: Purchased. Sold 1805.

Massachusetts: Topsail schooner. Sold 1816.

St. Mary's: Lateen galley. Ex-USN.

Governor Williams: Lateen galley. Ex-USN. Lost off Ocracoke, N.C., Sep 1806.

General Greene: Sold at Charleston, 1808.

Jefferson: USN 1812–17. Sold 1817.
  Ships captured: Schr *Patriot*, brig *Ariadne*, 1812.

New Hampshire: Sold May 1816.

Vigilant: Sold 1807.

Diligence: Lost in hurricane, 1806.

Louisiana: At New Orleans, Dec 1804. Sold 1812.
  Ships captured: Recaptured schr *Felicity* from pirates, 11 Apr 1805.

Argus: Sold 1809.

Dolly: Sold 1807.

Surveyor: Schooner. Battery: 6–6pdr. Captured by British on York River, Va., 12 Jun 1813, and taken into service.

Gallatin: Purchased at Charleston, 1807. USN 1812–13. Sunk by accidental explosion at Charleston (3+ killed), 1 Apr 1813.
  Ship captured: Brig *General Blake* (LofM), 1812.

James Madison: Captured by HM Frigate *Barbadoes* near Savannah, 24 Nov 1812.
  Ship captured: Brig *Shamrock*, 6, Jul 1812.

Mercury: USN 1812. Out of service, 1820.

The revenue cutter *James Madison*, built in 1807. Print by C. J. A. Wilson. (U.S. Naval Historical Center)

Name	Builder	L	Dimensions	Tonnage	Principal station
Sally		1808*			Newport, R.I.
Thorn		1808*			Boston
Union		1808*			
Argus		1809			New York
Eagle		1809*			Boston
Independence		1810*			
Pilgrim		1811*			Wilmington, N.C.
General Greene	Philadelphia	1811	60′ × 21′ × (U)		
Vigilant	Newport, R.I. (Marble)	1812	60′7″ × 18′9″ × 6′8″	65	Newport
Active		1812*		38	New London
Commodore Barry		1812*			Passamaquoddy, Maine
George		1812*			Newport
Lynx		1814*			
Dallas	New York (Brown)	1816	56′8″ × 17′ × 6′	51	Savannah
Surprise	New York (Brown)	1816	56′8″ × 17′ × 6′	51	Norfolk
Detector	Newport, R.I. (Cook & Gyles)	1815	60′7″ × 16′9″ × 6′8″	65	Portland, Maine
Search	Newport, R.I. (Cook & Gyles)	1815	60′7″ × 16′9″ × 6′8″	65	Boston
Gallatin	Baltimore	1815			Charleston
South Carolina	Baltimore	1815			
Active		1816*		38	Chesapeake Bay
Eagle	New York	1816			New Haven, Conn.
Monroe	Norfolk, Va. (Servant)	1817			Norfolk
Alert	New York (Bergh)	Apr 1818	58′ × 19′ × 6′6″	75	Eastport, Maine
Alabama	New York (Bergh)	Jun 1819	52′ × 18′6″ × 5′9″	56	Mobile, Ala.
Louisiana	New York (Bergh)	1819	52′ × 18′6″ × 5′9″		New Orleans
Search	Boston (Wade)	1820			Boston
Crawford	New York	1821			Savannah
Florida	New York	1822	63′3″ (bp) × 17′5″ × 6′4″	73	Florida
Vigilant	Baltimore (Flannigin)	1824		75	Chesapeake Bay; New Orleans

Notes and service records:

Argus: Sold 1812.

Eagle: Battery: 4–4pdr, 2–2pdr. Captured by British brig *Dispatch*, 18, after being forced aground in Long Island Sound, 11 Oct 1814.

General Greene: Sold 1815.

Vigilant: Battery: 4–4pdr. USN 1813–14. Sold 13 May 1842.

   Ship captured: Privateer sloop *Dart*, 4, off Newport, 4 Oct 1813; armed brig *B of Bristol*, 11 Oct 1817; Spanish brig *Belle Corunnes*, 17 May 1818.

Active: USN 1812. Sold 1817.

Commodore Barry: USN 1812. Captured by British vessels off Maine, 3 Aug 1812.

Lynx: Returned to owner, 1819.

Dallas: Sold Dec 1821.

   Ships captured: Privateer *Young Spartan*, 17 Jun 1818; brig *General Ramirez*, 8 Jul 1820.

Surprise: Sold Jun 1817.

Detector: Sold Dec 1825.

Search: Sold 1820.

Gallatin: Out of service, 1824.

Active: SE, 1823.

   Ships captured: Ship *Margaret*, 12 Aug 1817; privateer *Hornet*, 21 Dec 1818; pirate *Irresistible*, 16 Apr 1819.

Eagle: Sold 1829.

Monroe: Sold 30 Jun 1825.

   Ships captured: Venezuelan brig *Columbia*, 23 Oct 1818; privateer *General Artigas*, 16 Mar 1819.

Alert: Sold 1829.

Alabama: Sold Aug 1833.

   Ship captured: (With *Louisiana*) Pirate *Bravo*, 31 Aug 1819.

Louisiana: Sold Mar 1824.

   Later history: Probably renamed *Cecil.*

   Ships captured: (With *Alabama*) Pirate *Bravo*, 31 Aug 1819. (With *Peacock*) Schr *Carmen*, 5 others in W. Indies, 28–30 Sep 1822.

Search: Battery: (1830) 2–6pdr, 2–4pdr. SE 1830.

Crawford: Lost off St. Mary's, Ga., 27 Mar 1829.

Florida: Sold 1831.

   Ship captured: Recaptured schr *Nuestra Señora de los Angeles* in Florida Keys.

Vigilant: Renamed **Dallas** Jan 1830. Seminole War, 1832–33. Lost at Tampico, Mexico, while attempting to cross bar during war between Texas and Mexico, 21 Sep 1836.

Name	Builder	L	Dimensions	Tonnage	Principal station
Marion	Baltimore	Sep 1825	78′8″ × 19′6″ × 9′3″	115	Charleston; New London; Norfolk
Pulaski	Baltimore	1 Sep 1825	78′8″ × 19′6″ × 9′6″	115	Key West; Mobile
Swiftsure	New York	1825		110	Eastport, Maine
Detector	N. Yarmouth, Maine (Fisher & Webster)	1825	52′ (bp) × 18′3″ × 6′2″	62	Portland, Maine
Wasp	N. Yarmouth, Maine (Fisher & Webster)	1825	52′ (bp) × 18′3″ × 6′2″	62	Norfolk
Louisiana	New York	1825			New Orleans
Benjamin Rush	Erie, Pa.	13 Sep 1828		39	Erie, Pa.
Alert		1829	74′3″ × 20′6″ × 7′9″	120	New York; Eastport, Maine
Portsmouth ex-*Hiram*	Connecticut	1829*	60′6″ × 17′5″ × 6′8″	61	

* Purchased

Notes and service records:
Marion: Seminole War, 1832–33. Renamed *James Madison* 1833. In USN, 1837–38. Seminole War, 1841–42. To Coast Survey, 6 Dec 1850. Sold 1858.
Pulaski: Sold 1833.
Swiftsure: Renamed *Crawford*, 21 Dec 1835. Sold 1 Apr 1839.
Detector: Sold 1832.
Wasp: Sold 7 Jan 1831.
Louisiana: Sold Jun 1830.
   Ship captured: Pirate *Bolivia* (*Bolivar?*), 11 May 1827.
Benjamin Rush: Sold 1833.
Alert: Nullification Crisis, Charleston, 1833. Sold Apr 1853.
Portsmouth: Battery: 2–4pdr. Sold 1 May 1833.

MORRIS-TANEY CLASS

Name	Builder	L	Dimensions	Tonnage	Principal station
Crawford	New York (Webb & Allen)	1830		112	Norfolk; Savannah
Dexter	New York	1830		112	Norfolk; Mobile
Gallatin	New York NYd	1830	80′6″ × 21′ × 7′1″	112	Wilmington, NC
Alexander Hamilton	New York NYd	1830	78′ × 21′3″ × 7′8″	112	Boston; Charleston
Ingham	New York (Webb & Allen)	1830		112	New Orleans
Andrew Jackson	Washington NYd	1832		112	various
Jefferson	New York (Webb & Allen)	1832		112	
McLane	New York (Webb & Allen)	1832	72′ (deck) × 20′ × 7′7″	112	Charleston
Morris	New York NYd	30 Jun 1831		112	Portland, Maine
Richard Rush	New York (Webb & Allen)	1831	71′ dk × 20′2″ × 6′8″	112	New York
Roger B. Taney	New York (Webb & Allen)	26 Dec 1833	71′ (deck) × 19′6″ × 7′2″	112	Norfolk; Eastport, Maine
Washington	New York	1832		112	Key West
Oliver Wolcott	New York	1831	71′4″ × 20′6″ × 7′	112	various

Notes and service records:
Crawford: Sold 27 Jul 1835.
Dexter: Nullification Crisis, Charleston, 1833. Seminole War, 1836–37. Sold 25 Feb 1841.
Gallatin: Nullification Crisis, Charleston, 1833. Trfd to USCS, 1840. Returned to USRCS, 1848–49. Seized by Confederates at Savannah, 1861; became Confederate privateer.
Alexander Hamilton: Foundered in gale at Charleston (1 survivor), 9 Dec 1853.
Ingham: Sold 14 Jan 1836.
   Later history: Texan *Independence*. Captured by Mexicans, 17 Apr 1836; renamed *Independencia*.
Andrew Jackson: Nullification Crisis, Charleston, 1833. Seminole War, 1833 and 1836. Sold 31 Oct 1865.
Jefferson: Damaged in collision, Jan 1833. USN 1836–37; Seminole War. Reconditioned and rebuilt, 1839. Renamed *Crawford* Apr 1839. Wrecked at Gardiners Point, N.Y., 15 Dec 1847.
McLane: Nullification Crisis, Charleston, 1833. Capsized in tornado at Hadleys Harbor, Mass., 1 Sep 1837; salved. Sold 21 Oct 1840.
Morris: Mexican War. Wrecked in hurricane at Key West, Fla., 11 Oct 1846; sold and salved.
Richard Rush: Severely damaged by ice, Jan 1840. Trfd to Lighthouse Service, 30 Mar 1840.
Roger B. Taney: Capsized at New York, 3 Aug 1852; repaired. Trfd to USCS, 1847–50. Sold 5 Jan 1858.
Washington: Seminole War, 1836. Sold 26 Jun 1837.
Oliver Wolcott: Driven ashore on Florida coast, 23 Jan 1846. Sold Jan 1851.

U.S. Coast Survey Schooner *Gallatin*, built in 1830 as a revenue cutter and seized by the Confederates at Savannah in 1861. (U.S. Naval Historical Center)

Name	Builder	L	Dimensions	Tonnage	Principal station
Campbell	New York	1830		60	Norfolk
Argus	Surrey, Maine	1830	39′7″ × 10′ × 5′		
Veto	Blue Hill, Maine	1832	49′6″ × 13′6″ × 6′2″	45	Castine, Maine
Erie	Presque Isle, Pa.	1833		60	Erie, Pa.
Campbell	Oxford, Md.	1834*		40	New Orleans
Washington	Baltimore (McCulley)	Aug 1837	91′2″ (bp) × 21′2″ × (U)	190	

Notes and service records:
Campbell: Sold 30 Jun 1834.
Argus: Sold 1834.
Veto: Sold 1850.
Erie: Sold 13 Jul 1849.
Campbell: Battery: 2–6pdr. Second Seminole War, 1837. Sold Jun 1839.
Washington: With USCS, summer 1838, summer 1839, 1840–52. Damaged in hurricane (11 killed), 1847; repaired at Philadelphia. Trfd from Treasury Dept. Employed principally on survey of coast. Gulf of Mexico during Mexican War. Seized by Confederates at New Orleans, 31 Jan 1861. Ship captured: Slaver schr *Amistad*, off New London, Conn., which had been taken over by slaves, 26 Aug 1839.

Name	Builder	L	Dimensions	Tonnage	Principal station
Levi Woodbury	Baltimore (Duncan)	27 Mar 1837		120	Gulf of Mexico
Jefferson	Baltimore (McCulley)	1 Jan 1839	84′6″ (bp)		Mobile
Van Buren	Baltimore	1839			Charleston
Ewing	Baltimore	1841	91′6″ × 22′9″ × 9′2″	170	New York; New London
William J. Duane		1841			Mobile
Walter B. Forward	Washington, D.C. (Easby)		89′ × 21′2″ × 8′6″	139	Baltimore; Wilmington, N.C.; Beaufort, S.C.
Nautilus	Baltimore	1843*	76′ × 19′ × 7′		Key West
Vigilant	New York (Webb & Curtis)	1843	56′ (bp) × 18′5″ × 4′8″	50	Key West
Lawrence	Washington, D.C. (Easby)	1848			San Francisco

* Purchased

Notes and service records:
Levi Woodbury: Battery: 4–12pdr, 1–6pdr. Mexican War. Sold 1 Jun 1847.
Jefferson: Brigantine. Battery: 4–12pdr crde. USN 1841–42. Sold 22 May 1843.
Van Buren: USN 2 Aug 1841–18 Aug 1842; Seminole War. Mexican War. Sold 1 Jun 1847.
Ewing: Mexican War. Trfd to USCS, Oct 1848. Decomm 1876.
William J. Duane: Sold Nov 1844.
Walter B. Forward: Battery: (1845) 1–18pdr, 4–9pdr. Comm 23 Apr 1842. USN 1846–47. Sold 30 Nov 1865.
Nautilus: Trfd from USCS; returned 13 Jun 1844. Again trfd to USRCS, 30 Oct 1847; returned to USCS, 5 Mar 1848. SE 1859.
Vigilant: Lost in hurricane off Key West (2 survivors), 5 Oct 1844.
Lawrence: Lost at entrance to San Francisco Bay, 25 Nov 1851.

CAMPBELL CLASS

Name	Builder	L	Dimensions	Tonnage	Principal station
Campbell	Portsmouth, Va. (Graves)	30 Jul 1849	102′ × 23′ × 8′8″	155	Astoria, Oreg.
Crawford	Philadelphia (Tees)	1849	102′ × 23′ × 8′8″	155	Charleston; Key West; Newport
William J. Duane	Philadelphia (Tees)	1849	102′ × 23′ × 8′8″	155	Norfolk
Morris	Baltimore (Brown)	26 Apr 1849	102′ × 23′ × 8′8″	155	Boston; Baltimore

Notes and service records:
Campbell: Severely damaged in collision with schr during gale, 27 Aug 1851. Renamed *Joseph Lane* 1855. Sold 20 Jul 1869.
Crawford: Trfd to USCS, 21 Jun 1852–31 May 1861. Sold 21 Jun 1869.
William J. Duane: Seized by Confederates at Norfolk, 18 Apr 1861.
Morris: Sold 10 Dec 1868.

The revenue cutter *Morris*, one of several sister ships built in 1849. (U.S. Naval Historical Center)

HARRISON CLASS

Name	Builder	L	Dimensions	Tonnage	Principal station
Harrison	Erie, Pa. (Carrick)	1849	(U)	115	Oswego, N.Y.
Ingham	Erie, Pa. (Carrick)	1849	(U)	115	Erie, Pa.; Detroit

Notes and service records:
Harrison: Sold 6 Oct 1856.
Ingham: Sold 24 Sep 1856.

CUSHING CLASS

Name	Builder	L	Dimensions	Tonnage	Principal station
James Campbell	Somerset, Mass. (Hood)	9 Jul 1853	91′ × 21′ × 8′6″	152	New London
Caleb Cushing	Somerset, Mass. (Hood)	12 Jul 1853	93′7″ × 21′8″ × 9′		Portland, Maine
Jefferson Davis	Bristol, R.I. (Hood)	1853			West Coast
James C. Dobbin	Somerset, Mass. (Hood)	13 Jul 1853	93′9″ × 22′6″ × 10′	174	Wilmington, N.C.; Savannah; Portland, Maine; Baltimore
William L. Marcy	Bristol, R.I. (Hood)	Jun 1853	94′ × (U)		San Francisco
Robert McClelland	Somerset, Mass. (Hood)	11 Jul 1853			Mobile; New Orleans

Notes and service records:
James Campbell: Sold 8 Jul 1875.
    Later history: Merchant *Pedro Varela.* Lost 1916.
Caleb Cushing: Captured at Portland, Maine, by CSS *Archer,* 27 Jul 1863; burned.
Jefferson Davis: Pacific Coast, 1854–62. Hospital ship, 1862. FFU.
James C. Dobbin: Sold 6 Apr 1881.
    Later history: Merchant *John L. Thomas.*
William L. Marcy: Trfd to USCS, 5 Mar 1862.
Robert McClelland: Seized by Louisiana, 18 Feb 1861.
    Later history: CSS *Pickens.*

Name	Builder	Acquired	Dimensions	Tonnage	Principal station
William Aiken ex-*Eclipse* (pilot boat)	Charleston?	1855*		82	Charleston

Service record:
William Aiken: Seized by Confederates at Charleston, 27 Dec 1860.
    Later history: Confederate privateer *Petrel.* Sunk by USS *St. Lawrence,* 28 Jul 1861.

ALLEN CLASS

Name	Builder	L	Dimensions	Tonnage	Principal station
Philip Allen	Portsmouth, Va. (Page & Allen)	1856	80′ (oa) × 23′ × 5′6″	93	Baltimore
Lewis Cass	Portsmouth, Va. (Page & Allen)	1856	80′ (oa) × 23′ × 5′6″		Mobile
Henry Dodge	Portsmouth, Va. (Page & Allen)	1856	80′ (oa) × 23′ × 5′6″		Galveston, Tex.

Notes and service records:
Philip Allen: SE 1865.
Lewis Cass: Seized by Alabama, 31 Jan 1861.
    Later history: CSS *Lewis Cass.*
Henry Dodge: Seized by rebels at Galveston, 2 Mar 1861.

LEGARE-CLASS STEAMERS

Name	Builder	Laid down	L	Comm
Bibb ex-*Tyler*	Pittsburgh (Knapp)	(U)	10 Apr 1845	(U)
Dallas	New York (Stillman; Stratton)	(U)	4 Apr 1846	(U)
McLane	Boston (Alger)	(U)	1845	(U)
Spencer	New York (West Point Foundry)	(U)	1845	(U)

Dimensions	160' × 24' × 9'3"
Tonnage	*Bibb:* 409 tons
	Dallas: 391 tons
	McLane: 368 tons
	Spencer: 398 tons
Machinery	Hunter wheel, engine (24" × 3', except *Spencer:* 36" × 2')
Complement	60 (est.)
Battery	*Bibb:* 1–long 18pdr, 4–32pdr

Notes: Iron hulls.

Service records:

Bibb: Leaked; beached during trials to prevent sinking. Converted to side wheels at Cincinnati, 1845. Mexican War. Trfd to USCS, Jul 1847. Rebuilt with wood hull at Boston NYd. Launched 12 May 1853.

Dallas: Laid down at Buffalo. Converted to side wheels during construction. Trfd to USCS, 1848. No service. Sold 4 Mar 1851.

McLane: Converted to side wheels prior to launching. Mexican War. Sold 3 Dec 1847. Converted to lightship.

Spencer: Modified to Loper propellers, 1846. Boilers failed, May 1846. Converted to lightship, 1848.

Name	Builder	Laid down	L	Comm
Jefferson	Pittsburgh (Knapp)	(U)	1845	(U)
Legare	New York (Schuyler)	(U)	(U)	May 1844

Dimensions	*Jefferson:* 160' × 24' × 9'9"
Tonnage	*Jefferson:* 343 tons
	Legare: 364 tons
Machinery	1 screw, (36" × 2'8")
Complement	58
Battery	*Legare:* 1–18pdr, 1–12pdr, 1–9pdr, 2–4pdr

Notes and service records:

Ordered 1839.

Jefferson: Ericsson's propellers replaced with Loper propellers, Sep 1845. Re-erected at Oswego, N.Y., 23 Jun 1847. Operated on Great Lakes. Trfd to New York, 1848. Trfd to USCS but did not serve. Sold 1861.

Legare: Ericsson's propellers replaced with Loper propellers. Trfd to USCS, 12 Nov 1847. Converted to lightship, 1857.

Name	Builder	Laid down	L	Comm
Polk	Richmond, Va. (Anderson)	(U)	1846	Jan 1847
Walker	Pittsburgh (Tomlinson)	(U)	Nov 1847	(U)

Dimensions	(U)
Tonnage	400 tons
Machinery	side wheels
Complement	(U)
Battery	(U)

Notes: Iron hulls.

Service records:

Polk: Sailed to Gulf under Navy orders, Mar 1847, but returned, leaking badly. Returned to USRCS, May 1847. Converted to bark, 1848. San Francisco 1850. Sold at San Francisco, 29 Dec 1854.

Walker: Trfd to USCS, Jan 1848. Sunk in collision off Absecon, N.J., 21 Jun 1860.

5
TEXAS NAVY

Settlement of Texas by Americans started in 1821 and negotiations with Mexico led to Texas becoming part of the republic of Mexico. In 1830 the Mexican Congress enacted legislation that the settlers regarded as violating their rights. Relations worsened until in 1835 armed violence broke out, leading to the siege of the Alamo, which fell on 27 March 1836. On 21 April the Mexicans were defeated at the Battle of San Jacinto and the independence of Texas was established. Texas's request for annexation was denied by the U.S. Congress.

Some small vessels were armed and fought under the Texas flag during this period. In 1838 a sloop and two brigs were ordered to be built and some other vessels were acquired. Relations with Mexico were poor and Texas participated in the Mexican civil war against the central government, helping the Yucatan faction. Without sufficient funds, the ships of the navy deteriorated and by 1843 the navy ceased to exist. Texas was finally annexed by the United States on 1 March 1845; the surviving ships were taken into the U.S. Navy on 11 May 1846 but were of no use and were quickly sold.

Name	Builder	Laid down	L	Comm (Texas)
Austin	Baltimore (Schott & Whitney)	1839	1839	5 Jan 1840
ex-*Texas*				

Rate	18 guns
Dimensions	130'2" (bp) × 31'9" × 15'10"; also reported as 125' × 31' × 12'6"
Tonnage	589 tons
Complement	174
Battery	16–24pdr, 4–18pdr; (1840) 2–18pdr, 18–24pdr crde

Notes: Sloop. Designed by Francis Grice. Built for Texas Navy. Taken into USN, 11 May 1846; never used in active service.
Service record: (In Texas Navy) Supported Yucatan in Mexican civil war, Dec 1841. Captured Mexican brig *Progreso*, 6 Feb 1842; schr *Doloritas*, 1 Apr 1842; and schr *Dos Amigos*, 3 Apr 1842. Action with Mexican sqn off Campeche, 30 Apr 1843. Hit 17 times and damaged during second action with Mexican sqn off Campeche (3 killed), 16 May 1843. Decomm at Galveston, Jul 1843.

(In USN) Receiving ship, Pensacola, 1846–48. BU 1848.

Name	Builder	Laid down	L	Comm (Texas)
Colorado	Baltimore (Schott & Whitney)	1838	1838	Oct 1839
Galveston	Baltimore (Schott & Whitney)	1838	1838	25 Apr 1840

Rate	18 guns
Dimensions	112' × 29' × 11'
Tonnage	419 tons
Complement	86
Battery	16–18pdr; (1842) 15–18pdr, 1–9pdr

Notes: Brigs. Too rotten for USN service, never comm. Trfd 11 May 1846.
Service records:
Colorado: Renamed **Wharton** 1840. Damaged in action with Mexican sqn off Campeche (2 killed), 30 Apr 1843. Damaged in second action off Campeche (2 killed), 16 May 1843. Decomm at Galveston, 14 Jul 1843. Sold 30 Nov 1846.
Galveston: Renamed **Archer** 1840. Sold 30 Nov 1846.

Name	Builder	Built	Comm
Zavala	Philadelphia	1836	23 Mar 1839
ex-*Charleston*			

Dimensions	201' × 24' × 12'
Tonnage	569 tons
Machinery	side wheels
Complement	126
Battery	4–12pdr, 1–9pdr

Notes: Steamer.
Service record: Sank at mooring at Galveston, Jun 1842; beyond repair.

MISCELLANEOUS VESSELS

Name	Type	Acquired	Tonnage	Battery	Crew
Brutus	schr	Jan 1836	160	1–18pdr, 9 others	40
Independence		Jan 1836	112	9 guns	
ex-USRC *Ingham*					
Invincible	schr	Jan 1836	100	1–9pdr, 6 crdes	40
Liberty	schr	9 Jan 1836	70	6 guns	40
ex–*William Robbins*					
Potomac	brig	1838			
San Antonio	schr	7 Aug 1839	170	6–12pdr	82
San Bernard	schr	31 Aug 1839	170	6–12pdr	82
San Jacinto	schr	27 Jun 1839	170	4–12pdr, 1–9pdr	

Notes and service records:

Brutus: Lost rudder and went aground during engagement at Galveston, 27 Aug 1837; total loss.

Ships captured: (With *Invincible*) schr *Telegrafo*, schr *Adventure* at Sisal, 25 Jul 1836; schr *Eliza Russell*, 8 Aug 1836; *Correo de Tobasco*, 12 Aug 1836; schr *Rafaelita*, 17 Aug 1836.

Independence: Captured by Mexican ships *Vencedor del Alamo*, 7, and *Libertador*, 16, 17 Apr 1837.

Ship captured: Brig *Pocket*, Mar 1836.

Later history: Mexican *Independencia*.

Invincible: Ran aground after engagement at Galveston, 27 Aug 1837; total loss.

Ships captured: (With *Brutus*) schr *Telegrafo*, schr *Adventure* at Sisal, 25 Jul 1836; schr *Eliza Russell*, 8 Aug 1836; *Correo de Tobasco*, 12 Aug 1836; schr *Rafaelita*, 17 Aug 1836.

Liberty: Former privateer. Sold Oct 1836.

Ships captured: schr *Pelicano*, 3 Jan 1836; brig *Durango*, Mar 1836.

Potomac: Useless, never converted to warship. Served as receiving ship, Galveston.

San Antonio: Supported Yucatan in Mexican civil war, Dec 1841. Captain, Lt. Fuller, killed in mutiny at New Orleans, 11 Feb 1842. Missing in Gulf of Mexico, Oct 1842.

San Bernard: Supported Yucatan in Mexican civil war, Dec 1841. Went aground in gale, Sep 1842; repaired. Trfd to USN, 11 May 1846. Sold 30 Nov 1846.

San Jacinto: Went aground in Arcas Islands, 30 Oct 1840. Wrecked in gale, 25 Nov 1840.

APPENDIX
ROYAL NAVY LOSSES IN NORTH AMERICAN WATERS

The following are chronological lists of losses of Royal Navy ships in North American waters during the American Revolution and the War of 1812. Ships preceded by an asterisk (*) were taken into U.S. service. Dates in parentheses, unless otherwise noted, signify date built.

LOSSES DURING THE REVOLUTION

Enterprise, 10, tender. Taken by Americans at St. Johns, Richelieu River, 14 May 1775.

Diana, 6, schr (purchased 1775). Abandoned and burned at Boston, 28 May 1775.

Margaretta, schr. Taken by eight small American vessels near Machias, Maine, 12 Jun 1775.

Diligent, 6, schr. Taken by Americans at Machias, Maine, 15 Jul 1775.

Hunter, 10, sloop (1756). Taken by American privateer off Boston, 23 Nov 1775 (later retaken).

Gaspe, 6, brig. Taken by Americans in the St. Lawrence, Nov 1775 (retaken Apr 1776).

Hawk, schr (1775). Captured by Americans, 4 Apr 1776.

Bolton, 12, gun brig. Captured by Americans, 4 Apr 1776.

Edward, tender. Taken by USS *Lexington*, 16, off Virginia, 17 Apr 1776.

Actaeon, 28, 6th rate (1775). Grounded and burned during attack on Charleston, S.C., 29 Jun 1776.

Despatch, 6. Taken by American privateer *Tyrannicide*, 14, 12 Jul 1776.

Cruizer, 8, sloop (1782). Wrecked and burned off South Carolina, 2 Oct 1776.

George, tender. Wrecked near Piscataqua River, 26 Dec 1776.

Repulse, 32, 5th rate (ex-French *Bellone*, taken 1759). Foundered off Bermuda with all hands, Dec 1776.

Racehorse, 8, bomb sloop (ex-French *Marquis de Vaudreuil*, 1757) Taken by American *Andrew Doria*, 14, off Puerto Rico, Dec 1776.

Fox, 28, 6th rate (1773). Taken by USS *Hancock*, 32, 7 Jun 1777 (retaken 8 Jul 1777).

Augusta, 64, 3rd rate (1763). Accidentally burned in Delaware River, 24 Oct 1777.

Merlin, 18, sloop (1757). Abandoned and burned in Delaware River, 23 Oct 1777.

Vestal, 20, 6th rate (1777). Foundered in gale off Newfoundland with all hands, Oct 1777.

Pegasus, 14, sloop (1776). Foundered in gale off Newfoundland with all hands, Oct 1777.

Siren, 28, 6th rate (1773). Wrecked off Rhode Island, 10 Nov 1777.

Charity, sloop (1770). Lost in Lake Niagara, 1777.

Liverpool, 28, 6th rate (1758). Wrecked on Long Island, N.Y., 11 Feb 1778.

Drake, 14, sloop (ex-*Resolution*, purchased 1777). Taken by USS *Ranger*, 18, off Belfast, 24 Apr 1778.

Spy, 16, sloop (1776). Wrecked off Newfoundland, 6 Jun 1778.

Mermaid, 28, 6th rate (1761). Driven ashore by French sqn in Delaware Bay, 8 Jul 1778.

York, 12, brig-sloop (1777). Taken by French off North America, 10 Jul 1778 (retaken 23 Aug 1778, lost 1779).

Alarm, armed ship ex-galley (purchased 1777). Destroyed to prevent capture at Rhode Island, 1 Aug 1778.

Falcon, 16, sloop (1771). Sunk as blockship in Narragansett Bay, 5 Aug 1778.

Kingfisher, 16, sloop (1770). Destroyed to prevent capture at Rhode Island, 7 Aug 1778.

Juno, 32, 5th rate (1757). Destroyed to prevent capture at Rhode Island, 7 Aug 1778.

Lark, 32, 5th rate (1762). Destroyed to prevent capture at Rhode Island, 7 Aug 1778.

Cerberus, 28, 6th rate (1758). Destroyed to prevent capture at Rhode Island, 7 Aug 1778.

Flora, 32, 5th rate (ex-French *Vestale*, captured 1761). Destroyed to prevent capture at Rhode Island, 7 Aug 1778 (salved by Americans, returned to France, and became privateer *La Flore*, retaken 1798).

Somerset, 64, 3rd rate (1748). Wrecked near Cape Cod, 12 Aug 1778.

Senegal, 14, sloop (1760). Taken by French *L'Hector*, 74, off Rhode Island, 14 Aug 1778 (retaken 2 Nov 1780).

Orpheus, 32, 5th rate (1773). Burned to prevent capture at Rhode Island, 15 Aug 1778.

Thunder, 8, bomb (ex-merchant *Racehorse* purchased 1771). Taken by French *Le Vaillant*, 64, off Rhode Island, 17 Aug 1778.

Zephyr, 14, sloop (ex-*Martin*, 1756). Taken by French *La Gracieuse*, 24, off Newport, R.I., 23 Aug 1778.

Otter, 14, sloop (1767). Wrecked on coast of Florida, 25 Aug 1778.

Minerva, 32, 5th rate (1759). Taken by French *Concorde*, 32, off Santo Domingo, 28 Aug 1778.

Stanley, 10. Taken by French *Le Cesar*, 74, Aug 1778.

Active, 28, 6th rate (1758). Taken by French *La Charmante*, 38, and *La Dedaigneuse*, 26, off Santo Domingo, 1 Sep 1778.

Pigot, 8, galley (purchased 1778). Run ashore to prevent capture at Rhode Island, 28 Oct 1778.

Grampus, 32, storeship (ex–3rd rate *Buckingham*, 1751). Foundered off Newfoundland, Nov 1778.

Swift, 14, sloop (1777). Wrecked off Cape Henry and burned, Nov 1778.

Dispatch, 14, sloop (1777). Capsized in the St. Lawrence, 8 Dec 1778.

Ceres, 18, sloop (1777). Taken by French *L'Iphigénie*, 32, off St. Lucia, 19 Dec 1778.

Cupid, 14, sloop (purchased 1777). Foundered off Newfoundland, 28 Dec 1778.

Mercury, 24, 6th rate (1756). Wrecked near New York, 1778.

Enterprise, 10, tender. Taken by the Americans and burned, 1778.

Weazle, 16, sloop (purchased 1745). Taken by French *La Boudeuse*, 32, near St. Eustatius, 30 Jan 1779.

Diligent, 10, sloop (purchased 1776). Taken by USS *Providence*, 14, 7 May 1779.

Egmont, 10, schr (purchased 1770). Taken by American privateer *Wild Cat*, 14, off Newfoundland, 14 Jul 1779.

Haerlem, 10, sloop (1778). Taken by American privateer *Impertinent*, 16 Jul 1779.

York, 12, brig-sloop (ex-*Betsy*, purchased 1777). Captured by French sqn in West Indies, Jul 1779.

Thorn, 16, sloop (1779). Taken by an American frigate, 25 Aug 1779 (retaken 20 Aug 1782).

Ariel, 20, 6th rate (1777). Taken by French *L'Amazone*, 26, off South Carolina, 10 Sep 1779.

Rose, 20, 6th rate (1757). Sunk as blockship at Savannah, 16 Sep 1779.

Savannah, 14, brig-sloop (purchased 1779). Sunk as blockship at Savannah, 16 Sep 1779.

Serapis, 44, 5th rate (1779). Taken by USS *Bonhomme Richard*, 42, off Flamborough Head, 23 Sep 1779.

Countess of Scarborough, 20, armed ship. Taken by USS *Pallas* off Flamborough Head, 23 Sep 1779.

Experiment, 50, 4th rate (1774). Taken by French *Sagittaire*, 50, off Georgia, 24 Sep 1779.

Champion, storeship. Taken by French *Sagittaire*, 50, off Georgia, 24 Sep 1779.

Myrtle, victualler. Taken by French *Sagittaire*, 50, off Georgia, 24 Sep 1779.

Tortoise, 26, transport (ex-merchant *Grenville*, purchased 1777). Foundered off Newfoundland, Sep 1779.

Sphinx, 20, 6th rate (1775). Taken by French *L'Amphitrite*, 32, in West Indies, 20 Oct 1779.

Hussar, 28, 6th rate (1763). Wrecked in Hell Gate, N.Y., Nov 1779.

North, 20, armed ship. Wrecked near Halifax, N.S., 1779.

Hope, 14 (comm 1764). Taken by an American privateer, 1779.

West Florida, 14. Taken by American *Morris* at Pensacola, 1779.

Leviathan, 50, storeship (ex–3rd rate *Northumberland*, 1750). Foundered on passage from Jamaica, 1779.

Defiance, 64, 3rd rate (1772). Wrecked on Savannah bar, 18 Feb 1780.

Fortune, 14, sloop (1778). Taken by French *L'Iphigénie*, 32, and *Gentille*, 32, in West Indies, 26 Apr 1780.

Courier, 8, lugger (ex-French *Le Coureur* taken 1778). Taken by two American privateers off Newfoundland, 21 Jun 1780.

Unicorn, 20, 6th rate (1776). Taken by French *L'Andromaque* off Tortuga, 4 Sep 1780.

Rover, 18, sloop (ex-American *Cumberland*, taken 1777). Taken by French *Junon*, 32, in West Indies, 13 Sep 1780.

Phoenix, 44, 5th rate (1759). Lost in hurricane off Cuba, 4 Oct 1780.

Stirling Castle, 64, 3rd rate (1775). Wrecked on Silver Key near Hispaniola in hurricane, 5 Oct 1780.

Scarborough, 22, 6th rate (1756). Wrecked on Silver Key near Hispaniola in hurricane, 5 Oct 1780.

Thunderer, 74, 3rd rate (1760). Wrecked on Silver Key near Hispaniola in hurricane, 5 Oct 1780.

Victor, 10, sloop (1777). Wrecked on Silver Key near Hispaniola in hurricane, 5 Oct 1780. *Laurel*, 28, 6th rate (1779). Lost in hurricane at Martinique, 10 Oct 1780.

Viper, 12, cutter (1762). Wrecked in the Gulf of St. Lawrence, 11 Oct 1780.

Blanche, 32, 5th rate (French prize, taken 1779). Wrecked in hurricane at Martinique, 11 Oct 1780.

Andromeda, 28, 6th rate (1777). Wrecked in hurricane at Martinique, 11 Oct 1780.

Deale Castle, 24, 6th rate (1756). Wrecked in hurricane at Puerto Rico, 11 Oct 1780.

Barbadoes, 14, brig-sloop (1778). Wrecked in hurricane at Puerto Rico, 11 Oct 1780.

Chameleon, 14, sloop (1777). Wrecked in hurricane at Puerto Rico, 11 Oct 1780.

Beavers Prize, 16, sloop (ex-American privateer *Oliver Cromwell*, taken 1778). Wrecked in hurricane at Puerto Rico, 11 Oct 1780.

Endeavour, 14, sloop (purchased 1763). Wrecked in hurricane at Jamaica, 11 Oct 1780.

Ontario, 16, sloop (1780). Foundered on Great Lakes, 1 Nov 1780.

Active, 14 (purchased 1776). Taken by Americans near New York, 1780.

Scorpion, 16, brig-sloop (ex-merchant *Borryon*, purchased 1771). Damaged in North America, 1780, and sold.

Shark, 28, 6th rate. Foundered in storm off North America, 1780.

Tapageur, 14, cutter (taken 1779). Wrecked in West Indies, 1780.

Vigilant, 20, armed ship (ex-merchant *Empress of Russia*, purchased 1777). Burned as unfit at Beaufort, S.C., 1780.

Culloden, 74, 3rd rate (1776). Wrecked off Long Island, N.Y., 23 Jan 1781.

Delight, 14, sloop (1778). Foundered on passage to North America, 25 Jan 1781.

Romulus, 44, 5th rate (1777). Taken by French *Eveille*, 74, off Virginia Capes, 19 Feb 1781.

Rover, 14 (ex-American *Cumberland*, taken 1777). Wrecked on North American coast, Feb 1781.

Atalanta, 16, sloop (1775). Taken by USS *Alliance*, 36, in North Atlantic, 28 May 1781.

Trepassy, 14, brig-sloop. Taken by USS *Alliance*, 36, in North Atlantic, 28 May 1781.

Snake, 14, sloop. Taken by American privateers *Pilgrim* and *Rambler*, 13 Jun 1781.

Loyalist, 14, sloop. Taken in Chesapeake Bay by French *Le Glorieux*, 74, 30 Jul 1781.

Pelican, 24, 6th rate (1777). Foundered in hurricane off Jamaica, 2 Aug 1781.

Sandwich, 24, armed ship (1780). Taken off Charlestown, Mass., by French fleet, 24 Aug 1781.

Cormorant, 14, sloop (1776). Taken off Charlestown, Mass., by French fleet, 24 Aug 1781.

Swallow, 14, sloop (1779). Driven ashore by four American privateers off Long Island, 26 Aug 1781.

Savage, 14, sloop (1778). Taken off Charleston by USS *Congress*, 24, 6 Sep 1781 (retaken Sep 1781).

Iris, 32, 5th rate (ex-American *Hancock*, taken 1777). Taken in Chesapeake Bay by French fleet, 11 Sep 1781.

Richmond, 32, 5th rate (1757). Taken in Chesapeake Bay by French fleet, 11 Sep 1781.

Terrible, 74, 3rd rate (1762). Burned as unserviceable after action with French off Chesapeake Bay, 11 Sep 1781.

Fowey, 24, 6th rate (1749). Sunk by American shore batteries at Yorktown, Va., or in action with the French in Chesapeake Bay, 10 Oct 1781.

Guadeloupe, 28, 6th rate (1763). Sunk to avoid capture by the French in Virginia, 10 Oct 1781 (salved by French).

Charon, 44, 5th rate (1778). Burned at Yorktown, 10 Oct 1781.

Vulcan, 8, bomb (ex-*Vesuvius*, 1776). Burned and sunk by red-hot shot at Yorktown, 10 Oct 1781.

Bonetta, 14, sloop (1779). Taken by French fleet in Chesapeake Bay, 10 Oct 1781.

Fly, 14, cutter (1778). Taken by French off U.S. coast, 1781.

Duchess of Cumberland, 16 (purchased 1781). Wrecked off Cape St. Mary, Nfld., 1781.

Hope, 14, brig-sloop (purchased 1780). Wrecked off Savannah, 1781.

Blonde, 32, 5th rate (French, taken 1760). Wrecked off Nantucket, 21 Jan 1782.

LOSSES DURING THE WAR OF 1812

*Oxford, 18, collier (purchased 1804). Taken by USS *Essex* off U.S. coast, 13 Aug 1812.

Guerriere, 38, 5th rate (1799, French, taken 1806). Captured by USS *Constitution* in Western Atlantic, 19 Aug 1812.

*Macedonian, 38, 5th rate (1810). Taken by USS *United States*, 25 Oct 1812.

Southampton, 32, 5th rate (1757). Wrecked near Conception Island, Bahamas, 27 Nov 1812.

Subtle, 12, schr (purchased 1807). Foundered with all hands off St. Barthélemy, 30 Nov 1812.

Plumper, 12, gun-brig (1807). Wrecked off New Brunswick, 5 Dec 1812.

Java, 38, 5th rate (1805, French *Renommee*, taken 1811). Taken by USS *Constitution* off San Salvador, 29 Dec 1812.

Sarpedon, 10, brig-sloop (1809). Foundered with all hands, 1 Jan 1813.

Rhodian, 10, brig-sloop (1809). Wrecked at Port Royal, Jamaica, 21 Feb 1813.

Peacock, 18, brig-sloop (1806). Taken by USS *Hornet* off Demerara, Guyana, and sunk, 24 Feb 1813.

Gloucester, 10, brig (1807). Taken by Americans at York, Lake Erie, 27 Apr 1813.

Algerine, 10, cutter (1810). Wrecked in Bahamas, 20 May 1813.

Persian, 18, brig-sloop (1809). Wrecked on Silver Keys, West Indies, Bahamas, 16 Jun 1813.

Dominica, 10, schr (1805, French *Duc de Wagram*, taken 1809). Taken by U.S. privateer *Decatur* off Charleston, S.C., 5 Aug 1813.

Colibri, 18, brig-sloop (1808, French prize, taken 1809). Wrecked at Port Royal, Jamaica, 22 Aug 1813.

Boxer, 12, gun-brig (1812). Taken by USS *Enterprise* off Portland, Maine, 5 Sep 1813.

Highflyer, 8, schr (American privateer, taken 1813). Taken by USS *President* off Nantucket, 9 Sep 1813.

*Queen Charlotte, 16, sloop (1812). Taken by Americans at Battle of Lake Erie, 10 Sep 1813.

*Detroit, 18, sloop (1813). Taken by Americans at Battle of Lake Erie, 10 Sep 1813.

*Hunter, 10, brig (1812). Taken by Americans at Battle of Lake Erie, 10 Sep 1813.

*Lady Prevost, 12, schr (1812). Taken by Americans at Battle of Lake Erie, 10 Sep 1813.

*Little Belt, 3, sloop (1812). Taken by Americans at Battle of Lake Erie, 10 Sep 1813.

*Chippeway, 2, schr (1812). Taken by Americans at Battle of Lake Erie, 10 Sep 1813.

Bold, 12, gun-brig (1812). Wrecked on Prince Edward Island, 27 Sep 1813.

Hamilton, 2, schr (ex–USS *Growler*). Taken by Americans on Lake Erie, 5 Oct 1813.

Confiance, 2, schr (ex–USS *Julia*). Taken by Americans on Lake Erie, 5 Oct 1813.

Detroit, 6, brig (USS *Adams*, taken 1813). Recaptured on Lake Erie and burned, 9 Oct 1813.

Laurestinus, 22, 6th rate (ex–*Laurel*, 1806). Wrecked on Silver Keys, West Indies, 22 Oct 1813.

Tweed, 18, sloop (1807). Wrecked in Shoal Bay, Nfld., 5 Nov 1813.

Woolwich, 44, storeship, ex-5th rate (1785). Wrecked off Barbuda, 6 Nov 1813.

Atalante, 18, sloop (1808). Wrecked off Halifax, N.S., 10 Nov 1813.

Dart, 10, cutter (1810). Foundered with all hands in Atlantic, Dec 1813.

Pictou, 10, brig-sloop (American *Bonne Foi*, purchased 1813). Taken by USS *Constitution* in West Indies, 15 Feb 1814.

*Epervier, 18, brig-sloop (1812). Taken by USS *Peacock* off Cape Canaveral, Fla., 29 Apr 1814.

Ballahou, 4, schr (1804). Taken by U.S. privateer *Perry* off U.S. coast, 29 Apr 1814.

Halcyon, 18, brig-sloop (1813). Wrecked in Anato Bay, Santo Domingo, 19 May 1814.

Reindeer, 18, brig-sloop (1804). Taken by USS *Wasp* in English Channel, 28 Jun 1814.

Leopard, 50, transport, ex–4th rate (1790). Wrecked on Anticosti Island, Gulf of St. Lawrence, 28 Jun 1814.

Landrail, 4, schr (1806). Taken by U.S. privateer *Syren* in English Channel, 12 Jul 1814.

Magnet, 10, brig (ex–*Sir Sidney Smith*, ex–*Governor Simcoe*, 1806). Burned to avoid capture on Lake Champlain, 5 Aug 1814.

Avon, 18, brig-sloop (1805). Sunk in action with USS *Wasp* in English Channel, 27 Aug 1814.

Peacock, 18, sloop (ex-American *Loup Cervier*, taken 1812). Foundered with all hands off southern U.S. coast, 29 Aug 1814.

Confiance, 36, 5th rate (1814). Taken at Battle of Lake Champlain, 11 Sep 1814.

Linnet, 16 (1813). Taken at Battle of Lake Champlain, 11 Sep 1814.

Chubb, 10 (ex–USS *Eagle*, taken 1813). Taken at Battle of Lake Champlain, 11 Sep 1814.

Finch, 8, brig (ex–USS *Growler*, taken 1813). Taken at Battle of Lake Champlain, 11 Sep 1814.

Hermes, 20, 6th rate (1811). Damaged by American batteries at Mobile, grounded, and burned, 15 Sep 1814.

Crane, 18, brig-sloop (1809). Foundered with all hands in West Indies, 30 Sep 1814.

Racer, 14, schr (ex-American *Independence*, taken 1812). Wrecked in Gulf of Florida, 10 Oct 1814.

Elizabeth, 10, schr (1806, former French, captured 1806). Foundered while chasing American privateer in West Indies, Oct 1814.

Fantome, 18, brig-sloop (1809, French privateer, taken 1810). Wrecked at mouth of St. Lawrence River, 24 Nov 1814.

Cuttle, 4, schr (1807). Foundered with all hands off Halifax, 1814.

Herring, 4, schr (1804). Foundered with all hands off Halifax, 1814.

Sylph, 18, sloop (1812). Wrecked on Southampton, Long Island, N.Y., 17 Jan 1815.

*Cyane, 22, 6th rate (1806). Taken by USS *Constitution* near Madeira, 20 Feb 1815.

Levant, 22, 6th rate (1813). Taken by USS *Constitution* near Madeira, 20 Feb 1815 (retaken).

Statira, 38, 5th rate (1807). Wrecked off Cuba, 26 Feb 1815.

St. Lawrence, 12, schr (ex-American *Atlas*, taken 1813). Taken by U.S. privateer *Chasseur* off Havana, 26 Feb 1815.

Cygnet, 16, sloop (1804). Wrecked off French Guiana, 7 Mar 1815.

Penguin, 18, brig-sloop (1813). Taken by USS *Hornet* off Tristan da Cunha, 23 Mar 1815.

Penelope, 36, transport, ex–5th rate (1798). Wrecked on coast of Newfoundland, 30 Apr 1815.

BIBLIOGRAPHY

SERIAL PUBLICATIONS

American Neptune
Annual Reports of the Navy Department
Journal of the Franklin Institute (1845–55)
Warship International

BOOKS

Bauer, K. Jack. *Ships of the Navy, 1775–1969.* Troy, N.Y.: Rensselaer Polytechnic Institute, 1969.

Bennett, Frank M. *The Steam Navy of the United States.* Pittsburgh, Pa.: Warren & Co., 1896.

Canney, Donald L. *U.S. Coast Guard and Revenue Cutters, 1790–1935.* Annapolis, Md.: Naval Institute Press, 1995.

Chapelle, Howard I. *The History of the American Sailing Navy.* New York: Bonanza, 1949.

Colledge, J. J. *Ships of the Royal Navy: An Historical Index.* Vol. 1. Newton Abbot, England: David & Charles, 1969.

Cooney, David M. *Chronology of the United States Navy, 1775–1965.* New York: Franklin Watts, 1965.

Emmons, George F., comp. *The Navy of the United States, from the Commencement, 1775–1853; with a Brief History of Each Vessel's Service and Fate as Appears upon Record.* Washington: Gideon & Co., 1853.

Fowler, William M., Jr. *Jack Tars and Commodores: The American Navy, 1783–1815.* Boston: Houghton Mifflin, 1984.

Heyl, Erik. *Early American Steamers.* 6 vols. Buffalo, N.Y.: author, 1953–69.

Neeser, Robert W. *Statistical and Chronological History of the United States Navy, 1775–1907.* New York: Macmillan, 1909.

U.S. Coast Guard. *Record of Movements, Vessels of the U.S. Coast Guard.* 1935.

U.S. Navy. *Dictionary of American Naval Fighting Ships.* 8 vols. Washington, D.C.: Naval Historical Center, Department of the Navy, 1959–91.

U.S. Navy. *The Texas Navy.* Washington, D.C.: Naval History Division, Department of the Navy, 1968.

INDEX

CN = Continental Navy
USRCS = United States Revenue Cutter
    Service

Accomac (Virginia), 20
Active, 56
Active (CN), 15
Active (1816) (USRCS), 82
Active (1812) (USRCS), 82
Active (Massachusetts), 19
Active (1791) (USRCS), 79
Adams, 32
Adams (Lake Erie), 64
Advance, 63
Adventure (Virginia), 20
Alabama, 24
Alabama (USRCS), 82
Albany, 43
Alert, 62
Alert (1818) (USRCS), 82
Alert (1829) (USRCS), 83
Alexander Hamilton (USRCS), 83
Alfred (CN), 6
Allegheny, 74
Allen (Lake Champlain), 72
Alliance (CN), 4
Alligator (1813), 55
Alligator (1820), 52
Alligator (ex-gunboat 166), 55
Amelia (Maryland), 18
America (CN), 2
American Congress (Virginia), 20
Andrew Doria (CN), 6
Andrew Jackson (USRCS), 83
Annapolis (Maryland), 18
Anthony (South Carolina), 20
Archer (Texas Navy), 89
Arctic, 78
Argo (1779) (CN), 15
Argo (ex-HMS *Pigot*) (CN), 13
Argo (Rhode Island), 20
Argus (1814), 39

Argus (1803), 46
Argus (1804) (USRCS), 81
Argus (1809) (USRCS), 82
Argus (1830) (USRCS), 84
Argus (1791) (USRCS), 79
Ariel (CN), 11
Ariel, 54
Ariel (Lake Erie), 65
Asp, 55
Asp (Lake Ontario), 69
Augusta, 46
Austin (Texas Navy), 88
Aylwin (Lake Champlain), 72

Bainbridge, 49
Ballard (Lake Champlain), 72
Ballony (South Carolina), 20
Baltimore, 34
Baltimore (CN), 15
Baltimore (Maryland), 18
Beagle, 61
Beaufort, 57
Beaufort (brigantine) (South Carolina), 20
Beaufort (galley) (South Carolina), 20
Bee (USRCS), 81
Benjamin Rush (USRCS), 83
Bibb (USRCS), 87
Bonhomme Richard (CN), 11
Bonita, 54
Borer (Lake Champlain), 72
Boston (CN), 2
Boston (1825), 40
Boston (Lake Champlain) (CN), 17
Boston (1799), 32
Bourbon (CN), 5
Boxer (1815), 49
Boxer (1831), 53
Brandywine, 36
Bricole (South Carolina), 20
Brutus (Texas Navy), 89
Buffalo, 55
Bull Dog, 55

Bulldog (Pennsylvania), 19
Bulloch (Georgia), 18
Burke (Pennsylvania), 19
Burrows (Lake Champlain), 72

Cabot (CN), 7
Caledonia (Lake Erie), 65
Camden (Pennsylvania), 19
Camel, 55
Campbell (1849) (USRCS), 85
Campbell (1830) (USRCS), 84
Campbell (1834) (USRCS), 84
Carolina, 51
Carolina (South Carolina), 20
Caswell (North Carolina), 19
Caswell (Virginia), 20
Centipede (Lake Champlain), 72
Champion (CN), 15
Charleston, 57
Chatham (Pennsylvania), 19
Chesapeake, 30
Chester (Maryland), 18
Chippewa, 49
Chippewa (Lake Erie), 66
Chippewa (Lake Ontario), 66
Collector (USRCS), 81
Colonel Harney, 77
Colorado (Texas Navy), 88
Columbia, 36
Columbus (CN), 6
Columbus (1819), 24
Columbus (1799), 23
Comet, 55
Comet (South Carolina), 20
Commerce (South Carolina), 20
Commodore Barry (USRCS), 82
Concord, 40
Confederacy (CN), 5
Confiance (Lake Champlain), 72
Congress (CN), 4
Congress (1841), 38
Congress (Georgia), 18

Congress (Lake Champlain) (CN), 16
Congress (Pennsylvania), 19
Congress (1799), 28
Congress (South Carolina), 20
Connecticut, 33
Connecticut (Lake Champlain) (CN), 17
Conqueror (Maryland), 18
Conquest (Lake Ontario), 68
Consort, 56
Constellation (1854), 44
Constellation (1797), 28
Constitution, 26
Convention (Pennsylvania), 19
Corporation, 55
Count de Kersaint (South Carolina), 20
Crane (Connecticut), 18
Crawford (1849) (USRCS), 85
Crawford (1830) (USRCS), 83
Crawford (1821) (USRCS), 82
Crawford (ex-*Jefferson*) (1839) (USRCS), 83
Crescent, 30
Cumberland, 36
Cyane (1815), 36
Cyane (1837), 42

Dale, 42
Dallas (1846) (USRCS), 87
Dallas (1816) (USRCS), 82
Dallas (ex-*Vigilant*) (1830) (USRCS), 82
Deane (CN), 10
Decatur, 42
Decoy, 62
Defence (brig) (Maryland), 18
Defence (Maryland), 18
Defence (Massachusetts), 19
Defence (South Carolina), 20
Defense (Connecticut), 18
Delaware (CN), 4
Delaware (1820), 25
Delaware (Pennsylvania), 19
Delaware (1798), 35
Despatch, 55
Despatch (CN), 15
Detector (1815) (USRCS), 82
Detector (1825) (USRCS), 83
Detroit (Lake Erie), 64
Dexter (USRCS), 83
Dickinson (Pennsylvania), 19
Diligence (1802) (USRCS), 81
Diligence (1797) (USRCS), 80
Diligence (1792) (USRCS), 79
Diligence (Virginia), 20
Diligent (CN), 13
Diligent (Massachusetts), 19
Dolly (USRCS), 81
Dolphin (CN), 12
Dolphin (1836), 49
Dolphin (1821), 52
Dolphin (Maryland), 18
Dolphin (Virginia), 20
Dragon (Virginia), 20
Duc de Lauzun (CN), 12

Eagle, 52
Eagle (1809) (USRCS), 82
Eagle (1816) (USRCS), 82
Eagle (ex-HMS *Bulldog*) (Lake Champlain), 70
Eagle (ex-*Surprise*) (Lake Champlain), 70
Eagle (1797) (USRCS), 80
Eagle (1793) (USRCS), 79
Edith, 77
Effingham (CN), 4
Effingham (Pennsylvania), 19
Electra, 63
Engineer, 76
Enterprise (CN), 15
Enterprise (1831), 53
Enterprise (Lake Champlain) (CN), 16
Enterprise (1799), 50
Epervier, 47
Erie (1842), 62
Erie (1813), 39
Erie (USRCS), 84
Eshe (South Carolina), 20
Essex (1813), 35
Essex (1799), 34
Essex Junior, 54
Etna (1847), 60
Etna (1806), 59
Etna (1813), 60
Ewing (USRCS), 85
Experiment (1831), 53
Experiment (Maryland), 18
Experiment (Pennsylvania), 19
Experiment (1799), 50
Experiment (Virginia), 20

Fair American (Lake Ontario), 68
Fair American (South Carolina), 20
Fairfield, 40
Falcon, 54
Falmouth, 41
Fame (CN), 15
Fearnought (Maryland), 18
Fenimore Cooper, 63
Ferret (1806), 51
Ferret (1812), 55
Ferret (1822), 61
Firebrand, 52
Firefly, 48
Flambeau, 47
Flirt, 61
Florida (USRCS), 82
Fly (CN), 15
Fly (Virginia), 20
Flying Fish, 56
Fox (1817), 56
Fox (1822), 61
Frances (Lake Champlain), 71
Franklin (CN), 14
Franklin (Pennsylvania), 19
Franklin (1815), 24
Franklin (1805), 62
Fredonia, 62

Freedom (Massachusetts), 19
Frolic, 39
Fulton (1851), 75
Fulton (1814), 73
Fulton (1837), 73

Gallatin (1815) (USRCS), 82
Gallatin (1807) (USRCS), 81
Gallatin (1830) (USRCS), 83
Gallinipper, 61
Galveston (Texas Navy), 88
Ganges, 31
Gates (Lake Champlain) (CN), 17
General Arnold (CN), 15
General Gates, 13
General Greene, 32
General Greene (1811) (USRCS), 82
General Greene (1802) (USRCS), 81
General Greene (1791) (USRCS), 79
General Greene (1797) (USRCS), 79
General Lincoln (South Carolina), 20
General Mifflin (CN), 15
General Moultrie (South Carolina), 20
General Pike (Lake Ontario), 67
General Putnam (New York), 19
General Schuyler (CN), 15
General Schuyler (New York), 19
General Taylor, 77
General Washington (CN), 15
General Washington (North Carolina), 19
George (USRCS), 82
George Washington, 34
Georgiana, 54
Georgia Packet (CN), 15
Germ, 76
Germantown, 44
Ghent (Lake Erie), 66
Gloucester (Virginia), 20
Gnat, 61
Governor Davie, 57
Governor Gilman (USRCS), 80
Governor Jay (USRCS), 80
Governor Tompkins (Lake Ontario), 68
Governor Williams, 57
Governor Williams (USRCS), 81
Grampus, 53
Greenwich, 62
Greyhound, 61
Greyhound (Virginia), 20
Growler (Lake Champlain), 70
Growler (Lake Ontario), 68
Guerriere, 35
Guilford (Connecticut), 18

Hague (CN), 10
Hamilton (Lake Ontario), 68
Hampden (CN), 9
Hampden (New Hampshire) 19
Hampton (Virginia), 20
Hancock (1775) (CN), 14
Hancock (1776) (CN), 2
Hancock (Pennsylvania), 19

Hannah (CN), 13
Harrison (CN), 14
Harrison (USRCS), 86
Hassan Bashaw, 30
Hawke (CN), 15
Hazard (Massachusetts), 19
Hazard (USRCS), 81
Hecla, 60
Helen, 55
Henry (Virginia), 20
Henry Dodge (USRCS), 86
Herald, 35
Hero (Virginia), 20
Hornet (CN), 8
Hornet (1805), 47
Hornet (1804), 38
Hornet (1813), 55
Hornsnake (CN), 15
Hudson, 37
Hunter (Lake Erie), 65
Hyder Aly (Pennsylvania), 19

Independence, 23
Independence (CN), 8
Independence (Maryland), 18
Independence (Massachusetts), 19
Independence (Texas Navy), 89
Independence (USRCS), 82
Ingham (1849) (USRCS), 96
Ingham (1830) (USRCS), 83
Insurgent, 35
Intrepid, 59
Intrepid (Maryland), 18
Invincible (Texas Navy), 89
Iris, 78

Jackall, 61
James Campbell (USRCS), 86
James C. Dobbin (USRCS), 86
James Madison (1808) (USRCS), 81
James Madison (ex-*Marion*) (1833) (USRCS), 83
Jamestown, 44
Java, 35
Jefferson (1845) (USRCS), 87
Jefferson (1839) (USRCS), 85
Jefferson (1832) (USRCS), 83
Jefferson (1802) (USRCS), 81
Jefferson (Lake Ontario), 68
Jefferson (Virginia), 20
Jefferson Davis (USRCS), 86
Jersey (Lake Champlain) (CN), 17
John Adams (1830), 40
John Adams (1799), 33
John Hancock, 78
John P. Kennedy, 63
Johnson (Maryland), 18
Jones (Lake Ontario), 68
Joseph Lane (ex-*Campbell*) (USRCS), 85
Julia (Lake Ontario), 69

Katy (Rhode Island), 20
King Tammany (North Carolina), 19

Lady of the Lake (Lake Ontario), 69
Lady Prevost (Lake Erie), 65
Lady Washington (CN), 15
Lawrence, 50
Lawrence (Lake Erie), 64
Lawrence (USRCS), 85
Lee (CN), 14
Lee (Georgia), 18
Lee (Lake Champlain) (CN), 17
Lee (South Carolina), 20
Legare (USRCS), 87
Lelah Eisha, 30
Levant, 42
Levi Woodbury (USRCS), 85
Lewis (Virginia), 20
Lewis Cass (USRCS), 86
Lexington, 40
Lexington (CN), 8
Libertad, 57
Liberty (Lake Champlain) (CN), 16
Liberty (Texas Navy), 89
Liberty (Virginia), 20
Lincoln (Massachusetts), 19
L'Indien (CN), 10
Linnet (Lake Champlain), 72
Little Belt (Lake Erie), 65
Louisiana, 38
Louisiana (1804) (USRCS), 81
Louisiana (1819) (USRCS), 82
Louisiana (1825) (USRCS), 83
Lovely Julia (South Carolina), 20
Ludlow (Lake Champlain), 72
Lynch (CN), 14
Lynx, 55
Lynx (USRCS), 82

Macedonian (1836), 38
Macedonian (1812), 35
Machias Liberty (Massachusetts), 19
Madison (Lake Ontario), 67
Mahonese, 57
Malek Adhel, 57
Manly (Virginia), 20
Marion, 42
Marion (USRCS), 83
Marquis de Bretigny (South Carolina), 20
Mars (Massachusetts), 19
Maryland, 38
Massachusetts, 78
Massachusetts (1801) (USRCS), 81
Massachusetts (Massachusetts), 19
Massachusetts (1791) (USRCS), 79
Massachusetts (1793) (USRCS), 79
McLane (1845) (USRCS), 87
McLane (1832) (USRCS), 83
Mercury (ketch) (CN), 15
Mercury (schr) (CN), 15
Mercury (USRCS), 81
Merrimack, 33
Michigan, 75
Midge, 61
Mifflin (Connecticut), 18

Minerva (Connecticut), 18
Mississippi, 73
Missouri, 73
Mohawk (Lake Ontario), 66
Monroe (USRCS), 82
Montezuma, 35
Montgomery (CN), 4
Montgomery (Lake Champlain), 71
Montgomery (New York), 19
Montgomery (Pennsylvania), 19
Morris, 57
Morris (CN), 15
Morris (1849) (USRCS), 85
Morris (1831) (USRCS), 83
Morris (schr) (CN), 15
Mosquito, 61
Mosquito (CN), 15
Mosquito (Virginia), 20

Nancy (South Carolina), 20
Natchez, 40
Nautilus, 51
Nautilus (USRCS), 85
Nettle (Lake Champlain), 72
New Hampshire (USRCS), 81
New Haven (Lake Champlain) (CN), 17
New Orleans (Lake Ontario), 66
New York (1800), 32
New York (1820), 25
New York (Lake Champlain) (CN), 17
Niagara (Lake Erie), 64
Nicholson (Virginia), 20
Nonata, 57
Nonsuch, 52
Norfolk, 45
Norfolk (Virginia), 20
North Carolina, 24
North Carolina (USRCS), 79
Northampton (Virginia), 20
Norwich, 55
Notre Dame (South Carolina), 20

Ohio, 26
Ohio (Lake Erie), 65
Oliver Cromwell (Connecticut), 18
Oliver Wolcott (USRCS), 83
Oneida (Lake Ontario), 67
On-ka-hy-e, 57
Ontario, 39
Ontario (Lake Ontario), 69
Oregon, 57
Otsego, 56

Page (Virginia), 20
Pallas (CN), 12
Patapsco (1813), 55
Patapsco (1799), 38
Patriot (USRCS), 81
Patriot (Virginia), 20
Paul Jones, 38
Peacock (1813), 39
Peacock (1828), 41

Peggy (South Carolina), 20
Pennsylvania, 26
Pennsylvania Farmer (North Carolina), 19
Perry, 50
Pert (Lake Ontario), 69
Petrel, 54
Petrita, 77
Philadelphia, 31
Philadelphia (Lake Champlain) (CN), 17
Philip Allen (USRCS), 86
Phoenix, 61
Phoenix (CN), 15
Pickering (USRCS), 80
Pigot (Rhode Island), 20
Pilgrim (USRCS), 82
Pilot, 56
Pinckney, 46
Pinckney (USRCS), 81
Pioneer, 56
Plater (Maryland), 19
Plattsburg (Lake Ontario), 66
Plymouth, 44
Poinsett, 77
Polk (USRCS), 87
Polly (South Carolina), 20
Porcupine (Lake Erie), 65
Porpoise (1836), 49
Porpoise (1820), 52
Portsmouth (1843), 43
Portsmouth (1798), 33
Portsmouth (USRCS), 83
Potomac, 36
Potomac (Texas Navy), 89
Powhatan, 74
Preble, 42
Preble (Lake Champlain), 71
President, 26
President (Lake Champlain), 71
Princeton (1851), 76
Princeton (1843), 76
Prometheus, 55
Prosper (South Carolina), 20
Protector (Maryland), 18
Protector (Massachusetts), 19
Protector (Virginia), 20
Providence (frigate) (CN), 3
Providence (Lake Champlain) (CN), 17
Providence (sloop) (CN), 7
Pulaski (USRCS), 83

Queen Charlotte (Lake Erie), 64
Queen of France (CN), 10

Racehorse (CN), 13
Raleigh (CN), 3
Raleigh (Virginia), 20
Randolph (CN), 4
Ranger, 55
Ranger (CN), 5
Ranger (Lake Ontario), 70
Ranger (Pennsylvania), 19

Raritan, 36
Rattlesnake, 47
Rattlesnake (South Carolina), 20
Raven (Lake Ontario), 69
Reefer, 54
Reformation (Maryland), 18
Release, 63
Relief, 62
Reprisal (CN), 8
Republic (Massachusetts), 19
Repulse (CN), 15
Rescue, 63
Resistance (CN), 10
Resolution (Maryland), 18
Retaliation, 50
Retaliation (CN), 15
Revenge (CN), 12
Revenge (1806), 51
Revenge (1813), 55
Revenge (gunboat), 55
Revenge (Lake Champlain) (CN), 16
Revenge (Maryland), 18
Revenge (South Carolina), 20
Revenge (Virginia), 20
Richard Rush (USRCS), 83
Richmond, 45
Rising Empire (Massachusetts), 19
Roanoke, 55
Robert McClelland (USRCS), 96
Roger B. Taney (USRCS), 83
Rover (Rhode Island), 20
Royal Savage (Lake Champlain) (CN), 16
Rutledge (South Carolina), 20

Sabine, 37
Sachem (CN), 12
Safeguard (Virginia), 20
Sally (South Carolina), 20
Sally (USRCS), 83
San Antonio (Texas Navy), 89
San Bernard (Texas Navy), 89
San Jacinto, 75
San Jacinto (Texas Navy), 89
Sandfly, 61
Santee, 37
Saranac (1815), 49
Saranac (1848), 74
Saratoga, 43
Saratoga (CN), 6
Saratoga (Lake Champlain), 70
Savannah (1842), 36
Savannah (1799), 57
Scammel (1798) (USRCS), 80
Scammel (1791) (USRCS), 79
Schuyler (Connecticut), 18
Scorpion (1847), 77
Scorpion (1812), 55
Scorpion (Lake Erie), 66
Scorpion (Virginia), 20
Scourge (1804), 47
Scourge (1846), 77

Scourge (Lake Ontario), 69
Sea Gull (1838), 56
Sea Gull (1822), 76
Search (1815) (USRCS), 82
Search (1820) (USRCS), 82
Senator Ross, 57
Shark, 52
Shark (Connecticut), 18
Skjoldebrand, 30
Somers, 49
Somers (Lake Erie), 65
Somerset (Maryland), 18
South Carolina, 57
South Carolina (1815) (USRCS), 82
South Carolina (1798) (USRCS), 81
South Carolina (1793) (USRCS), 79
South Carolina (South Carolina), 20
South Edisto (South Carolina), 20
Southampton, 62
Spark (1814), 48
Spark (1831), 54
Spencer (USRCS), 87
Spitfire (CN), 15
Spitfire (1805), 59
Spitfire (1846), 74
Spitfire (1814), 52
Spitfire (Lake Champlain) (CN), 17
Spitfire (Rhode Island), 20
Spy (CN), 15
Spy (Connecticut), 18
St. Lawrence, 36
St. Louis, 40
St. Mary's (1844), 44
St. Mary's (1801) (USRCS), 81
St. Mary's (1799), 57
Stromboli, 60
Success (Lake Champlain) (CN), 17
Superior (Lake Ontario), 66
Supply, 63
Surprise, 55
Surprise (USRCS), 82
Surprize (CN), 12
Surveyor (USRCS), 81
Susquehanna, 74
Swiftsure (USRCS), 83
Sylph, 54
Sylph (Lake Ontario), 69
Syren, 46

Tampico, 54
Taney, 61
Tartar (Massachusetts), 19
Tartar (Virginia), 20
Tchifonta, 54
Tempest (Virginia), 20
Terrible (Maryland), 18
Terrier, 61
Thexis (Virginia), 20
Thorn (USRCS), 82
Three Friends (South Carolina), 20
Tickler, 55

Ticonderoga (Lake Champlain), 70
Tigress (Lake Erie), 66
Tom Bowline, 62
Torch, 52
Torpedo, 55
Trippe (Lake Erie), 64
Troup, 54
Truite (South Carolina), 20
Trumbull, 33
Trumbull (CN), 3
Trumbull (Lake Champlain) (CN), 16
Truxtun, 50
Turtle (CN), 16
Tyrannicide (Massachusetts), 19

Union (1846), 54
Union (1842), 73
Union (USRCS), 82
United States, 26

Van Buren (USRCS), 85
Vandalia, 40
Vengeance, 60
Vengeance (CN), 12
Venus (Maryland), 18
Vermont, 24
Vesuvius (1846), 60
Vesuvius (1806), 59
Veto (USRCS), 84
Vigilant (1843) (USRCS), 85

Vigilant (1812) (USRCS), 82
Vigilant (1824) (USRCS), 82
Vigilant (1802) (USRCS), 81
Vigilant (1791) (USRCS), 79
Vincennes, 40
Viper, 51
Viper (Lake Champlain), 72
Virginia, 24
Virginia (CN), 4
Virginia (1807) (USRCS), 81
Virginia (1791) (USRCS), 79
Virginia (1797) (USRCS), 79
Virginia (Virginia), 20
Vixen (1846), 74
Vixen (1813), 47
Vixen (1803), 51

Walker (USRCS), 97
Walter B. Forward (USRCS), 85
Warren (1826), 40
Warren (Pennsylvania), 19
Warren (1799), 34
Warren (1775) (CN), 14
Warren (1776) (CN), 3
Washington, 23
Washington (1837) (USRCS), 84
Washington (1832) (USRCS), 83
Washington (frigate) (CN), 4
Washington (galley) (CN), 15
Washington (galley) (Rhode Island), 20

Washington (Lake Champlain) (CN), 16
Washington (Georgia), 18
Washington (North Carolina), 19
Washington (Pennsylvania), 19
Washington (schr) (CN), 14
Washington (sloop) (Rhode Island), 20
Washington (Virginia), 20
Wasp (CN), 10
Wasp (1806), 47
Wasp (1813), 39
Wasp (1825) (USRCS), 83
Wasp (Lake Champlain), 72
Water Witch (1852), 75
Water Witch (1844), 74
Wave, 61
Weasel, 61
West Florida (CN), 15
Wharton (Texas Navy), 89
Whiting (Connecticut), 18
Wild Cat, 61
William Aiken (USRCS), 96
William J. Duane (1849) (USRCS), 85
William J. Duane (1841) (USRCS), 85
William L. Marcy (USRCS), 86
Wilmer (Lake Champlain), 72
Winthrop (Massachusetts), 19

Yorktown, 42

Zavala (Texas Navy), 88

ABOUT THE AUTHOR

Paul H. Silverstone is an internationally recognized naval authority known for his many books and articles on warships. His earlier works on U.S warships in the twentieth century are being rewritten as part of the Naval Institute U.S. Navy Warship Series. Silverstone edits the naval notes column of *Warship International,* the quarterly journal of the International Naval Research Organization, and he has also written and lectured on the subject of Jewish clandestine immigration to Palestine by ship between 1938 and 1948.

A resident of New York City where he is a travel consultant, Silverstone has been an avid student of naval history for many years. He holds an undergraduate degree from Yale University and a law degree from Harvard and became a member of the New York Bar in 1958.

The Naval Institute Press is the book-publishing arm of the U.S. Naval Institute, a private, nonprofit, membership society for sea service professionals and others who share an interest in naval and maritime affairs. Established in 1873 at the U.S. Naval Academy in Annapolis, Maryland, where its offices remain today, the Naval Institute has members worldwide.

Members of the Naval Institute support the education programs of the society and receive the influential monthly magazine *Proceedings* and discounts on fine nautical prints and on ship and aircraft photos. They also have access to the transcripts of the Institute's Oral History Program and get discounted admission to any of the Institute-sponsored seminars offered around the country.

The Naval Institute also publishes *Naval History* magazine. This colorful bimonthly is filled with entertaining and thought-provoking articles, first-person reminiscences, and dramatic art and photography. Members receive a discount on *Naval History* subscriptions.

The Naval Institute's book-publishing program, begun in 1898 with basic guides to naval practices, has broadened its scope in recent years to include books of more general interest. Now the Naval Institute Press publishes about one hundred titles each year, ranging from how-to books on boating and navigation to battle histories, biographies, ship and aircraft guides, and novels. Institute members receive discounts of 20 to 50 percent on the Press's more than eight hundred books in print.

Full-time students are eligible for special half-price membership rates. Life memberships are also available.

For a free catalog describing Naval Institute Press books currently available, and for further information about subscribing to *Naval History* magazine or about joining the U.S. Naval Institute, please write to:

Membership Department
U.S. Naval Institute
291 Wood Road
Annapolis, MD 21402-5034
Telephone: (800) 233-8764
Fax: (410) 269-7940
Web address: www.usni.org